STUDY GUIDE

for J. Gresham Machen's

New Testament Greek for Beginners

by David L. Thompson

Asbury Theological Seminary
Wilmore, Kentucky

MACMILLAN PUBLISHING CO., INC.
New York
COLLIER MACMILLAN PUBLISHERS
London

Macmillan Publishing Company
113 Sylvan Avenue, Englewood Cliffs, NJ 07632

Collier Macmillan Canada, Ltd.

ISBN 0-02-420650-4
Printing Number: 10 9 8
Printed in the United States of America

Cover design by Jim Anderson

The exercises from J. Gresham Machen's New Testament Greek for
Beginners, copyright Macmillan Publishing Co., Inc., 1923, copyright
renewed, 1951, by Arthur W. Machen, are reproduced here in translated
form by permission of Westminster Theological Seminary and Macmillan
Publishing Co., Inc.

FOREWORD

It would be difficult to find a Grammar of any language that makes learning easier for the student and teaching less demanding for the instructor than Machen's New Testament Greek for Beginners. Its clarity, precision, and simplicity of expression, its stress on the regular and the normal in usage, its high-frequency Greek vocabulary, and the abundance and character of its exercises have contributed to its success in firmly planting in the student's mind the basics of New Testament Greek. In fact, when the student has worked through Machen's Grammar, on his own, he should be at least as familiar with the fundamentals of New Testament Greek as he is with the elements of his native language. Here is a textbook that goes far toward teaching itself.

This is not to say, however, that a teacher's guidance is not beneficial and at times even necessary if one is to obtain the best results from the study of Machen's Grammar. Many students will have questions about matters not dealt with in the Grammar and which are beyond its scope, and these will benefit from supplementary information; everyone can profit from an instructor's suggestions as to study methods and from his morale-building encouragement and exhortation; and all will need to have their exercises competently checked.

A very large contribution toward meeting these needs can be made by the Study Guide which Professor Thompson has prepared. The work of one who is sensitive to the problems and needs of students, it reduces the area in which the services of a teacher are required, and it should prove especially helpful to those who are studying Machen's Grammar without benefit of an instructor. It provides substantial teaching support for a Grammar that has already been unusually successful in teaching itself.

John H. Skilton
Westminster Theological Seminary

PREFACE

A significant number of college and seminary instructors of beginning New Testament Greek have found it advantageous to retain a generally deductive structure in their teaching of the language. This is true in spite of the appearance within the last decade of several excellent grammars based on an inductive study of the New Testament Greek text itself. For many of these instructors J. Gresham Machen's New Testament Greek for Beginners, a classic first published in 1923, remains by far the most acceptable, traditional presentation available.

Nevertheless, Machen's text presents several deficiencies which must usually be met with supplementary notes or exercises. The more obvious of these are: 1) the almost total lack of exposure to the Greek text of the New Testament until the final lessons; 2) the neglect of some points of grammar and syntax quite usefully learned in first year study; 3) the delayed presentation of the perfect tense and the mi-verbs; and 4) the minimal emphasis on sentence structure.

To these and other problems in an otherwise highly useable text this Study Guide addresses itself. Written to be used paragraph by paragraph with Machen's grammar, the Study Guide contains four major divisions in every lesson.

1. Notes on Greek vocabulary, grammar and syntax to supplement New Testament Greek for Beginners, keyed to Machen's paragraph numbers.
2. Aids to the exercises with questions, diagrams, and constant reference to New Testament Greek for Beginners, to lead the student in more efficient analysis of the exercise sentences.
3. New Testament Greek readings to introduce immediately actual examples of what the student is learning in the grammar and to increase motivation for study.
4. Translations of all exercise sentences in Machen, gathered in the Appendix to the Study Guide.

Designed to be used as a companion to Machen's text, in many cases the supplementary materials make sense only in light of Machen's presentation.

The aids to the exercises lead the student in the analysis of the exercise sentences. It is not intended that every student will write out an answer to all the questions asked. The majority of the aids are questions which students with a clear understanding of the materials in the text would ask and answer almost automatically. At the same time they are questions which one must usually be able to answer if not automatically, then with help, if one is to translate intelligently. Thus, the student who cannot answer them will in most cases also be unable to understand the exercise. References in the aids lead such students to the information needed to do the sentences, while they provide constant review to the student who knows the answers.

Aids to the English to Greek exercises are omitted after Lesson III. The main objective, to teach Greek reading (not Greek composition), supports this omission and the addition of other reading opportunities, especially in the Greek New Testament itself. Additional bulk involved in their inclusion is also a consideration.

The appended translations are intended as _aids_ to _learning_, to maximize the effectiveness of persistent study. They enable the student to check his own work immediately, when correction has the most potential as a stimulus to learning. In some cases, consulting the "answer" in the process of working the exercise can also assist in understanding a particularly difficult item, although this should be a most exceptional use of the translations. The use of the translations as a crutch to prop up faulty study habits or compensate for lack of diligent work can only prove disastrous. The _Appendix_ is also intended to make the _Study Guide_ useful for completely independent study of Machen's text.

If the student is not already aware of it, he will soon discover that no single translation exhausts the possible ways of rendering one language into another. Especially in later lessons the student may prefer alternative renderings. In those cases it is more important that the student understand _why_ the suggested translation may have been given and that he be able to defend his own translation than that he agree with the phrasing offered here.

The author expresses his deep appreciation to the secretaries of the Division of Religion and Philosophy of Marion College, Marion, Indiana, especially Mrs. Maxine Haines, and to Mrs. Lyn Miller, Asbury Theological Seminary, for their patient and careful typing of these esoteric pages. The author also thanks the Macmillan Company for permission to reproduce Machen's exercise sentences in the _Study Guide_, and Professor Bruce Metzger for permission to adapt materials from his _Lexical Aids for Students of New Testament Greek_, New edition. A special debt is gratefully acknowledged to Dr. Philip S. Clapp of Western Evangelical Seminary for his meticulous reading of the entire manuscript. His many corrections and helpful suggestions have proved of inestimable value in preparing this work for publication.

David L. Thompson
Asbury Theological Seminary
Wilmore, Kentucky

CONTENTS

LIST OF ABBREVIATIONS

AG   Arndt, William F., and F. Wilbur Gingrich. _A Greek-English Lexicon of the New Testament and Other Early Christian Literature_. Chicago: The University of Chicago Press, 1957.

CEG   Greenlee, J. Harold. _A Concise Exegetical Grammar of New Testament Greek_. Third edition, revised. Grand Rapids: Wm. B. Eerdmans Publishing Co., 1963.

DM   Dana, H. E., and Julius R. Mantey. _A Manual Grammar of the Greek New Testament_. New York: The Macmillan Co., 1927.

Lexical Aids   Metzger, Bruce M. _Lexical Aids for Students of New Testament Greek_. New edition. Princeton, New Jersey: By the author, 1974.

NT   _The New Testament_

NTGFB   Machen, J. Gresham. _New Testament Greek for Beginners_. New York: The Macmillan Co., 1951.

1.1[1]   Notice Machen's footnotes on the alphabet. Examples of the γ combined with following γ, κ, ξ, or χ, and pronounced "ng" in that combination are:

ἄγγελος, angelos, φάραγξ, pharanx, ἤνεγκα, ēnenka, ἐγχρίω, enchriō

All other consonant combinations are pronounced giving each consonant its normal value.

φθαρτός, phthartos, πνεῦμα, pneuma, not with "silent" pi as in English.

1.2   When the characters of one language are transcribed into the practically equivalent characters of another language, the characters are said to be transliterated (not translated).

The Greek alphabet is transliterated with the obvious English alphabetic correspondent (e.g., α = a, β = b), with the following exceptions:

ζ = z; η = ē; υ = y, except in diphthongs where it is transliterated "u," e.g., αυ = au, ευ = eu, ηυ = ēu; χ = ch; ω = ō.

Note the following: ζωή = zōē, ψυχή = psychē.

The consonant combinations noted above are transliterated;

γγ = ng, γκ = nk, γξ = nx, γχ = nch

The student need not master the transliteration values now. They may be learned by reference. Transliteration is often used in works in the field of biblical literature, making it a necessary part of the student's knowledge of the language.

4.1   What is the iota subscript, and what phonetic combination gives rise to it?

4.2   When a diphthong with iota subscript is written in capital letters, the iota is written after the long vowel rather than under it, and is called iota adscript.

8.1   For further study on the Greek alphabet, consult the following:

On the Semetic origin of the Greek alphabet:
Lambdin, T. O. "The Alphabet." Vol. I of The Interpreter's Bible Dictionary. Edited by George A. Buttrick et. al. Nashville: Abingdon Press, 1962. pp. 89-96.

---

[1]The paragraph numbers indicate first the paragraph being considered in Machen, NTGFB, then the paragraph of discussion in the Study Guide. Thus, "1.2" indicates the second paragraph in the Study Guide pertaining to Machen's paragraph 1.

On pronunciation of Koine:

> Robertson, A. T. <u>A Grammar of the Greek New Testament in the</u>
> <u>Light of Historical Research</u>. Nashville, Tenn.: Broadman
> Press, 1934. p. 71ff., and 236-241.

8.I   There is a striking correlation between a student's ability to pronounce a foreign language and his mastery of it. Thus, this first
exercise in writing and pronouncing Greek letters, words and sentences (even
though they are not now intelligible) is the beginning of a discipline whose
importance can scarcely be over emphasized.

8.II   NEW TESTAMENT GREEK READING,   Jn. 1.1-6

Beginning at John 1.1 and proceeding as far as your time will allow,
do the following exercises.

1. <u>Spell</u> the words aloud, <u>writing</u> the characters as you spell them.

   E.g., "<u>epsilon</u>, <u>nu</u>" (ἐν), "<u>alpha</u>, <u>rho</u>, <u>chi</u>, <u>eta-iota</u> subscript"
   (αρχῆ), and so on.

2. <u>Transliterate</u> the Greek characters into English characters (see
   para. 1.2). E.g., <u>en archei</u> (ἐν ἀρχῇ), and so on. Again, spell
   as you go.

3. <u>Read</u> the words aloud, pronouncing them according to the phonetic
   values given in paragraph 1.

Verse six should not be considered a limit for this exercise, even
though all the letters of the Greek alphabet except <u>xi</u> and <u>psi</u> appear in John
1.1-6.

10.1   Which syllables are long, which short?

11.1   The "domain" of the three accents may be graphed as follows (rule 1).

antepenult   penult   ultima

                                     grave – only when no punctuation
                                                separates next word
                                   circumflex – on long syllable only
                                   acute

11.2   The length of the ultima affects general accent.

        1. The ultima is long?
            a. The antepenult cannot be accented.
            b. The penult, if accented, must have acute.

        2. The ultima is short?
            a. Any syllable may receive appropriate accent.
            b. A long penult, if accented, must have circumflex.

12 -14.1 Note carefully Machen's explanation (para. 12) that the general rules do not in themselves specify how a given word is to be accented. They provide the frame of reference within which verbs, with their recessive accent (para. 13), and nouns, with their retentive accent (para. 14) are to be accented. For example, rule 4 does not say that when the ultima is short and the penult long, the penult must have the circumflex accent. Rather, it states that if the penult is to be accented at all (because of the accent demands of a verb or noun), that penult must have the circumflex if it is long and the ultima is short.

13.1   Why is it unnecessary to have any information beyond a knowledge of the general rules (para. 11) in order to accent a given verb form? Illustrate.

14.1   Why must one learn the accent position of the nominative singular of noun forms in order to accent other forms of the word? Illustrate.

15.I   Aids to exercise I.

        1. What two facts of accent combine to indicate the syllable upon which the accent will rest in Greek verbs? See para. 13 and general rules 3 and 4.

        2. Why is it unnecessary for you to know the length of the upsilon in ἐλυσω (I.1) or of the alpha in ἐλυσαμην (I.2)? See the general rules.

        3. On λυσαι (I.5), check para. 10 again.

15.II   Aids to exercise II.

1. Why does Machen give you the nominative singular form of the nouns to be accented? See para. 14.

2. Knowing the nominative singular with its accent, what other fact will affect the <u>position</u> of the accent? See general rule 3.

3. Review 10.1 before accenting such pairs as ἀποστολοις/αποστολοι, and κωμαις/κωμαι.

15.III

1. ἔδιδομεν, no.

   a. No accent appears farther back than the antepenult; rule 1.
   b. Considering <u>only</u> the general rules, not whether it is a verb or noun, it could be accented:

   ἐδίδομεν, ἐδιδόμεν, ἐδιδομέν (rules 1 and 2).

   ὦραι, no.

   a. When the ultima is short, a long penult, <u>if</u> it is accented, should have a circumflex, not an acute; rule 4.
   b. Could be accented ὦραι (rule 4) or ὡραί (rules 1 and 5), according to the general rules above.

   πρόφηταις, no.

   a. The long ultima allows accent only on the ultima or the penult; rule 3(a).
   b. προφήταις (rule 3 a, b), προφηταίς or προφηταῖς (rule 5).

2. δόξη, yes; rule 3(b) and 2, could also be δοξή or δοξῆ (rule 5).

   ἐρῆμου, no.

   a. If the ultima is long, the penult, if accented al all, should have the acute, not the circumflex; rule 3(b).
   b. ἐρήμου. (rules 1 and 3b), ἐρημοῦ or ἐρημού (rules 1 and 5).

   οὔρανον, no.

   a. The circumflex cannot appear farther back than the penult; rule 1.
   b. Considering only the general rules (cf para. 12), the word could be accented:

   οὖρανον, οὐράνον, οὐρανόν (rules 1 and 2) and ουρᾶνον (if α is long; rule 4).

3. ἔρημος, yes; rule 1.

Could also be ερῆμος (rule 4), or ἐρημός (rules 1 and 2).

Βουλαί, yes; rules 1 and 2. Could also be Βοῦλαι (rule 4).

λὺε, no.

 a. The grave stands only on the ultima.
 b. No, if one recalls 15:I, 4 where one is told that the <u>upsilon</u> here is long. Then should be λῦε (rule 4).
 c. Could also be λυέ (rules 1 and 2) or λύε (rule 1).

15.IV NEW TESTAMENT READING, Jn. 1.6-9

1. Study each word in these verses, explaining their accents <u>as well</u> as you are able with the information you have. Where you can, specify whether the word could or could not be a verb (paras. 13-14).

2. Pronounce each word, giving proper emphasis to accented syllables.

3. Review any letters of the alphabet which are not familiar to you by now.

16.1   Supplementary study in vocabulary may be profitably pursued in such tools as:

        Metzger, Bruce M. LEXICAL AIDS FOR STUDENTS OF NEW TESTAMENT
          GREEK. Princeton: By the Author, revised edition, 1974.

Included here are words listed according to their frequency in the New Testament and then grouped by roots in families of related words.

16.2   Many words you already know are related to Greek words. Associate these known derivatives with the Greek words you are studying. It will help you master vocabulary, both Greek and English.

        Note: gnostic, gnosticism   γινώσκω (γνω-)
              graphic, (phono)graph   γράφω
              didactic   διδάσκω

17.1   <u>Tense</u> in Greek, as in many languages, has to do not so much with <u>time</u> of action as with <u>kind</u> of action. The Greek present tense in the indicative mood does refer generally to present time and will be translated in the following exercises by the English present. But the student should also know that the basic meaning of the Greek present is <u>continuing</u> action, whatever the time indicated by the context.

17.2   <u>Voice</u> indicates the relation of the subject to the action in a verbal clause.

      <u>Active voice</u>   The subject is acting, usually upon or in
                             reference to some other person or thing.

          "I   -   see   - the man."
      Subject - active verb - object

      <u>Passive voice</u>   The subject is being acted upon by some
                             person (agent) or thing (instrument).

          "I   - am being seen- by the man."
      Subject - passive verb - agent (prep. phrase)

      <u>Middle voice</u>   The subject is acting upon itself or in
                             its own interests, or with intimate in-
                             volvement in the action.

The middle voice is, of course, not found in English. Both the Greek passive and middle will be studied later and need not concern the student now, except as they contrast with the active voice.

17.3   Mood indicates the verbal idea's relation to reality. It tells
         whether the verb is a statement of fact (indicative), or probability
or possibility (subjunctive), or simply of wish (optative) or command (imperative).

<u>Indicative mood</u>: A statement of fact--may be true or false.

18.1   The paradigm may be readily learned by a period of concentrated
         writing and rewriting with pronunciation, perhaps done best after
the chapter as a whole has been understood.

19.1   Every verb identification should include tense, voice, mood, person,
         number and vocabulary form (lexical form; the form in the word list
or a standard Greek-English dictionary). For example, βλέπεις, is "the present
active indicative, second person singular, of βλέπω."

<u>Number</u> designates the verb as singular or plural.

19.2   Although there is nothing sacred about that order of identification,
         an identification including all of this information must become
automatic in a short time. An adoption of some order by the class is
recommended.

Complete identifications every time foster accuracy in learning and save
valuable time. Some system of abbreviation will probably be helpful for the
student's notes, such as P.A.I., 2 sg., for the above identification.

20.1   The <u>present stem</u> is called the <u>tense stem</u>. The tense stem of a
         verb indicates (1) the nature of the act itself (is it "seeing," or
"knowing") and (2) the tense of the action (present, aorist). How do you find
the present stem of any verb?

20.2   The student must learn immediately the <u>primary active endings</u> they
         are:

Singular		Plural	
1. -ω	"I"	1. -μεν	"we"
2. -εις	"you"	2. -τε	"you (pl.)"
3. -ει	"he, she, it"	3. -ουσι	"they"

The primary endings appear only on non-past tenses. The "original" endings
given by Machen are of interest in a more historical study of Greek grammar.
But they are of little importance in understanding the present active indicative.

The personal endings indicate:

    1. Voice (here active)
    2. Person and number (1 sg., 1 pl., etc.)

20.3   A _variable vowel_ connects the personal ending and the tense stem.
In the case of the primary active endings, – ω, – ειϛ, – ει, and
– ουσι, the variable vowel and the personal ending have become inseparably
joined by contraction in the development of the language and so are to be
learned as given above.

Where possible the ending should be learned without the variable vowel (-μεν and
-τε, rather than -ομεν and -ετε) in anticipation of the pattern to be used in
learning the three other major sets of personal verb endings.

What is the variable vowel before μ/ν? _____
Before other consonants? _____

Careful observation of the variable vowel is necessary, since the variable
vowel helps to indicate the verb's mood. Short o/ε here indicate indicative
mood.

20.4   Be able to "dissect" any verb as follows:

λύομεν: λυ   o   μεν

Tense stem –	_variable vowel_ –	_personal ending_
(present stem)	(indicative mood)	(primary active, 1 pl.)

23.1   Learn the vocabulary (para. 16), the primary active endings (20.2),
and the present active indicative paradigm (18) before you do the
exercises. The student will find it possible to do some of the early exercises without doing this, or course. But doing _any_ exercise as a substitution
for a reasonable, preliminary mastery of the main items in the chapter can only
prove disastrous in a short time.

23.2   Review and learn the meaning of the following terms before doing
the exercise: tense, voice, mood, person, number, tense stem,
present, active, indicative.

23.3   Aids to exercise I, Lesson III

In _each_ case:

A. Analyze the form by identifying
    1. the tense stem
    2. the personal ending
    3. the variable vowel, if possible

This may be done graphically: λυ/ο/μεν

B. Identify the form completely:

     tense
     voice
     mood
     person
     number
     lexical form

     For example, βλέπεις = P.A.I. 2 sg. of βλέπω

C. Translate from Greek to English.

D. The paragraph citations are intentionally included as teaching aids. Unless the connections and answers are obvious to you, look them up!

23.I   Write the Greek words from the exercises in the blanks provided. Use remaining room for identification, translation and other notes.

1. _____, _____, _____.

  a. What is - εις (para 20)?
  b. How do you know they are active verbs (20.2)?
  c. How do you know they are verbs making a statement of fact and not giving a wish or a command (20.3)?

2. _____, _____, _____.

  a. Identify - ει (para. 20).
  b. How do you know these are present tense verbs (20.1)?
  c. Does your translation reflect the Greek tense?

3. _____, _____, _____.

  a. Why accented on the penult with acute (para. 11, rule 3b, and para. 13)?
  b. All items in 23.3 noted?

4. _____, _____, _____.

  a. Present stem = _____, _____, _____ (20).
  b. Variable vowel (20.3) = _____?
  c. Personal ending (20.2) = _____?
  d. How do you know these are present tense verbs (20.1)?
  e. How do you know they are active verbs (20.2)?
  f. How do you know they are verbs making a statement of fact and not giving a wish or a command (20.3)?

5. _____, _____, _____.

    a. Why accented with acute on antepenult (para. 13 and rule 1)?
    b. Variable vowel (20.3)? _____
    c. Primary personal ending (20.2)? _____
    d. How do these verbs contrast most consistently with those in sentence 1?

6. _____, _____, _____.

    a. Singular or plural verbs? How do you know (20.2)?
    b. Active or passive? How do you know (20.3)?

7. _____, _____, _____.

    All items in 23.3 observed?

8. _____, _____, _____.

9. _____, _____, _____.

23.II   NEW TESTAMENT GREEK READING, Jn. 1.1-9

Verses 5 and 9 contain present active indicative verbs. Locate them, parse them, and look up their meaning in a lexicon.

Conjugate (i.e., write the six conjugational forms) of each one.

Figure out the meanings of as many of the words as you can in Jn. 1.1-5, perhaps using an English version as an aid.

24.1 Learn the accent position of the nominative singular (the lexical form) of each noun in the vocabulary. Why so (para. 14)?

24.2 The nouns should be learned with the article, since in the vocabulary the article indicates the gender of the noun (see 28 below). Thus, ὁ ἀδελφός, "the brother," but τὸ ἱερόν, "the temple."

25.1 A declension is a group of formally similar nouns. English hat and bat might be said to belong to the same "declension," because their plurals are both formed by adding -s. On the other hand, box and fox and foot and goose would belong to other "declensions," forming their plurals in the first case by adding -es, and in the other by internal vowel change, -oo- to -ee-.

26.1 Recall that English has both indefinite (a, an) and definite articles (the) which function by marking certain constructions, often by specifying something in the case of "the."

26.2 Summarize the use of the Greek article or the lack of it. How translated?

28.1 The "genders" referred to as "masculine," "feminine," and "neuter" are of course grammatical genders and not basically related to sexual differentiation. However, in most cases obvious sexual distinction will coincide with grammatical gender: ὁ ἀδελφός is "the brother" (not "the sister") and ἡ γυνή (feminine) is "the woman."

28.2 What is the usual gender of the -ος and -ον words of the second declension?

30.1 In Greek, as in English, words performing certain functions in a sentence regularly appear with a characteristic form (inflexion) and are said to be in a certain "case."

30.2 Recall that the case of some English pronouns signals (with word order) their function in a sentence. Thus, an English pronoun in the subjective (nominative) case is known to be the subject of a sentence, in the objective (accusative) case is labelled as the object of a sentence or of a preposition, and in the possessive (genitive) case is marked as a possessor with the function "of."

subjective (nominative)	objective (accusative)	possessive (genitive)
he	him	his
she	her	her
it	it	its
they	them	their
who	whom	whose

Thus

"She hit him on his head," or "Who hit whom on whose head?"

but not

"His hit her on him head," or "Whom hit whose on who head?"

Even in some cases of unusual word order the case of the English pronouns labels their function and renders the sentence intelligible.

"<u>Him</u> she hit on his head," or even "On his head him she hit."

30.3   This familiar practice of allowing word form to signal word function must be observed even more extensively in Greek. Whereas few nouns in English have full case inflection, nearly all Greek nouns do, enabling them to indicate by their <u>form</u> whether they are

subject	(nominative case)
possessor	(genitive case)
indirect object	(dative case)
direct object	(accusative case)
direct address	(vocative case).

30.4   Paragraphs 34-37 give <u>representative</u> functions signaled by each case. These are by no means exhaustive, but are convenient places for the beginning student to start his mastery of the Greek cases and their many uses.

For a more extended presentation of the cases and their use, see H. E. Dana and Julius R. Mantey , A MANUAL GRAMMAR OF THE GREEK NEW TESTAMENT (New York: The Macmillan Co., 1927), pp. 65-95 (hereafter as DM).

For a presentation of Greek cases using the insights of contemporary linguistic analysis, see Goetchius, THE LANGUAGE OF THE NEW TESTAMENT, (New York: Charles Scribner's Sons, 1965), pp. 36-39, 56-67, and 108-112.

30.5   Traditional (though frequently inadequate) definitions of the parts of the sentence are:

Subject: the actor, or the person said to be in a given state.
Direct object: the person/thing receiving the action or the result of the action.
Indirect object: the person/thing to whom or for whom an act is done.

Learn these representative functions and the paradigms in this chapter now!

31, 39.1 Paragraphs 31 and 39 do not give <u>different</u> declensions. They both contain common second declension <u>masculine</u> nouns. The nouns differ only in the syllable accented in the nominative singular (see the discussion in para. 40).

32.1 Note para. 31.

Why may ἄνθρωπος be accented on the antepenult (para. 11, rule 1)?

Given the antepenult accent of the nominative singular ἄνθρωπος, explain the accents of the genitive and dative singular, and the genitive, dative, and accusative plural (para. 11, rule 3a).

32.2 Notice in para. 40 the <u>special rule</u> of <u>accent</u> for second declension nouns. What is that rule?

Illustrate it.

33.1 Review the paradigms in paragraphs 31, 39 (masculine) and 41 (neuter).

33.2 For practical purposes it may be acceptable to learn the endings as Machen has suggested, with the final vowel of the stem included.

33.3 It is also helpful to study the endings themselves <u>without</u> the stem vowel, since these endings will appear again and again in the entire Greek noun system.

Masculine	Neuter
Sg.	Sg.
Nom. - ς	N. - ν
Gen. - ου	G. - ου
Dat. - ¯. (length of stem vowel plus iota)	D. - ¯.
Acc. - ν	A. ν
Voc. - #[1]	V. - ν
Pl.	Pl.
N. - ι	N. - α
G. - ¯ν	G. - ¯ν
D. - ις	D. - ις
A. - ους	A. - α
V. - ι	V. - α

33.4 In spite of the extensive inflectional system, word order and/or context will often be the deciding factors in accurate identification and accurate translation.

34.1 How do you know that Machen's example can not mean "He knows an apostle" or "Apostles know"?

---

[1] # = lack of a case ending as a morpheme in itself. i.e., a "zero morpheme."

35.1   How do you know Machen's example does not mean
        "An apostle of words" (i.e. full of words or characterized by
        words), or "Words of an apostle," or "A word of apostles"?

36.1   Why can the example not mean "Apostles say a word," or even "I say a
        word to an apostle"?

37.1   The vocative case frequently precedes commands or questions.
        "Lord (vocative for direct address), Save us!"
        "Lord, to whom shall we go"?

37.2   Why can Machen's example not mean "We see a brother"?

42.1   Learn this second "all" statement. Cf. 28.2.

45.1   General suggestions for the exercises.

        A. Learn both the vocabulary (para. 24, with review of previous
            vocabulary) and the two paradigms of the second declension
            (para. 31 and 41) before you work the exercises.

            The exercises reinforce your learning and sharpen your under-
            standing of the concepts and data learned. But you do not
            have time to learn only by use. Take the caution in para.
            23.1 seriously. It's true!

        B. Identify every word fully in every sentence. The identifica-
            tion of a noun should include (in this order) gender, case,
            number, and lexical form (N. sg.), e.g., ἄνθρωπους is the
            masculine accusative plural of ἄνθρωπος, or M. A. pl. Abbrevia-
            tions can save much time in these frequent identifications. And,
            after a number of sentences in which you are obviously showing
            facility in identification, you may simply do it mentally,
            making notes only on difficult or unfamiliar forms.

            However, it is done, every form must be accurately and completely
            identified. If you cannot do this, you do not fully understand
            the material and need to review. You will find constant identifi-
            cation to be an irreplaceable aid to language learning of the
            sort you are engaged in.

        C. In the aids below, space for your translation has been left
            immediately beneath the Greek sentence. It is recommended that
            you review the analytical aids before beginning your translation
            of each sentence.

D. Write out the translation and as much of your grammatical analysis as necessary.

Note: In several early lessons the Greek sentences are begun with capital letters to assist the student's mastery of them. Early New Testament manuscripts do not exhibit this practice.

45.I   Aids to Exercise I, Lesson IV.

1. Ἀδελφὸς βλέπει ἄνθρωπον.
   Translation:

   a. What function does ἀδελφός have in the sentence?
      How do you know (31 and 34)?
   b. Can ἄνθρωπον be the subject? Why not (31, 34)?
   c. Identify the verb fully?
      Why is the verb singular (29)?
   d. Are the nouns definite or indefinite (26)?

2. Δοῦλος γράφει λόγους.

   a. How does sentence 2 differ from sentence 1 (beyond vocabulary change)?
   b. Why is δοῦλος accented with circumflex on the penult and λόγους with acute (para. 11, rules 3 and 4)?

3. Ἀπόστολοι διδάσκουσιν ἄνθρωπον.

   a. - οι signals what function for ἀπόστολοι (31,34)?
   b. - ον signals what function for ἄνθρωπον (31,34)?
   c. Is the form ἄνθρωπον ambiguous?
      Why not? Compare the neuter nouns (41), where -ον may signal either _____, _____, or _____, depending on the context.
   d. Is διδάσκουσιν sg. or pl? Why?
   e. What is the difference between διδάσκουσι and διδάσκουσιν (44)?

4 Ἀπόστολοι λύουσι δούλους.

   Explain the accent change from δοῦλος to δούλους (11, rule 3b).

5. Δοῦλος λαμβάνει δῶρα.

    a. Without a context, what functions could -α on δῶρα signal (41)?

    b. Why must it be the accusative case and thus the direct object here (33.4)?

    c. Judging from the accent of δῶρα, the final -α is long or short (11, rule 4)? _____

    d. Are all items in 45.1 cared for?

6. Λαμβάνουσιν υἱοὶ οἴκους.

    a. Why the movable <u>nu</u> on λαμβάνουσιν (44)?

    b. Is the verb singular or plural (18)?
       How do you know?
       Why that number here (29)?

    c. Diagram the Greek sentence using the following pattern:

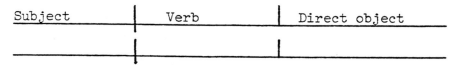

Subject	Verb	Direct object

    d. Verb-subject-object would not be acceptable word order in English. Translate into acceptable English regardless of the Greek word order.

       Recovery of the significance of word order in the Greek New Testament, often completely obscured in any translation, is simply <u>one</u> of the many reasons why you are taking New Testament Greek.

7. Δούλους καὶ οἴκους λαμβάνουσιν ἀδελφοί.

    a. Diagram this sentence using the pattern:

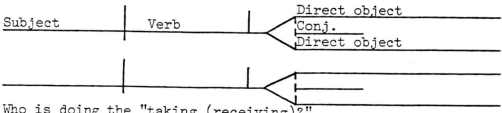

    b. Who is doing the "taking (receiving)?"
       How do you know?

8. Βλέπομεν ἱερὰ καὶ ἀποστόλους.

    a. Diagram the sentence.

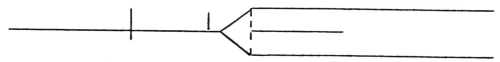

    b. Remember to "dissect" the verbs, identifying all the parts (at least mentally) and finally identifying the verb itself.

       Βλέπομεν: What are the parts (20.4)? _____

    c. Joined by καί in a compound construction with ἀποστόλους, ἱερά is most likely to be identified as the _____ of _____.

9. Δούλους βλέπετε καὶ ἀδελφούς.

    a. Don't be fooled by word order. Δούλους is to be joined with _____ as a compound _____.
    b. Are the words fully identified?
    c. What is the tense of this verb?
       How do you know (20.1)?
    d. Is the verb indicative or some other mood?
       How do you know (20.3)?
    e. Verb singular or plural (20.2)?

10. Γράφεις λόγον ἀποστόλῳ.

    a. Diagram the sentence. Subj. | Verb | D. Obj. \ Indirect Obj.

    b. ἀποστόλῳ: long stem vowel and <u>iota</u> subscript indicate the _____ case and the function of _____ _____ in the sentence (31, 36).
    c. Verb is singular or plural? active or passive? present or past? indicative or subjunctive? How do you know?

11. Διδάσκει ἄνθρωπον.

    a. How does this sentence differ from No. 1?
    b. Is it at all ambiguous?

12. Ἀδελφὸς λέγει λόγον ἀποστόλῳ.

    a. Is the apostle or the brother doing the action?
       How can you tell for sure (31, 34, 36)?
    b. Are λέγει and λόγον correctly accented?
       Explain the accentuation of each (11, rules 1 and 3b;
       remember recessive and retentive accents).
    c. Diagram the sentence (see pattern in No. 10).

13. Ἀδελφὸς ἀποστόλων γινώσκει νόμον.

    a. Identify all the words fully (45.1.B).
    b. Who knows what?
    c. Ἀποστόλων qualifies ἀδελφός with what additional information
       (35)?
    d. Ἀποστόλων could be related to νόμον with reasonable sense.
       Why are you prone to take it with ἀδελφός?
    e. Diagram (see No. 6) the sentence, attaching the modifier
       beneath the word it modifies.

14. Δοῦλοι γινώσκουσι νόμον καὶ λαμβάνουσι δῶρα.

    a. This is a compound sentence, with two verbs joined by the
       conjunction καί.
       The subject is not repeated (=ellipsis) but is to be under-
       stood as _____.
    b. In addition to the conjoined structure of the verbs, what else
       supports taking δοῦλοι as the subject of both clauses?
    c. Is δῶρα subject, object, or noun of direct address (41)?
       How do you know?
    d. Diagram·

```
                           V.              | D.C.
              _____
         S.  |            |cj.
              _____
                          |V              | D.O.
```

15. Γινώσκουσιν ἄνθρωποι θάνατον.

    a. All items fully identified (cf. 45.1)?
    b. Diagram:

16. Λαμβάνομεν δῶρα καὶ ἔχομεν ἀδελφούς.

    a. Contrast δῶρα and ἀδελφούς.
    b. Why can δῶρα not be subject (20.2)?

17. Ἀποστόλοις καὶ δούλοις λέγομεν λόγους θανάτου.

    a. Who is doing what to whom? Full identification is always
        necessary.
    b. Ἀποστόλοις and δούλοις are said to be in "emphatic position."
    c. Judging by word order, what noun does θανάτου modify (33.4)?
        Is it possessive?
          This is an example of the genitive case used to qualify
        another noun by the "of" relationship which is much broader
        than possession. Here "words" is somehow qualified, character-
        ized by "death."
    d. Diagram. See No. 10 for pattern.

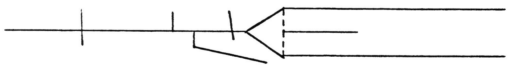

18. Ἀδελφοὶ καὶ δοῦλοι γινώσκουσιν καὶ βλέπουσιν ἱερὰ καὶ δῶρα.

    a. Why the antepenultimate accent on the verbs (13)?
    b. Is the -ιν long or short (11, rule 3a)?

19. Γράφει ἀπόστολος νόμον και λέγει λόγους υἱοῖς δούλου.

    a. Fully identified all words?
    b. Diagram this compound sentence.

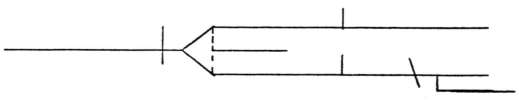

20. Ὑιοὶ ἀποστόλων λέγουσι λόγους καὶ λύουσι δούλους.

    a. What is the subject of λύουσι (compare No. 14)?
    b. Why no movable <u>nu</u> on λέγουσι and λύουσι (44)?

45.II   NEW TESTAMENT GREEK READING, Jn. 1.1-9

1. Locate all the second declension, masculine or neuter forms you
can in these verses. Identify them fully(gender, number, case
and lexical form) and look up their meaning in a lexicon if the
word is new to you.

ἀπεσταλμένος and ἐρχόμενον: participles which use second
declension endings (see para. 230).

φωτός. A third declension neuter noun φῶς (see 212).

2. As much as you can with your present information, explain the
functions of these nouns in their contexts by the case indicators.
Several which are presently beyond you are explained by paras.
81 and 85. Note, but don't linger.

3. What articles do you recognize (28; 63)?

46.1   The vocabulary of lesson V contains several words with obvious English derivatives or near derivatives (derived from other closely related Greek words).[1] Fill in the Greek words.

basilica

_____
Compare closely related
_____
cardiograph
Greek kappa becomes c in English
when derived through Latin.

doxology
_____+_____

ecclesiology
_____+_____

zoology
_____+_____
Contrast βίος, "the course of life;"
cf. biology.

parable
_____

phonology
_____+_____

psychology
_____+_____
Do you see why it is spelled with
"ps" and "y" and "ch" (review 1.2)?

Proper name, Aletheia
_____

46.2   Note the "alpha-privative" or "negative alpha" in ἀλήθεια, alpha + formation based on the root, λαθ, "conceal" = "the unconcealed." Compare English "amoral" with the related morpheme a-. See Lexical Aids, p. 47.

46.3   Note also the compound words:

ἐκκλησία: preposition ἐκ, "out of" + word formed on the root, καλ, "to call."

παραβολή: preposition παρά, "along side of" + word formed on root, βαλ, "to put," hence "something put along side (for comparison)."

48.1   Observe that three main paradigms for feminine first declension nouns are presented in this lesson, not four. Paragraphs 48 and 53 differ only in the length of the alpha in the N., A., and V. sg.

In this connection paragraph 50 can be misleading. The paragraph refers only to the long alpha in the paradigm of para. 48 not to the first declension in general. (Note the accent with acute on the long penult. Had the alpha been short, what accent would have been on the accented penult? para. 11, rule 4.)

_____

[1]Etymological information is available in such lexicons as Joseph H. Thayer's Greek-English Lexicon of the New Testament (Grand Rapids: Zondervan, 1962), a reprint of C. L. Grimm's Wilke's Clovis Novi Testament, 1862.

Notice that the nouns in para. 53 have short <u>alpha</u> in the N., A., and V. sg. Does the accent tell you that? It should (para. 11, rule 1).

Paragraphs 54 and 56 present the two additional patterns.

48.2   Of course, a noun belongs to only one of the three, depending on its nominative singular vowel (-α or -η) and its stem ending (para. 55 and 57).

The three sets are as follows:

Nouns with:
1.   Nominative singular -α preceded by a vowel or ρ (48 and 53).
2.   Nominative singular -α preceded by any consonant other than ρ (54-55).
3.   Nominative singular -η (56-57).

49.1   Compare the discussion here with para. 28. Listed <u>with</u> the stem vowels α/η of the first declension feminine nouns, the endings are:

	-α		-α after consonant except ρ		-η
	Sg.		Sg.		Sg.
N.	- α		- α		- η
G.	- ας		- ης		- ης
D.	- ᾳ		- ῃ		- ῃ
A.	- αν		- αν		- ην
V.	- α		- α		- η

	Pl.	
N.	- αι	
G.	- ων	
D.	- αις	
A.	- ας	
V.	- αι	

All three are:

What patterns do you see?

49.2   It will be helpful to compare the noun endings learned so far without the stem vowels to see the patterns they exhibit.

		1st declension	2nd declension	
		Feminine	Masculine	Neuter
Sg.	N.	– #	– ς	– ν
	G.	– ς	– ου	– ου
	D.	– $\bar{\ }_{.}$	– $\bar{\ }_{.}$	– $\bar{\ }_{.}$
	A.	– ν	– ν	– ν
	V.	– #	– #	– ν
Pl.	N.	– ι	– ι	– α
	G.	– $\bar{\ }$ν	– $\bar{\ }$ν	– $\bar{\ }$ν
	D.	– ις	– ις	– ις
	A.	– ας	– ους	– α
	V.	– ι	– ι	– α

What patterns do you see?

Note that the vowel differences in the singular patterns of the feminine first declension nouns do not alter the basic endings. E.g., length and iota subscripts remain the morphemes of the dative singular, whether –ᾳ or –ῃ (or –ῳ in the second declension).

51.1 What special rule for the accenting of first declension nouns is given here?

51.2 Comparing the accents of the paradigms in paras. 48 and 53. What endings appear always to have <u>long alpha</u> (review 11, the general rules of accent if you cannot tell)?

53.1 Note the link between the N., A., and V. sg. in vowel length.

54.1 Why does δόξα change to δόξης and δοξῃ (see 55)?

56.1 Why is γραφή accented with circumflex in the G. and D. sg. and pl. (see 58)?

59.1 Aids to exercise I, Lesson V.

General suggestions:

A. Continue full and accurate identification of <u>all</u> words.
Verbs: tense, voice, mood, person, number
Nouns: gender, case, number
   Also lexical forms in all cases must be known. Remember helpful abbreviations.

B. Review the parts of the sentence (30.4) if these are not clear by now. If any major questions exist in this regard see the instructor immediately.

C. Review the meanings of the cases (34-37), which, of course, remain the same in all the noun declensions, even though the morphemes signaling the cases may differ.

59.I

1. Ψυχὴ βλέπει ζωήν.

    a. What is the subject? How do you know (56, 34)?
    b. The object? How can you be sure (56, 34)?
    c. Why is the verb singular (29)?
    d. Diagram the Greek sentence (Cf. 45.I.6c).

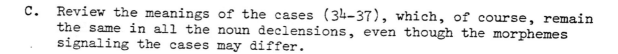

2. Βασιλεία γινώσκει ἀλήθειαν.

    a. Explain the accents of (para. 11, rules 1 and 3b):
         Βασιλεία
         ἀλήθειαν
    Recessive or retentive accent (14)?
    b. How do βασιλεία and ψυχή differ other than accent?
    c. Why can the sentence not be translated "He knows truth for a kingdom"?

3. Ἄνθρωπος γράφει ἐντολὰς καὶ νόμους.

    a. Compare ἐντολάς and νόμους.
    Both are 1.
             2.
    One is _____.
    The other is _____.
    b. Why do you identify ἐντολάς as F.A. pl. of ἐντολή and not F. G. sg.?
    Does νόμους help, too?
    c. Diagram (Cf. 45.I.6c):

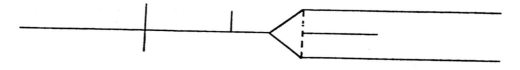

4. Ἀπόστολοι λαμβάνουσι δούλους καὶ δῶρα καὶ ἐκκλησίας.

    a. Compare δούλους, δῶρα and ἐκκλησίας.
       All three are 1.
                2.
       They differ in _____
    b. How do ἀπόστολοι and λαμβάνουσι agree (29)? _____.
    c. What prevents you from identifying δῶρα as F.N.sg. (33.4)?

       as N.N. pl.?

5. Ἀπόστολοι καὶ ἐκκλησίαι βλέπουσι ζωὴν καὶ θάνατον.

    a. Note the compound subject and compound object.
    b. What is the tense stem of βλέπουσι?
       What does it tell you (20.1)?
    c. -ι on ἀπόστολοι and ἐκκλησίαι signals what (49.2)?
    d. -ν on ζωήν and θάνατον signals what (49.2)?

6. Υἱὸς δούλου λέγει παραβολὴν ἐκκλησίᾳ.

    a. How is υἱός qualified?
    b. παραβολήν must have nominative singular -η. How do you know?
       Review the patterns in 48, 54 and 56 if you don't see it.
    c. Diagram (Cf 45.I.10). Note that qualifying words (genitives,
       adjectives, adverbs) are placed beneath the unit they qualify
       and are linked to that head of the construction.

| S. | V. | DO | IO |

7. Παραβολὴν λέγομεν καὶ ἐντολὴν καὶ νόμον.

    a. The subject of the sentence is _____
       How do you know (20.2)?
    b. Short variable vowel tells what about the mood (20.3)?
    c. παραβολήν, ἐντολήν, νόμον are all:
       1.
       2.
       They differ only in _____

8. Βασιλείας γινώσκετε καὶ ἐκκλησίας.

    a. βασιλείας . . . καὶ ἐκκλησίας is, of course, <u>formally</u> ambiguous, the words could be either:
         1.
    or
         2.
    What makes you settle on one of these?
    b. How do you know γινώσκετε is an <u>active</u> verb, not passive (20.2)? Present, not imperfect (20.1)? Indicative, not subjunctive (20.3)?

9. Ἐκκλησίαν διδάσκει ἀπόστολος καὶ βασιλείαν δοῦλος.

    a. Don't be fooled by the word order. Watch the morphemes. Case, not order, is the basic clue to function in the sentence.
    b. Translate ἐκκλησίαν διδάσκει ἀπόστολος.
    c. What has been <u>orthographically</u> omitted in the second clause, assuming the reader will supply the word: βασιλείαν [_____]δοῦλος ? Use parallel structure of clauses as the clue. If you have subject and object, what is assumed?

10. Νόμον καὶ παραβολὴν γράφει ἄνθρωπος ἐκκλησίᾳ.

    a. γράφει assumes a subject in the singular or in the plural? Why? This helps spot subject.
    b. ἐκκλήσιᾳ. Feminine dative singular; case signals what function (36)?
    -ᾳ on a noun means the nominative singular ends how (48, 53)?
    -ῃ could have nominative singular as either _____ or _____, depending on what (55, 57)?
    c. Note emphatic position of the object.
    d. Diagram (variation of No. 6 above):

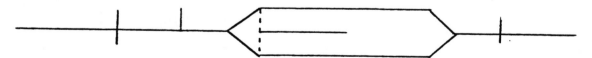

11. Καρδίαι ἀνθρώπων ἔχουσι ζωὴν καὶ εἰρήνην.

    a. Is καρδίαι singular or plural (40) _____? What else in the sentence would lead you to expect a plural subject (20)?
    b. How is καρδίαι modified?

c. Knowing only the form ἀνθρώπων you could not give its N. sg.? Why not?
In this case you must know the vocabulary to know the lexical form.
d. All identifications complete and translation given in good English?

12. Φωνὴ ἀποστόλων διδάσκει ψυχὰς δούλων.

a. Word order leads you to associate the genitive nouns with what other words?
b. How do you know ψυχάς is F.A. pl. and not F.G. sg.?
1. Form (56-57)?
2. Syntax (how the sentence goes together; function most likely)?
c. Is "the voice of the apostles" correct?
d. Diagram.
Remember to attach qualifiers to the "head of the construction" as in No. 6 above.

13. Ὥρα ἔχει δόξαν.

Contrast ὥρα and δόξαν in as many ways as you can (34, 46, 48, 55).

14. Φωναὶ ἐκκλησιῶν διδάσκουσι βασιλείας καὶ ἀνθρώπους.

a. ἐκκλησιῶν: explain the accent (58).
How can accent in this case be a clue to the form of the nom. sg. (cf. 55)?
b. Compare and contrast βασιλείας and ἀνθρώπους.

15. Βλέπεις δῶρα καὶ δόξαν.

a. Why can δῶρα not be the subject?
1.
2.
b. What is the subject and how are you certain (20.2)?

16. Γράφει ἐκκλησίᾳ λόγον ζωῆς.

    a. Ζωῆς modifies what? how?
       Cf. note on 45.I.17
    b. Subject named only where (20.2)?
    c. Diagram.

17. Λέγει καρδίαις ἀνθρώπων παραβολὴν καὶ νόμον.

    a. The indirect object is (30.4;36) _____?
    b. Why accented ἀνθρώπων with nom. sg. ἄνθρωπος
       (para. 11, rule 3a; para. 14)?
    c. Accusative sg. in -ην (παραβολήν) can only have
       _____ as nom. sg. (56, 58).

18. Γράφει ἐκκλησίᾳ υἱὸς ἀποστόλου.

    a. Γράφει: tense stem (20.1)? _____
              personal ending (20.2)? _____
    b. Is the subject named more specifically than in the personal
       ending?
    c. No direct object, so verb is <u>intransitive</u>, i.e., the action is
       <u>not</u> "carried across" to a specified direct object.

       "Γράφει λόγον" would be a transitive use of γράφω.

59.II   NEW TESTAMENT GREEK READING, Jn. 1.1-11

    Locate all the first declension, feminine nouns in Jn. 1.1-11. Identify
them fully and look up their meaning in a lexicon if the word is new to you.
Translate 1.1-2 and 4 (omit v. 3 for now).

    1.1 ἐν ἀρχῇ   Remember para. 81.

          ἦν   Imperfect, past tense, indicative, 3 sg.
                         of the verb, εἰμί, "I am;" here, "he/she/it was."

    1.4 ἐν αὐτῷ   "In Him," See paras. 81 and 96.

When translation notes are not given for items in the text, one of two situations
obtains.

    1. The item may be looked up as is in a standard Greek-English vocabu-
       lary.
    2. The student, with his present skill, should be able to analyze and
       look up the word.
    3. Read paras. 63-67 <u>before</u> attempting to translate.

Lesson VI

60.1 What vocabulary words do you spot with obvious English derivatives? Relate the following to the appropriate words in the vocabulary.

allomorph (=another form) _____

eschatology _____ + _____

"micro" words _____

exodus, odometer _____ + _____

"proto-" words _____

The proper name, Agatha _____

60.2 ἀγαθός, ή, όν, in general denotes essential goodness, as in a good character, while καλός, ή, όν, is frequently non-essential goodness, e.g., "attractive," "good looking," "suitable."

60.3 How would you have known that ἡ ἔρημος and ἡ ὁδός were feminine, though second declension nouns (28)?

61.1 The learning of these Greek adjectives and the article (63) provides an excellent opportunity for the reinforcement of one's mastery of first and second declension forms, since these are the endings used in the declension of the articles now to be learned. If you don't see that readily, check para. 31, 41, 48 and 56, and MEMORIZE them NOW, before going any farther.

62.1 Notice that adjectives may be distinguished in the vocabulary (60) by the fact that they are listed with the nominative singular form of the word in all genders: thus, ἀγαθός, ή, όν, and μικρός, ά, όν.

62.2 In the feminine adjective:

1. Nominative singular is _____ after a vowel or rho (much like feminine nouns of the first declension, para. 48.2)

2. Nominative singular is _____ after any consonant but rho (cf. 48.2 and 55).

62.3 How are adjectives accented?

63-65.1 You already know the masculine, feminine and neuter articles in the nominative singular from their use in the vocabularies to indicate noun gender.

63-65.2 Note any differences between the article and the first and second
declension endings you already know and secure the entire paradigm
in your mind.

66.1   Adjectives exhibit endings in all cases and genders in order to show
relationship to any noun in any conceivable number, gender, case combination. This formal signal of relationship is called grammatical agreement.
With the exception of the vocative, the same is true of the article.

66.2   What is illustrated by the examples in para. 66(1)?

by 66(2)?
and 66(3)?
What is specifically illustrated by 66(4)?
Para. 66(5) moves from the agreement of the article and its noun to
what point?

66.3   Observe carefully that agreement is a matter of "grammatical" corres-
pondence and not necessarily of similar appearance.

68.1   An attributive adjective attributes some characteristic directly to
the noun it qualifies (modifies). Illustrate from English.

68.2   A predicate adjective qualifies the noun it modifies by making a
predication, i.e., by predicating or making a statement about that
noun. It is equivalent, then, to the English subject complement or predicate
noun/adjective.

Illustrate from English.

69.1   Believe Machen!

70.1   A Greek attributive adjective is said to appear in the attributive
position and may either precede or follow the noun. In either case,
what is the characteristic mark of the attributive adjective with the definite
noun?

70.2   The article goes with the noun, of course, specifying it (not the adjective). But it also serves to tie the attributive adjective to its
noun and so must be repeated if that adjective follows the noun it modifies.
Illustrate: _____.

70.3   ὁ ἀγαθὸς ἄνθρωπος and ὁ ἄνθρωπος ὁ ἀγαθός are equivalent expressions
(allomorphs) but are not identical. Even though the translator cannot
show the difference, the interpreter will always note it (Cf. DM, pp. 151-152,
for more extended comment). In the first the adjective is more prominent; in
the second the emphasis is distributed more over both words.

71.1   The Greek predicate adjective is said to appear in the predicate position
and may also either precede or follow the noun about which it makes a
predication. In either case, what is the characteristic feature of the predicate adjective with the definite noun?

71.2   Observe that a noun plus a predicate adjective <u>constitutes a full
        sentence</u>, a predication. As in many languages the verb "to be" (which
can also be written in Greek) is understood here, but omitted from the text,
making a "verbless clause."

74.1   Observe that 70.1 and 71.1 refer to the attributive and predicate ad-
        jectives <u>with the definite noun</u>. Why, according to para. 74, was that
qualification given?

74.2   If one cannot <u>formally</u> distinguish the predicate and attributive ad-
        jective when they appear with an <u>indefinite</u> noun, how then is one to
tell the difference and decide upon a translation?

75.1   Relate the <u>substantive</u> adjective to the attributive adjective (70) of
        which it is simply an extension. The substantive adjective attributes
characteristics to an <u>unexpressed noun</u> in the same way an attributive adjective
modifies a written noun. The substantive adjective virtually stands in place
of that unexpressed noun and takes its name from the fact that nouns are "sub-
stantives."

75.2   Observe that no <u>specific</u> noun can be supplied by the substantive ad-
        jective, except in a very clear context. Some general noun, easily
deduced from the gender and number of the adjective must usually be understood.
Illustrate from the examples in 75.

75.3   Observe also from the illustrations that this use of the adjective is
        also common to English.

76.1   Aids to the exercises, Lesson VI
        General observations

        A. By now the process of complete identification of all forms should
            be a habit. If it isn't, either acquire it now or forget about
            learning the language (23.3; 45.1, <u>B</u>).

        B. Make sure you understand the difference between the attributive
            and predicate uses of the Greek adjective (70 and 71) and how to
            distinguish them by their characteristic syntactic clues.

76.I   Aids to Exercise I, Lesson VI.

        1. ἀγαθή ἡ ἐκκλησία καὶ ἡ βασιλεία κακή.

            a. How can you be certain that ἀγαθή and κακή modify
                ἡ ἐκκλησία and ἡ βασιλεία respectively (66).
            b. Are they attributive (70.1-2) or predicate (71.1-2) adjectives?
                How can you tell?
            c. Diagram the compound sentence as follows:

76.I.1.c. (continued)

PA = predicate adjective. Note the slanted line does not intersect
the base as does the sign for the indirect object.

2. ἡ κακὴ καρδία τῶν ἀνθρώπων γινώσκει θάνατον.

    a. κακή modifies what noun? _____

       How do you know (66)?

    b. Is κακή modifying ἡ καρδία by <u>attribution</u> or <u>predication</u>

       (making a full statement) (70.1-2; 71.1-2)? _____

       How can you tell?

    c. "Of the bad men" would have been τῶν _____

       ἀνθρώπων.

3. οἱ ἀπόστολοι βλέπουσι τοὺς μικροὺς οἴκους κὰι τὰς κακὰς ὁδούς.

    a. Are μικρούς and κακάς functioning as attributive or predicate
       adjectives?
       What gives the clue?

    b. τὰς κακὰς ὁδούς illustrates what point (66.3)?

    c. Why the plural verb (29)?

4. οἱ δοῦλοι οἱ κακοὶ λύουσι τὸν οἶκον τοῦ ἀποστόλου.

    a. οἱ κακοί must modify οἱ δοῦλοι. Why (66)?

    b. Is it attributive or predicative (70-71)?

    c. Compare with a possible οἱ κακοὶ δοῦλοι (70.3).

    d. Explain the accents of δοῦλοι and οἶκον (para. 11, rule 4).
       λύουσι (para. 11, rule 1 and para. 13).
       ἀποστόλου (para. 11, rule 3b).

    e. Diagram

5. οἱ κακοὶ λύουσι τὸ ἱερόν.

    a. Verb fully identified (23.3B)?
    b. οἱ κακοί: identified fully by gender, case, and number?
    c. Is κακός, ή, όν a noun or a word that modifies or qualifies nouns?
    d. In what use does the adjective modify an unexpressed noun (75.1)? In what sense is this an "extension" of the attributive use?
    e. Are "the wicked" here men or women? How do you know (75.2)?

6. ὁ κύριος τῆς ζωῆς ἐγείρει τοὺς νεκρούς

    a. Good place to start identifications is with the verb, since it will tell you what person and number to expect in the subject and whether to expect a direct object or not.
    b. Why is ὁ the article with κύριος and not ἡ or τό (66)?
    c. τοὺς νεκρούς modifies what "noun" (75.1-2)?
    d. ὁ κύριος is modified how (in addition to the article)? See note on sentence 45.I.17.

7. οἱ λόγοι τῆς ἀληθείας διδάσκουσι τοὺς ἄλλους ἀποστόλους.

    a. How can you be confident in identifying οἱ λόγοι as the subject of διδάσκουσι (34; 29)?
    b. Why must ἄλλους be related to τοὺς ... ἀποστόλους (66)? Why related _attributively_ (68.1 and especially 70.1-2)?
    c. ἀληθείας could formally be either G. sg. or A. pl. What does the context dictate (33.4)? How does the article help decide this? Is it ambiguous, (63)?
    d. Full identifications of every word? Smooth translation?

8. οἱ δίκαιοι λαμβάνουσι τὰ δῶρα τοῦ κυρίου τὰ καλά.

    a. Again, probably best to start identification with verb for the several clues it can give.
    b. Why must οἱ δίκαιοι be a substantive use of the adjective (75.1-2)?
    c. What adjective modifies τὰ δῶρα? How do you know (66)? Attributively or predicately (70.1-2)?

9. ὁ κακὸς βλέπει τὴν ἔρημον καὶ τοὺς ἐσχάτους οἴκους.

    a. Contrast the uses of the two adjectives in the sentence
       (70.1-2; 75.1).
    b. Remember to look for grammatical agreement and not necessarily
       similar appearance (τὴν ἔρημον; para. 60)

10. πρῶτοι οἱ δοῦλοι· ἔσχατοι οἱ κύριοι.

    a. Is πρῶτοι an adjective or noun (60)?
    b. Is it modifying οἱ δοῦλοι attributively (70.1-2), predicatively
       (71.1-2) or substantively (75.1)?
       Why so?
    c. Would οἱ δοῦλοι πρῶτοι be equivalent or quite different
       (71.1 on word order)?

11. τῇ ἐκκλησίᾳ τῇ μικρᾷ γράφει ὁ κύριος λόγον ἀγαθόν.

    a. Sentence begins with what grammatical unit, τῇ . . . μικρᾷ
       (36)?
    b. Why is the article repeated in this construction (70.2)?
    c. Note λόγον ἀγαθόν.
       In spite of the caution in 74, and 74.1-2, the predicate ad-
       jective construction will be in the nominative case, almost with-
       out exception.

12. τοὺς πιστοὺς βλέπει ὁ πιστός.

    a. How do you know that the subject of the act is "the faithful
       (one, man, person)" whereas the "the faithful" as direct object
       must be "the faithful (ones, men, persons)" (75.2)?
    b. How are the adjectives used here (75)?

13. ἔσχατοι οἱ δοῦλοι οἱ κακοί· πρῶτοι οἱ υἱοὶ οἱ ἀγαθοί

    a. In the first clause as in the second, what clue distinguishes
       the <u>differing</u> use of the two adjectives (70.2; 71.2)?
    b. Explain the accents of πρῶτοι, κακοί, and μικρᾷ (in No. 11)
       See paras. 11-13 if necessary and also 51 and 61).

14. ὁ υἱὸς τοῦ ἐσχάτου ἀδελφοῦ βλέπει τὰς καλὰς ἐκκλησίας τοῦ κυρίου.

    a. τοῦ ἐσχάτου ἀδελφοῦ could just as well be stated as
                    _____ (70.3).
    b. What two facts make you identify ἐκκλησίας as F. A. pl. (not
          G. sg.)? Check article.

15. ἄλλην παραβολὴν λέγομεν τῇ κακῇ βασιλείᾳ.

    Compare 76.I.11, note c.

16. πρώτη ἡ ἐκκλησία· ἐσχάτη ἡ ἄλλη βασιλεία.

    a. πρώτη: why not attributive (70-71)?
    b. Why not πρῶτα as F. N. sg. (62.2)?
          Same on ἄλλη.

17. ταῖς πισταῖς λέγει ὁ κύριος παραβολὴν καλὴν καὶ τοῖς πιστοῖς.

    a. ταῖς πισταῖς must be linked with _____
          as a compound _____.
    b. Why are both of these parts stated do you suppose?
    c. Diagram

18. ὁ ἀγαθὸς γράφει ἀγαθα· ὁ κακὸς κακά.

    a. Can κακά be related to ὁ κακός as a predicate adjective?
          Why not (66)?
    b. What has been omitted, and what part of the sentence, then, is
          κακά (see para. 59.I.9)?

19. ἀγαθὸς ὁ δοῦλος καὶ λέγει καλά.

20. ἡ ἀλήθεια πιστὴ καὶ ἡ ὥρα κακή.

    See para 75 for any troubles.

76.II   NEW TESTAMENT GREEK READING, Jn. 1.1-11

Review Jn. 1.1-11 with special attention to the definite articles, both their presence and their absence.

Translate Jn. 1.3 and 5

1.3   πάντα

"All things," (365). Subject of the singular verb here (145).

δι'

Short form of διά (85)

ἐγένετο

"Came into existence." Aorist (past tense) indicative, 3 sg., of the verb, γίνομαι, "I become, come into existence."

On the meaning of the aorist tense, see paras. 167-169, but don't worry about mastery now.

χωρίς

"Without." preposition with genitive.

οὐδὲ ἕν

"Not even one thing"

ὃ γέγονεν

"Which is come into existence"

1.5   τὸ φῶς

Third declension noun, N. N. sg., "the light" (212).

αὐτό

"It," i.e., the light. N.A. sg., (96)

οὐ

Negative, "no, not"

κατέλαβεν

"(did not) overcome" Second aorist (past tense) active indicative (193), 3 sg., of καταλαμβάνω, "I grasp, seize," either in the sense of "I understand" or "I overcome."

77.1   Use the obvious English derivatives from the vocabulary to help fix the Greek word in your mind.

77.2   Note also:

βάλλω	ballistic
λίθος	lithography, monolith
οὐρανός	Uranus (via Latin)
τόπος	Utopia οὐ τόπος
εἰς	eisegesis
ἐκ, ἐξ	exegesis
διά	diagram
μετά	metathesis

79.1   There is no new information here with respect to the names or the functions of the case endings. The forms are new and should be learned at once. (Compare the forms in chapter V.)

79.2   Note that the first declension masculine nouns have tau (-τ) before all their declensional endings (including the stem vowel in the ending). Thus -της, -του, -τῃ, -την, etc.

Just as in the case of ὁ προφήτης and ὁ μαθητής, nouns of this type (i.e., first declension masculine nouns) will be occupational. They will name a person characterized by a certain action, "a prophet" (built on the verb "to prophecy"), "a disciple" (built on the verb "to learn"). ὁ βαπτιστής, then, would mean what? Cf. CEG, p. 19; Lexical Aids, p. 42.

79.3   In the vocabulary, or in a context, what would identify nouns like προφήτης as masculine forms (28, 66)?

80.1   Recall correct English is "to him" "with him" (preposition and object in objective case; see para. 30.2) not "to he/his" or "with he/his." The "object" of a preposition is the word whose main function in the sentence is to be related to another word by that preposition (i.e., it does not also function as subject or object of the sentence itself).

·81. and 86.1
        The Greek preposition (1), the case demanded by the preposition (2), and the preposition's meaning with that case (3), must be learned as a unit, "ἐν-with-the dative: 'in,'" "εἰς-with-the-accusative: 'into.'"

82.1   Make a list of the prepositions, relating as far as possible their meanings to the basic ideas of the cases given in 82. Not all will make sense from your present vantage point.

85.1   How do the prepositions ἐκ, ἐν, εἰς, and ἀπό differ from διά, μετά?

85.2   In the case of διά and μετά (and others like them), both meanings must be carefully learned and related to the correct case (cf. 86).

87.1   Label the graph below, correlating the proper prepositions-case unit with the relationship designated by the graph. More prepositions will be added later.[1] Not all prepositions to be learned are so readily diagramed.

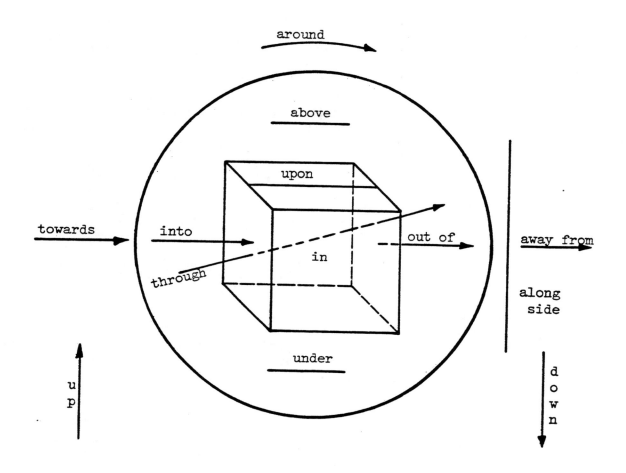

[1]Adapted from Lexical Aids, p. 80, and used with the permission of the author.

38

89.I. Aids to exercise I, Lesson VII.
Reread 23:1; 45.I.B.

1. οἱ μαθηταὶ τῶν προφητῶν μένουσιν ἐν τῷ κόσμῳ.

    a. All forms fully identified? Their function in the sentence located?
    b. Why the masculine nominative plural article, οἱ, with μαθηταί (66, 78-79)?
    c. "ἐν-with-the-dative" means what (77, 86)?
    d. ἐν τῷ κόσμῳ is a prepositional phrase. It modifies the verb by telling _____ the action "μένουσιν" is occurring. Show that adverbial function in a diagram as follows:

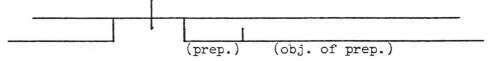

                  (prep.)   (obj. of prep.)

2. οἱ κακοὶ βάλλουσιν λίθους εἰς τὸν οἶκον τῶν μαθητῶν.

    a. οἱ κακοί: what use of the adjective (75)?
       What function in the sentence?
    b. Why connect τον οἶκον with εἰς as a prepositional phrase (77, 81, 86)?
       Why not make it the direct object of βάλλουσιν (33.4)?
    c. What information does the prepositional phrase give?
       Modifies what word in the clause?

3. ὁ θεὸς πέμπει τοὺς ἀγγέλους εἰς τὸν κόσμον.

    a. τοὺς ἀγγέλους εἰς τὸν οἶκον. The nouns on both sides of the preposition εἰς are accusative. Since the preposition normally <u>precedes</u> its object, connect τὸν οἶκον with εἰς and seek another function for τοὺς ἀγγέλους.
    b. Diagram.

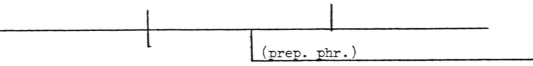

                             (prep. phr.)

4. ὁ προφήτης πέμπει τοὺς μαθητας τοῦ κυρίου ἐκ τῶν οἴκων εἰς τὴν ἐκκλησίαν.

    a. ὁ προφήτης/τοὺς μαθητάς. Make sure the first and second declension endings are clear to you, in order to avoid confusion on constructions like these.

    b. Why relate τῶν οἴκων with ἐκ (77,85)?

    c. The prepositional phrases are _____

    and _____; they qualify what other word in the sentence?

5. ὁ θεὸς ἐγείρει τοὺς νεκροὺς ἐκ θανάτου.

    a. τοὺς νεκρούς: what use of the adjective (75.1-2)? What function in the sentence?

    b. How do you know (34)?

6. λαμβάνετε τὰ καλὰ δῶρα ἀπὸ τῶν τέκνων.

    a. τὰ καλὰ δῶρα: what use of the adjective (70)?

    b. How else could the attributive construction be phrased (70 and 70.3)?

    c. Verb fully identified and understood (ch. III and 23.3)?

    d. Can ἀπό be used with any other case (81)?

7. ἄγομεν τὰ τέκνα ἐκ τῶν οἴκων.

8. μετὰ τοὺς ἀγγέλους πέμπει ὁ θεὸς τὸν υἱόν.

    a. The prepositional phrase is in "emphatic" position, but as elsewhere, other word orders are possible. In this case you can translate acceptably preserving <u>some</u> of the Greek order and emphasis.

    b. μετά here means "after" (85-86), not "with;" why? In the NT, μετά with the accusative expresses <u>time</u>, more than <u>place</u>.

VII
89.I.9

9. μετὰ τῶν ἀγγέλων ἄγει ὁ κύριος τοὺς δικαίους εἰς τὸν οὐρανόν.

    a. All forms <u>fully</u> identified?
    b. τοὺς δικαίους: what use of the adjective here (75)?
       What function in the sentence?
       How do you know (30.3; 34)?
    c. Diagram:

10. διὰ τῶν ὁδῶν τῆς ἐρήμου φέρουσιν οἱ δοῦλοι τὰ δῶρα εἰς ἄλλον τόπον.

    a. Why take τῆς with ἐρήμου (other than word order; 60.3)?
    b. Is ἄλλον τόπον an attributive or predicative construction
       (70, 71 and 74)? Only one (70) makes sense here.
    c. διὰ τῶν ὁδῶν modifies _____ by telling _____.

11. διὰ τῶν γραφῶν τῶν προφητῶν γινώσκομεν τὸν κύριον.

    a. διά-with-the-genitive means _____.
    b. What information does the prepositional phrase give in this
       sentence?
    c. Indicative verb? How do you know (17.3; 70.3)? Active?
       How do you know (20.2)?

12. διὰ τὴν δόξαν τοῦ θεοῦ ἐγείρει ὁ κύριος τοὺς νεκρούς.

    a. Why -αν on δόξαν (and not -ην)(48.2; 49.1)?
    b. Contrast the use of διά in Nos. 11 and 12 (85).

13. φέρουσιν τοὺς νεκροὺς εἰς τὴν ἔρημον.

    a. Fully identify and diagram:

(Where is the prep. phrase to be attached and why? See 1.d.)

41

14. οἱ μαθηταὶ διδάσκουσι τὰ ἀγαθὰ τέκνα ἐν τῇ ἐκκλησια.

    a. τὰ ἀγαθὰ τέκνα could also be expressed how (70.1-<u>3</u>)?
    b. Why call ἐν τῇ ἐκκλησία a "prepositional phrase of location?"

15. ὁ κύριος λέγει παραβολὴν τοῖς μαθηταῖς ἐν τῷ ἱερῷ.

    Are all these endings familiar to you? If not, immediate review
    is imperative.

ὁ κύριος	(ch. IV)	τοῖς μαθηταῖς, ἐν τῷ ἱερῷ
λέγει	(ch. III)	(chs. IV and VII)
παραβολήν	(ch. V)	

16. διὰ τὴν ἀλήθειαν βλέπουσιν οἱ προφῆται τὸν θάνατον.

    a. Does διὰ τὴν ἀλήθειαν give the <u>cause</u> or the <u>agency</u> of
       βλέπουσι (85)?
       Do you understand the question? If not, ask the instructor.
    b. Explain the accent on the subject (79, 11, rule 4), προφῆται.

17. ἀπό τῆς ἐρήμου ἄγουσιν οἱ μαθηταὶ τοὺς ἀγαθοὺς δούλους καὶ τοὺς
    υἱοὺς τῶν προφητῶν πρὸς τοὺς μικροὺς οἴκους τῶν μαθητῶν.

    a. The syntactic units here are the verb, subject, object (and any
       modifiers), and the two prepositional phrases. Separate these
       from one another by brackets and put them together again one
       by one, in an appropriate translation. Breaking the sentence
       up into its units simplifies the analysis considerably.
    b. ἀπό -with-the-genitive means _____. πρός-with-the-
       accusative means _____. What is their function here?
    c. ἀγαθούς: used attributively or predicatively (70-71)?
       How do you know?

18. διὰ τὴν βασιλείαν τοῦ θεοῦ φέρομεν τὰ κακά.

    a. διά gives the cause or the agent here (85)? How do you know?
    b. τὰ κακά modifies an unexpressed noun deduced from what (75.1-2)?

19. διὰ τὰς ψυχὰς τῶν ἀδελφῶν βλέπει κακά.

    a. τὰς ψυχάς is <u>not</u> F. G. sg. How do you know (53, 56)? What is it?

    b. Compare κακά with τὰ κακά (No. 18). How used here (75)?

20. καλὸς ὁ οὐρανός· κακὸς ὁ κόσμος.

The anarthrous (=without the article) adjective modifying a definite noun signals _____ use of the adjective (71.1-2).

89.II   NEW TESTAMENT GREEK READING, Jn.1.1-11

In light of paras. 80-87 analyze the prepositional phrases in these verses. Include χωρίς (v. 3), παρά (v. 6) and περί (vs. 7, 8).

Review your translation of 1.1-5 and translate 1.6-7

1.6 ἐγένετο	"There was," or "There came." See 76.II on Jn.1.3 and para. 522 also.
ἀπεσταλμένος	"Sent." an adjectival participle of the verb ἀποστέλλω. Modifies ἄνθρωπος.
ὄνομα	"A name," N. N. sg., of ὄνομα, -ματος (222).
1.7 ἦλθεν	"(He) came." Second aorist (past) active indicative 3 sg., ἔρχομαι, "I come." Remember paras. 167-169?
ἵνα	Find in NTGFB, p. 261.
(ἵνα) μαρτυρήσῃ	"(That) he might bear witness." Aorist active subjunctive, 3 sg., of μαρτυρέω, "I bear witness." See paras. 269.5 and 286.
πάντες	See para. 365. What function here (34)?
πιστεύσωσιν	"(They) might believe." Aorist active subjunctive, 3 pl., of πιστεύω, "I believe."

90.1   Learn the pronoun paradigms (para. 94-96) as part of the vocabulary study of this chapter.

91.1   Define postpositive.

92.1   What is an enclitic?

92.2   What is a proclitic and how is it accented?

93.1   The accenting of enclitics can be simplified greatly if one will conceive of the accents as having an "accent force" capable of "carrying" the pronunciation of the word and its enclitic for a certain number of syllables, something like the "domain" of the accents (11.1).

Thus conceived, the grave has no accent force, the circumflex has a two-syllable accent force, and the acute a three-syllable accent force. So, even in a single word, the acute may stand as far back as the antepenult, the circumflex only as far back as the penult (11).

93.2   Starting with this rather concrete (and, one may also say unscientific) visualization of the accents and their "accent force," accent any word-enclitic pronunciation unit as follows.

1. Treat the word and its enclitic as a single unit and accent the first word as usual. Then count the syllables, beginning at the accent.

    1 2 3 4   1 2 3
    ὁ ἄν/θρω/πος/μου   ὁ δοῦ/λος/μου

2. If there is an "overload" on the "accent force," there is one cure: accent the ultima with the acute. ("Accent overload:" the acute is carrying more than three syllables, or the circumflex is carrying more than two.)

    1 2 3 4   1 2 3
    ὁ ἄν/θρω/πός/μου   ὁ/δοῦ/λός/μου

3. Change no acutes to grave with an enclitic following. Accent the first of two succeeding enclitics (or enclitic-proclitic) with acute on the ultima.

4. Notice Machen's para. 92.II.(2) on emphasis by accent.

94-95.1   ἡμεῖς ("we") and ὑμεῖς ("you" pl.) are easily confused. Associating υ- in ὑμεῖς ("you") with English "you" (somewhat inaccurately) may help fix their meaning in mind.

94-95.2   Comparing 33.2 and 61 with the paradigms to be learned in this chapter, observe all the parallels and contrasts you possibly can to aid you in the memorization of the personal pronouns. Notice the iota in the dative, and -ας in the accusative plural.

94-95.3 Observe that the first and second person pronouns do not distinguish gender as the third person pronoun does.

97.1 What is the function of a pronoun? Illustrate.

97.2 What is an antecedent? Illustrate.

97.3 What feature of pronoun form assists in identification of its antecedent?

97.4 Think your way through all of Machen's examples on pp. 48-49. If you do not fully understand them, review para. 94-97. Ask the instructor if your confusion persists.

97.5 Why does the pronoun not agree with its antecedent in case as well as gender and number (see 97(3b))?

Notice: the pronoun gets its case from its own function in the sentence, not from its antecedent.

97.6 A personal pronoun in the nominative case almost always indicates _____(97(4)), caused by contrasting subjects.

97.7 Note "the word of me" = "my word." Frequently the noun qualified by the genitive and so specified by it, will be rendered sufficiently specific as to attract the Greek article.

97.8 After prepositions, μου, μοι and με should be ____, ____, and ____; σου, σοι, and σε should be ____, ____, and ____ (95).

98.1 Learn the present indicative of εἰμί. This is not normally called active, because it is the statement of a present condition/state, not an action.

99.1 The Greek predicate nominative is comparable to English:
   "I (subjective) am he/she (subjective also)," but not
   "I (subjective) am him/her (objective case)."

So also in Greek, the noun or adjective related to the subject by εἰμί will agree with that subject in case and number (and gender if possible). This will usually mean a predicate in the nominative case to agree with the subject.

99.2 Notice the only formal difference between the predicate adjective (71.1-2) and the adjective with εἰμί is the actual presence of the verb.

"The apostle is good." ὁ ἀπόστολος (ἐστιν) ἀγαθός.

The statements are virtually equivalent, though the presence of the verb allows more precision in the designation of the tense and mood than the verbless clause where these are understood from context.

99.3   <u>Identity/character</u> <u>signalled</u> <u>by</u> <u>article's presence/absence</u>. The example in para. 99.2 well illustrates a very important item in Greek syntax.

     (a)   <u>Articular</u> constructions <u>specify</u> or identify.

         ὁ ἀπόστολος (ἐστιν) ὁ ἀγαθός.   "The apostle is the good man."

     (b)   <u>Anarthrous</u> constructions <u>characterize</u> or describe.

         ὁ ἀπόστολος (ἐστιν) ἀγαθός.   "The apostle is a good man."

Note carefully that in the sentence under (a), the <u>articular</u> ὁ ἀγαθός <u>specifies which man</u> is the apostle, namely "the good one." In the sentence under (b), on the other hand, the <u>anarthrous</u> ἀγαθός <u>describes the kind</u> of a man the apostle is, namely "a good man," as opposed to a bad man or tall man. For more information see CEG, p. 22 and DM, pp. 137-140, 149.

100.1   Warm up review for the exercises. Don't skip this!

    Be able to define the following and explain their use briefly.

nominative (34)	active (17.2)
genitive (35)	mood (17.3)
dative (36)	indicative (17.3)
accusative (34)	person (19)
vocative (37)	subject (30.5)
tense (17.1)	object (30.5)
present (17.1)	indirect object (30.5)
voice (17.2)	

If there is <u>any</u> hesitation on the answers to these, check your answer with the paragraphs cited. These must be "stock-in-trade" items by now.

Full identifications continue to be important for <u>every</u> word. Abbreviated identifications are excellent for this continuing <u>discipline</u>.

100.I.　Aids to exercise I, Lesson VIII

1.　οἱ μαθηταί σου γινώσκουσι τὴν βασιλείαν καὶ ἄγουσι τοὺς
ἀδελφοὺς αὐτῶν εἰς αὐτήν.

　　　a.　οἱ μαθηταί σου: explain the accent of this unit (93.1-2).
　　　b.　What qualifies τοὺς ἀδελφούς? How?
　　　c.　αὐτῶν: why masculine plural (97(3))? Why genitive (97.5)?
　　　　　To what does this pronoun refer back (= antecedent) _____?
　　　d.　αὐτήν: Why feminine singular (97(3))? Why accusative (97.5;
　　　　　81)?
　　　e.　Note that frequently the word qualified by the genitive is
　　　　　thus made specific enough to require an article; so in both
　　　　　cases here (cf. 97(5) and 97.7).

2.　διδάσκω τοὺς ἀδελφούς μου καὶ λέγω αὐτοῖς παραβολήν.

　　　a.　τοὺς ἀδελφούς μου: explain the accent (93.1-2).
　　　b.　αὐτοῖς: identify. Why this gender and number (97(3))?
　　　　　Why this case (97.5)?
　　　　　Antecedent (97.2)?
　　　　　What function does this pronoun have in the sentence (36)?

3.　ἄγει με ὁ κύριος πρὸς τοὺς μαθητὰς αὐτοῦ.

　　　a.　με: identify fully. What function in the sentence (34)?
　　　b.　τοὺς μαθητὰς: why not τάς (78-79)?

4.　δι᾽ ἐμὲ βλέπεις σὺ τὸν θάνατον, σοὶ δὲ ἐγὼ λέγω λόγους κακούς.

　　　a.　Why "emphatic" ἐμέ (97.8)?
　　　b.　Why δι᾽ instead of διά? Did you catch the footnote on NTGFB,
　　　　　p. 49?
　　　c.　Would βλέπεις σύ normally accent the σύ? Why (95, bottom)?
　　　　　What apparently is implied by the presence of the pronoun?
　　　　　Note the contrasting subject in clause two (97(4b)).

5.　διὰ σοῦ ἄγει ὁ θεὸς τοὺς πιστοὺς εἰς τὴν βασιλείαν αὐτοῦ καὶ
δι᾽ αὐτῶν τοὺς ἄλλους.

　　　a.　διὰ σοῦ: cause or agency (85)?
　　　b.　Adjectives are used how here (75)?
　　　c.　αὐτοῦ: why masculine singular (97(3))?
　　　　　What function signaled by the genitive (35; 97.5)?
　　　　　Antecedent?

47

    d. αὐτῶν: What is the antecedent? How do you know (97.2-3)?
    e. What parts of the first clause are ellided in the second clause, and therefore to be assumed?

6. δι᾽ ἡμᾶς μένει ὁ κύριος ἐν τῷ κόσμῳ.

    a. Footnote on NTGFB, p. 49?
    b. Singular of ἡμᾶς would be _____.

7. ἐγὼ εἰμὶ δοῦλος, σὺ δὲ ἀπόστολος.

    a. Why δοῦλος, not δοῦλον (99 and 99.1)?
    b. Verb identified (98)?
       What is assumed in clause two?

8. ἀγαθός ἐστιν ὁ κύριος καὶ ἀγαθοί ἐστε ὑμεῖς.

    a. Explain the enclitic accents (or lack of accent).
    b. Would the statements be greatly altered by omission of the εἰμί verbs here (99.2)?
    c. Why nominatives ἀγαθός and ἀγαθοί (99.1)?
    d. Diagram

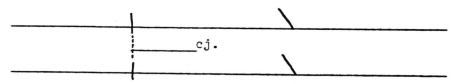

9. μαθηταί ἐστε τοῦ κυρίου καὶ ἀδελφοὶ τῶν ἀποστόλων αὐτοῦ.

    a. Subject is _____.
    b. αὐτοῦ: antecedent is _____ (97.3).
    c. Notice: anarthrous (without the article) μαθηταί speaks of the <u>kind</u> of person "you" are, namely a disciple and not an apostle. See 99.3 again.
    d. Diagram

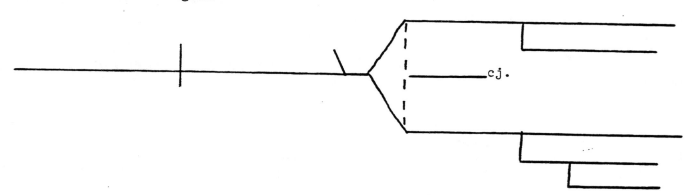

10.　ὁ ἀπόστολος πιστός ἐστιν, οἱ δὲ δοῦλοι αὐτοῦ κακοί.

    a.　What is the main formal difference between the two clauses (99.2)?
    b.　Why do you relate πιστός to ὁ ἀπόστολος (66)?
       What is that relationship here (99.1)?
    c.　αὐτοῦ: antecedent?

11.　ἡ ἐκκλησία πιστή ἐστιν, ἡμεῖς δὲ βλέπομεν αὐτήν

    a.　ἡμεῖς has what function in the sentence? How do you know (34 and 97(4b))?
    b.　αὐτήν: antecedent? Why accusative (97.5)?

12.　βλέπομέν σε καὶ λέγομέν σοι παραβολήν.

    a.　Contrast σε and σοι (95).
    b.　Explain the enclitic accents in the sentence (93.1-2).

      βλέ/πο/μέν/σε　　　　　　　　　λέ/γο/μέν/σοι

    c.　παραβολήν: what other first declension nouns follow the same paradigm (56, 46)?
    d.　Variable vowel, short o, tells what (20.3)?

13.　δοῦλοι ἐσμέν, δούλους δὲ διδάσκομεν.

    a.　Significance of the word order?
    b.　Why is ἐσμέν accented (92.II.(2))?

14.　οἱ δοῦλοι ἡμῶν βλέπουσιν ἡμᾶς, ἡμεῖς δὲ διδάσκομεν αὐτούς.

    a.　Identified ἡμῶν, ἡμᾶς and ἡμεῖς?
       Why are they in these cases (97.5)?
    b.　Antecedent of αὐτούς? How do you know (97.2-3)?
    c.　Note as elsewhere, the noun defined by the genitive of possession often becomes specific enough to require the article (97(5) and 97.7)

15. ἀφ'ὑμῶν λαμβάνει ὁ ἀδελφός μου δῶρα καλά, καὶ πέμπει αὐτὰ πρός με διὰ τῶν δούλων αὐτοῦ.

    a. Why ἀφ'instead of ἀπό?
       See footnotes on NTGFB, pp. 49 and 51.
    b. δῶρα καλά: attributive or predicative (70, 71)?
    c. αὐτά: identify carefully and find the antecedent (97.2-3).
       Don't confuse αὐτά and αὐτή (96).

16. γινώσκομεν τὴν ὁδόν, καὶ δι' αὐτῆς ἄγομέν σε εἰς τὸν οἶκον ἡμῶν.

    a. Note the gender of τὴν ὁδόν (60.3).
    b. Antecedent of αὐτῆς? Why feminine (97(3))?
    c. Accent of ἄγομέν (93.1-2)?

17. μετὰ τῶν ἀδελφῶν ἡμῶν βλέπομεν τοὺς μαθητὰς τοῦ κυρίου ἡμῶν.

    a. μετά-with-genitive means _____; modifies _____
       by telling _____.
    b. τοῦ κυρίου modifies what? ἡμῶν modifies what?
    c. Antecedent of ἡμῶν?

18. μετὰ τὰς ἡμέρας τὰς κακὰς βλέπομεν τὴν βασιλείαν τοῦ κυρίου ἡμῶν.

The object of μετά could also have been phrased how (70.1-3)?

19. ΜΕΘ ΗΜΩΝ ΒΛΕΠΕΙΣ ΑΥΤΟΝ.

Review para. 1 if necessary. Notice the footnote on ἡμῶν along with 97(6).

20. μεθ' ὑμῶν ἐσμὲν ἐν τοῖς οἴκοις ὑμῶν.

100.II   NEW TESTAMENT GREEK READING, John 1.1-11

Review these verses and study the personal pronouns. Identify their gender, number and case, and, where possible (some are beyond you now), their function in the sentence.

Translate Jn. 1.8-9

1.8   τὸ φῶς

Predicate noun, in nominative case following the verb, "I am;" ἦν from εἰμί; see above on this.
Look up if still unfamiliar with meaning.

ἐκεῖνος

Look up meaning. Declined like ἄλλος, η, ο. See para. 104 on use.
Why not translate, "He was not that light?"

ἀλλ'

A form of the conjunction, ἀλλά para. 108. A strong "but." On the loss of the final alpha before the vowel, in ἵνα, see NTGFB, p. 49, n.1.

ἵνα. . . φωτός

See notes on 1.7, same clause.

1.9   ἦν

Review paras. 133 and 98-99.

τὸ φῶς τὸ ἀληθινον

Look up ἀληθινός, ή, όν. The article and adjective with φῶς should aid in identifying it (66).

How is the adjective used here (72)?

ὃ φωτίζει

"Which lights, illuminates." Relative clause modifying τὸ φῶς, introduced by the neuter sg. relative pronoun, ὃ (395, 397) to tie it to that neuter word.

πάντα

See paras. 365, 369. Modifies ἄνθρωπος; how do you know?

ἐρχόμενον

"Coming." Present participle., introducing a participle construction whose relation to the context is a matter of some question among scholars. Check various translations to see how it is treated. We will return to this clause when you can analyze it yourself and make a decision. On the form see para. 230, if you wish.

Lesson IX

101.1 Give the Greek vocabulary words from which the following English terms are derived.

    hamartiology _____   evangel _____
    baptize   _____

101.2 Note the positive prefix ευ-. Thus, ευ + αγγελιον "good news." Cf. εὐλογία, εὐδοκία, and "ευ-" words in English. Cf. Lexical Aids, p. 47.

101.3 There are several adverbs in the vocabulary. What is an "ad-verb"? Check a dictionary if you do not know. Ask the instructor if mystery remains. -ως is a signal of the adverb function in Greek.

103.1 On the neuter ending -ο of ἐκεῖνος, -η, -ο and οὗτος, αὕτη, τοῦτο, compare the adjective, _____, from Lesson VI, para. 60.

104.1 Demonstrative pronouns modify nouns (expressed or unexpressed) by very pointed specification of the noun as either "this" or "that," "these" or "those."

104.2 οὗτος, αὕτη, τοῦτο is the near demonstrative, pointing to some person or thing close at hand ("this," pl. "these"), ἐκεῖνος, ἐκείνη, ἐκεῖνο is the far demonstrative, specifying a relatively distant person of thing ("that," pl. "those").

104.3 Do not be confused by the fact that the demonstratives never appear with the article (never ὁ οὗτος or ὁ ἐκεῖνος) and so may be said formally to be in the predicate position. Whether or not it serves as a predicate must be determined from context. (Cf. paras. 70-71).

104.4 Notice that the noun modified by these demonstrative pronouns is always rendered so specific by them as to require an article. "This man" = οὗτος ὁ ἄνθρωπος; never οὗτος ἄνθρωπος.

So (104.3-4), the demonstrative always modifies a definite noun but never has the article itself.

104.5 οὗτος, "this man," αὕτη, "this woman," τοῦτο, "this thing" are analogous to what use of the adjective (75)?

105.1 Review NTGFB, 97(4c), p. 49, before your study of this paragraph.

105.1 Standing without the article (predicate position), the third person pronoun αὐτός, αὐτή, αὐτό may intensify nouns, pronouns, or even unexpressed subjects of verbs. Such a pronoun then agrees in gender, number and case with the word (expressed or not) it intensifies. The intensive pronoun always means " -self" (i.e., itself, himself, myself, etc.).

105.2 The third person pronoun is also used attributively (70.1-2). When so used it always attributes the <u>same</u> characteristic to the noun modified, namely "same." Here the pronoun functions as an adjective.

Being attributive it agrees in gender, number and case with whatever noun (expressed or unexpressed) it modifies. Review para. 66 and use the endings in para. 96.

This attributive use of the third person pronoun is also extended to the modification of unexpressed nouns (i.e., a substantive use). ὁ αὐτὸς ἄνθρωπος and ὁ αὐτός both mean "the same man."

106.1 Each of the examples given by Machen in this summary paragraph is of basic importance in New Testament Greek. Are they all clear to you? They must be. If they are not, review para. 70-71 and also the <u>Study Guide</u> on those paragraphs for the first two ("the good word"/"the word is good."), para. 104 on the next two ("the word"/"that word"), para. 105 on sets five and six ("the word itself"/"the same word"), para. 94-97 on "my word," "his word" and "I see him." and para. 104.6 on the last two ("I see this man,"/"I see these things."). If confusion persists, ask the instructor for an explanation, here and on any other examples in NTGFB.

107.1 Two important reminders for translation technique.

    a. Continue indefinitely the habit of precise identification of every word in the sentence. Writing an abbreviated identification of any word that gives the slightest trouble is an excellent aid to learning. Whether you write out the identification or do it automatically in your head, it <u>must</u> be done. With this identification be able to state clearly the <u>function</u> of every word in its context.

    b. Guard carefully against the misuse of the answers, if you are using them. Read again the introduction to the answer sheets.

107.I. Aids to exercise I, Lesson IX.

    1. οὗτοι οἱ διδάσκαλοι κρίνουσιν αὐτον τον ἀπόστολον.

        a. Note the agreement in gender, number and case between the demonstrative οὗτοι and the noun it modifies, οἱ διδάσκαλοι (compare 66).

        b. Is the word order of the demonstrative expression here characteristic or exceptional (104.3-4)?

        c. τον ἀπόστολον is obviously the direct object, not αὐτόν. What function then has αὐτόν (105.)? Note the agreement of αὐτόν and ἀπόστολον in gender, number and case.

2. ὁ δὲ αὐτος διδάσκαλος ἔχει τὴν αὐτὴν χαρὰν ἐν τῇ καρδίᾳ αὐτοῦ.

    a. ὁ δὲ αὐτός = δὲ ὁ αὐτός why (91)?
    b. ὁ..αὐτὸς διδάσκαλος then has αὐτός in the _____
       position, modifying the noun and meaning _____
       (105.3; cf. 70).
    c. τὴν·αὐτὴν χαράν: why not "the joy itself" (compare 105.2
       and 3)? What is the syntactic clue?
    d. αὐτοῦ: cannot modify τῇ καρδίᾳ meaning "same;" why (105.2; 66)?
       Antecedent then is _____ (check gender and number,
       97.3).

3. νῦν λαμβάνω αὐτὸς τὸ αὐτὸ εὐαγγέλιον ἀπὸ τοῦ κυρίου μου.

    a. αὐτός cannot be subject; why? What person does the verb demand
       (20.2) as subject?
    b. Being in the nominative case, αὐτός must either intensify
       (105.2) the subject, "I," or be the subject. Which is it here?
       If there is difficulty, review the illustrations in NTGFB 105.3.
    c. αὐτό modifies εὐαγγέλιον, and does so attributively. How do
       you know (105.2)?
    d. Explain the accent of κυρίου μου (93.1-2).

4. οὗτος βλέπει ἐκεῖνον καὶ κρίνει αὐτόν.

    a. οὗτος and ἐκεῖνον modify what nouns here (104.5)?
       If this is not clear, review the substantive adjective (75.1-2).
    b. ἐκεῖνον: direct object? How do you know (34)?
    c. αὐτόν: why not used as intensifier of the subject "he" implicit
       in βλέπει (105.2)? What case necessary in that event? Why
       accusative (34)?

5. μετὰ ταῦτα ἔχετε αὐτοὶ τὴν ἀγάπην τοῦ κυρίου ἐν ταῖς καρδίαις ὑμῶν.

    a. μετά = "with" or "after?" How do you know (85)?
    b. ταῦτα used how here (104.5)?
    c. αὐτοί cannot be the subject. Why (cf. sentence 3)? Relates
       to the subject "you" pl. intensively (105.2) or attributively
       (105.3)? How can you tell?
    d. ταῖς·καρδίαις: why dative (81)?

6. οὗτοι ἔχουσι χαράν, ἐκεῖνοι δὲ ἔχουσιν ἁμαρτίαν.

    a. οὗτοι and ἐκεῖνοι are used how (104.5)?
    b. Notice the anarthrous χαράν and ἁμαρτίαν stating the <u>kind</u> of thing possessed by the subject, "joy" and "sin" as opposed to other kinds of qualities (cf. 100.2, sentence 9d). With the article these qualities would be specified in some sense to be defined by the context. See paragraph 99.3 again.

7. αὗτν δέ ἐστιν ἡ φωνὴ τοῦ κυρίου αὐτοῦ.

    a. Why is αὗτη feminine? What noun does it specify?
    b. τοῦ κυρίου αὐτοῦ without the context could mean "of his Lord." But then what would be the antecedent of αὐτοῦ?
    c. If αὐτοῦ is not functioning in the place of a noun (ch. VIII), what other use is probable (105.1)?
    d. Explain the enclitic accent, δέ ἐστιν (93.1-2).

8. αὗτως γινώσκομεν τοῦτον καὶ βλέπομεν τὸ πρόσωπον αὐτοῦ.

    a. Compare καλός, "good," καλῶς "well," οὗτος, "this," and οὗτως, "thus;" what is the signal of the Greek adverb (101.3)?
    b. τοῦτον modifies what noun in this substantive use (104.5)? Explain its accent (para. 11, rule 4).
    c. What would τὸ πρόσωπον αὐτό mean (105.1)?

9. λαμβάνομεν ταῦτα τὰ δῶρα ἀπὸ τοῦ αὐτοῦ καὶ βλέπομεν αὐτόν.

    a. Why relate ταῦτα to τὰ δῶρα (see note b on sentence 1).
    b. Why the article on (τὰ) δῶρα (104.4)?
    c. ἀπὸ τοῦ αὐτοῦ: third person pronoun following the article has to be what use (105.2)? Why genitive (85)?
    d. Can αὐτόν refer to τὰ δῶρα? Why not (97.3)?

10. αὐτὸς βαπτίζεις ἐκεῖνον καὶ εἶ ἀδελφὸς αὐτοῦ.

    a. Compare and contrast βαπτίζεις and εἶ (98 and 98.1).
    b. αὐτός cannot be subject; why? Compare 3a above. Used how then (105.1)?

11. εἰς τὴν αὐτὴν ἐκκλησίαν ἄγομεν τούτους τοὺς διδασκάλους ἡμῶν τοὺς ἀγαθούς.

    a. εἰς τὴν αὐτὴν ἐκκλησίαν: third person pronoun with article must mean what (105.2)?
       Why certainly related to ἐκκλησίαν?
    b. τοὺς ἀγαθούς: why M.A. pl.? Related to what? How (70)?
    c. What three elements modify τοὺς διδάσκαλους?

12. αὐτὸς ἐγὼ ἔχω ταύτην τὴν ἐπαγγελίαν τοῦ κυρίου μου.

    a. αὐτός is related to ἐγώ; how (105.1)?
       Would it be greatly changed without the ἐγώ?
       Compare Machen's examples in 105.
    b. By now the pattern with the demonstrative should be familiar: anarthrous demonstrative with definite noun.

13. αὕτη βλέπει τὸ πρόσωπον τοῦ κυρίου αὐτῆς.

    a. Subject is _____.
    b. Contrast αὕτη and αὐτῆς in case, accent, and word class (96; 102).

14. αὐτὴ γινώσκει αὐτὴν τὴν ἀλήθειαν

    a. "This woman knows," or "She herself knows?" What is the difference (104; 105.1)?
    b. αὐτήν is probably not the direct object. Why? Sense? Antecedent?
       Rather it agrees with τὴν ἀλήθειαν, and, standing without the article, functions how (105.1)?

15. ἀγαθή ἐστιν ἡ ἐπαγγελία σου καὶ ἀγαθὴ εἶ αὐτή.

    a. Is the subject, "you," masculine or feminine?
    b. Can αὐτή be subject? Why not (98)?
    c. How is αὐτή related to the subject (105.3 in NTGFB)?

16. ἐκεῖνοί εἰσιν μαθηταὶ τοῦ αὐτοῦ διδασκάλου.

    a. The accent of ἐκεῖνοί εἰσιν (93.1-2)?
    b. Attributive third person pronoun always means _____ (105.3)?

17. οὗτός ἐστιν διδάσκαλος ἐκείνου, ἐκεῖνος δὲ τούτου.

What is omitted in the second clause? Work by parallel clause structure.

18. οὗτος διδάσκει τοὺς ἀγαθοὺς καὶ αὐτός ἐστιν ἀγαθός.

a. Contrast the uses of the two adjectives here (75 and 71).
b. αὐτός is rarely just a subject. Here it intensifies what, judging by the gender, number and case (105.2)?

19. μετὰ τὰς ἡμέρας ἐκείνας διδάσκαλοί ἐσμεν τούτων τῶν δούλων.

a. By grammatical agreement ἐκείνας must go with what, in spite of the variant word order?
b. μετά with the accusative gives time or place?

20. μετὰ τῶν πιστῶν ἔχομεν ἐπαγγελίας ἀγαθάς, οἱ δὲ πονηροὶ βλέπουσιν ἡμέρας κακάς.

107.II   NEW TESTAMENT GREEK READING, John 1.1-11

Review again Jn. 1.1-11 and observe carefully the demonstrative pronouns (102-104), both their form and function.

Translate Jn. 1.10-11.

1.10	ἐγένετο	See translation notes 76.II on 1.3 Aorist indicative, 3 sg. form of γίνομαι, "I become, come into existence." Translate here, "He/she it came into existence."
		Review paras. 167-169 on the meaning of the aorist tense (in the indicative mood).
		On form, see para. 194 and then 116
	ἔγνω	Second (i.e., irregular) aorist active indicative, 3 sg., of γινώσκ See para. 601.
1.11	τὰ ἴδια. . . οἱ ἴδιοι	ἴδιος, α, ον. An adjective showing ownership, possession (473) Look up meaning in a lexicon.
		Why neuter first and then masculine? Check some translations at this point.
		What use of the adjective (75)?
	ἦλθεν	"Came." Second (i.e., irregular) aorist active indicative, 3. sg., of ἔρχομαι. On form see para. 193.
	παρέλαβον	"Received," "did receive." Second (i.e., irregular) aorist active indicative, 3 sg., of παραλαμβάνω. On form see 193. Singular or plural here?
		Remember 167-169?

108.1

ἀλλά : a conjunction which strongly reverses the direction of thought, or presents a strong contrast (adversative); built on the root αλλ-, "other." Cf. ἄλλος.

ἀκούω : several other verbs of sense may also take objects in the genitive case.

γίνομαι: a being verb with a wide range of meanings. γίνομαι denotes something as "coming into existence," εἰμί as "being in existence."

109.1 Voice refers to what (17.2)?
Name and define the three voices in Greek (109 and 17.2).

    1. _____

    2. _____

    3. _____

109.2 What formal distinction is there in the present indicative between the middle and the passive verb form (109(3))?

110-112.1 <u>Primary middle endings</u> are used to express both the present passive and the present middle. This completes the learning of the primary endings of the Greek verb.

Primary Active		Primary Middle	
Sg.	Pl.	Sg.	Pl.
1. - ω	1. - μεν	1. - μαι	1. - μεθα
2. - εις	2. - τε	2. - η/σαι	2. - σθε
3. - ει	3. - ουσι	3. - ται	3. - νται

110.-112.3 The second person singular ending -η developed by contraction of the variable vowel ε and the αι of the original ending - σαι after the loss of intervocalic <u>sigma</u>: -εϕαι>-εαι>-η. Both -η and -σαι should be learned (in that order).

Compare the third person endings of the primary middle, singular and plural. What is apparently the sign of the plural in the third person?

110-112.4 The variable vowel may be more consistently separated from the primary middle endings than from the primary active endings.

As in the active, before μ/ν the variable vowel is _____, elsewhere it is _____ (20.3).

Note the <u>short variable vowel</u> indicating <u>indicative mood</u> (20.3).

110-112.5 Be able to "dissect" the middle-passive forms just as you did the active verb forms.

λύομαι: λυ   -   ο   -   μαι

λύεσθε: λυ   -   ε   -   σθε

Tense stem   variable   personal ending
                      vowel   (Primary middle)

113.1 How should λύομαι be translated for the time being, in order to avoid confusion with other, similar sounding English statements?

113.2 <u>Transform</u> the following English <u>active</u> statements <u>into passive</u> statements. Make sure that the same essential information is being given (i.e., that the same person or thing is receiving the action, the same one doing the action as in the active statement).

    1.   A.   Christ is saving us.

         P.

    2.   A.   The house is sheltering us.

         P.

114-115.1 When the action is described passively the actor is said to be the <u>agent</u> if it is a person, the <u>means</u> if it is a thing (instrument). The <u>grammatical</u> subject then is not acting but is being acted upon.

114-115.2 How are the agent and the means expressed in Greek:

Direct personal agent = _____

Intermediary agent = (77) _____

Means/instrument = _____

Watch carefully for these syntactic units and label them accurately to enhance your interpretive skills.

116.1 Define <u>deponent verbs</u>.

116.2 Observe that many (though by no means all) <u>deponent</u> verbs are <u>intransitive</u>, i.e., the subject acts, but not directly upon an object as in a transitive verb.

Illustrate transitive and intransitive verbs in English to make sure the categories are clear to you.

    Transitive:

    Intransitive:

116.3   Locating deponent verbs. Note that deponent verbs are given in the <u>middle-passive</u> form in the vocabulary lists, as well as in the standard dictionaries.

117.1   Be sure to relate the compound forms of the verb to the simple verb from which they are built. Think of διέρχομαι, εἰσέρχομαι, and ἐξέρχομαι all as variations of ἔρχομαι.

119.1   ἀποκρίνομαι τῷ ἀποστόλῳ: this is apparently equivalent to the English expression "to give an answer to," even though it is usually translated simply "to answer."

119.2   For further study on verbs with objects in the genitive case see William Sanford LaSor, <u>et.al</u>, <u>Handbook of New Testament Greek</u>, vol. 2 (Grand Rapids: Eerdmans, 1973) p. B-169.

120.1   Exercises for Lesson X.

A.   The student will have noticed numerous questions in the aids which relate to the syntax of the sentence, not just the forms of words. One is asked to identify an expression as the agent or means, as a geographical, or temporal, or causal expression, for example. This habit of analyzing the <u>logic</u> of the sentence, the thought flow of the writer, is indispensable to productive textual interpretation later on.

B.   Precise and complete identifications of form and function continue to be necessary. They may be automatic for you in many cases, but make sure they are being made whether quickly or step by step.

120.I   Aids to exercise I, Lesson X.

1.   λύονται οὗτοι οἱ δοῦλοι ὑπὸ τοῦ κυρίου.

    a.   λύονται: identify fully. Present tense; why (20.1)?
        Middle/passive voice, why (20.2)?
        Indicative mood, why (20.3)?
        Third plural, why (20.2)?
    b.   The verb form out of context could be middle or passive. Context dictates which identification (114)?
    c.   Who is doing the act of λυ- (114)?
        With the passive this person (actor) is called the _____ (114-115.2).

2. τῷ λόγῳ τοῦ κυρίου ἀγόμεθα εἰς τὴν ἐκκλησίαν τοῦ θεοῦ.

    a. Go to the verb, ἀγόμεθα. Identify it and locate the
        subject (110-112.3). Corresponding active form would be
        _____?
    b. εἰς phrase tells what? Why τὴν ἐκκλησίαν in accusative
        (81)?
    c. τῷ λόγῳ (τοῦ κυρίου): Why dative case?
        Could either be indirect object(36) or the "dative of means"
        (115).
        Which makes most sense here?
        How does the passive verb help you decide?

3. οὐκ ἀκούετε τῆς φωνῆς τοῦ προφήτου, ἀλλ᾽ ἐξέρχεσθε ἐκ τοῦ
οἴκου αὐτοῦ.

    a. οὐκ negates what word (118)?
    b. τῆς φωνῆς: why genitive (119)?
        τοῦ προφήτου: why genitive (35)?
    c. Major or minor contrast between the two clauses (108.1)?
        Can you reflect that in your translation?
    d. ἐξέρχεσθε: include "deponent" in the identification of
        the verb: "Present-middle passive deponent indicative,
        2 pl. of ἔρχομαι."
        Reminder: If the verb is deponent its lexical form will
        be middle or passive (or middle-passive), not active.
    e. Notice also the Greek idiom which repeats the preposition
        after many compound verbs.
        "ἐξέρχομαι . . . εκ" and "διέρχομαι . . . διά"
    f. ἐκ τοῦ οἴκου αὐτοῦ is ambigious without a context; could
        either be
        1. (105.2)
            or
        2. (97.(5))
        In context it is most likely to be a pronominal use referring
        back to _____.

4. τῷ λόγῳ αὐτοῦ τοῦ κυρίου γίνεσθε μαθηταὶ αὐτοῦ.

    a. γίνεσθε. Parse fully (112, 116).
    b. Why nominative μαθηταί (108 and 98-99)?
    c. αὐτοῦ. . . αὐτοῦ. Contrast their uses (105.2 and 35).
    d. τῷ λόγῳ. Why dative (114-115.2)? Position tells what?

5. ἐκεῖνοι οἱ ἀγαθοὶ διδάσκαλοι οὐκ εἰσέρχονται εἰς τοὺς οἴκους τῶν ἁμαρτωλῶν.

    a. Why not this word order: οἱ ἐκεῖνοι ἀγαθοὶ διδάσκαλοι (104.3-4)?

    b. εἰσέρχονται. Parse fully.
       Why not middle in meaning (116)?
       How does vocabulary help there (116.3)?

6. οὐ βαπτίζονται οἱ ἁμαρτωλοὶ ὑπὸ τῶν ἀποστόλων, ἀλλ' ἐξέρχονται ἐκ τούτων τῶν οἴκων πρὸς ἄλλους διδασκάλους.

    a. Parse fully (112):
       βαπτίζονται
       εἰσέρχονται
       What indicates plural (110-112.3)?
       Voice functions how in each case (17.2; 113.2; 116)?

    b. ὑπό phrase supplies what information (114-115.2)?

7. λέγετε ἐκείνοις τοῖς ἁμαρτωλοῖς ὅτι σώζεσθε ὑπὸ τοῦ θεοῦ ἀπὸ τῶν ἁμαρτιῶν ὑμῶν.

    a. Parse fully:
       λέγετε
       σώζεσθε
       Both presents? How do you know (20.1)?
       How do the verbs most obviously contrast (109.1)?

    b. Direct object of λέγετε is what construction?

    c. Why not τῷ θεῷ (114-115.2)?

8. ἄρχει αὐτὸς ὁ θεὸς τῆς βασιλείας αὐτοῦ.

    a. ἄρχει. Parse fully.
       "Rules" or "begins"? How do you tell the difference (108)?

    b. αὐτός. Function (105.2)? Why probably not just the subject?

    c. τῆς βασιλείας. Why genitive (108)? Will possession make sense here?
       What does the genitive signal here?

9. εἰρήνην ἔχει ἡ ἐκκλησία, ὅτι σώζεται ὑπὸ τοῦ κυρίου αὐτῆς.

    a. Parse and transform into the corresponding (same tense, person, number) active or middle-passive.
       ἔχει
       σώζεται

    b. ὅτι clause here gives what infomration logically (time, place, cause, contrast, condition, concession)?

    c. αὐτῆς. Why feminine sg. (97(3))?

    d. ὑπὸ τοῦ κυρίου gives the agent (114) of what act?

10. οὐκ ἀποκρινόμεθα τῷ ἀποστολῳ ὅτι οὐ γινώσκομεν αὐτόν.

    a. Parse and contrast the verbs.
       ἀποκρινόμεθα (112; 116)
       γινώσκομεν
      Why indicative (20.3 end)?

    b. τῷ ἀποστόλῳ. English translation uses this as a direct object. The Greek expression was apparently like our expression, "to give and answer to." See 108 and 119.

    c. ὅτι clause gives what information logically? Modifies what word? Can you diagram this sentence (use left margin)?

11. οὐχ ὑπὸ τῶν μαθητῶν σώζῃ ἀπὸ τῶν ἁμαρτιῶν σου, ἀλλ' ὑπ' αὐτοῦ τοῦ θεοῦ.

    a. σώζῃ. Parse carefully (110; 112). Why not middle (114)?

    b. οὐχ . . . ἀλλ' signals the contrast of what two syntactic units (114 and 118)?

    c. ὑπ' αὐτοῦ τοῦ θεοῦ. Why not, "by the same God" (105.3)? Why not "by his God"?

12. οὐ πορεύῃ ἐν τῇ ὁδῷ τῇ κακῇ, ἀλλὰ σώζῃ ἀπὸ τῶν ἁμαρτιῶν σου καὶ οἱ ἀδελφοί σου ἀκούουσι τῆς φωνῆς τοῦ κυρίου..

    a. Parse fully.
       πορεύῃ
       σώζῃ

    b. τῇ κακῇ modifies τῇ ὁδῷ? Are you sure (60)? How does it modify (72)?

    c. τῆς φωνῆς. Why genitive (119)?

13. μετὰ τῶν ἀδελφῶν αὐτοῦ ἄγεται εἰς τὴν βασιλείαν τοῦ θεοῦ τῇ φωνῇ τῶν ἀποστόλων.

    a. ἄγεται. Parse and transform into the corresponding active form.

    b. Why not ὑπὸ τῆς φωνῆς (114-115.2)?

14. οὐ γίνῃ μαθητὴς τοῦ κυρίου, ὅτι οὐκ εἰσέρχῃ εἰς τὴν ἐκκλησίαν αὐτοῦ.

a. Parse fully. Remember 116.

γίνῃ

εἰσέρχῃ

b. μαθητής. Why nominative (108; 99)? Anarthrous form calls attention to identity or kind (99.3)?

c. ὅτι clause supplies what information logically (condition, purpose, time, place, cause, concession)?

120.II NEW TESTAMENT GREEK READING, John 1.12

Translate

ὅσοι "As many as." See vocabulary para. 403. Obviously M.N. pl. and subject of the verb.

ἔλαβον How is this different from παρέλαβον, 1.11 (whose notes see in para 107.II)?

ἔδωκεν "He gave." Aorist active indicative, 3 sg., of δίδωμι, a mi-verb. On the mi-verbs read carefully paras. 482-485 now! Then look over the paradigms in 596-597. Begin informally to learn the present tense forms of the mi-verbs.

ἐξουσία Look up meaning and also see Lexical Aids, pp. 41-42 and no. 4 on p. 43, on first declension nouns ending in -ια. Does the description by Metzger fit this word?

γενέσθαι "To become." Second (i.e., irregular) aorist middle deponent infinitive (296) of γίνομαι. Note the aorist tense stem, γεν-, in common with ἐγένετο (Jn. 1.3, 6, 10).

τοῖς πιστεύουσιν Not P. A. I., 3 pl. verb, but a present active participle construction to be translated, "to (dative) those who believe." Modifies αὐτοῖς. See 226 and 236 on form and use.

Lesson XI

121.1   What compound (117) forms do you see here.

_____	from	_____	+	_____
_____	from	_____	+	_____
_____	from	_____	+	_____
_____	from	_____	+	_____
_____	from	_____	+	_____
_____	from	_____	+	_____

The meaning of the compound is usually clear from the meaning of the separate elements; sometimes not.

121.2   Note the obvious English derivatives.

catalog
  (and other "cata-" words)

from κατάλουος. Greek κ is often English c through Latin

synchronize
  (and the other "syn-" or "sym-" words)

ούν + χρόνος ("time")
why "syn" with "y" (1.2)?

"para-" words

παρά-

121.3   Bring your chart in 87.1 up to date.

122.1   Recall the fact that even though the present stem (e.g. λυ-) does not differentiate between simple and continued action in the present, the **present stem** should be linked in the student's mind with **continued action** regardless of the time indicated by other aspects of the form or context.

122.2   Note carefully the statement on the meaning of the imperfect tense. Two elements are critical:

    1. <u>Continued</u> action
    2. <u>Past</u> time

The action may be repeated, or habitual or going on in the past, but in some sense it is continued action.

127.1   (Order deliberately reversed.)
The Greek <u>secondary</u> tenses are <u>past</u> tenses (at least in the indicative): imperfect, aorist, and pluperfect (p. 21, n.1).

127.2   The secondary active endings are given below. Fill in the correct primary endings as a review to complete the chart (20.2 and 110-112). Do it!

Primary Active		Primary Middle	
Sg.	Pl.	Sg.	Pl.
1. -	1. -	1. -	1. -
2. -	2. -	2. -	2. -
3. -	3. -	3. -	3. -

Secondary Active		Secondary Passive	
Sg.	Pl.	Sg.	Pl.
1. - ν	1. - μεν		
2. - ς	2. - τε	To be learned (138-139)	
3. - #	3. - ν		

123.1   The Imperfect verbs and the present verbs (active, middle, and passive) together comprise the present verb system. These verbs are a unit in both form and meaning, bound together by the present stem which is common to all of them and by the meaning of continued action carried by that present stem.

123.2   "Dissect" the imperfect forms as you have all of the preceding verbs (see 123).

ἔ	-	λυ	-	ο	-	ν	ἔλυον
ἐ	-	λύ	-	ε	-	τε	ἐλύετε

augment (indicates past time)	present tense stem (continued action)	variable vowel (indicative mood)	personal ending

123.3   One can easily see why the imperfect tense means "continued action in past time."

     1.   Present tense stem conveys continued action (17.1).
     2.   Augment (see 125-126) signals past time.

     This clear link of tense with time is possible only in the indicative mood, the only mood in which the imperfect appears.

123.4   Since all imperfects are built on the present stem, and no other past tense is so built, one may identify any verb with (1) augment and (2) secondary active endings as imperfect (3) if it is built on the present stem.

(For example, the aorist indicative also uses augment to indicate past time, and as a "past" tense uses secondary endings, but it is not built on the present stem and so need not be confused with the imperfect.

124.1   The _augment_ is a past tense indicator. Since it is only in the indicative mood that tense has temporal significance, the augment appears on the secondary tenses only in the indicative mood. (Cf. 123.3)

125-126.1   List the two methods of augment for the secondary tenses. See para. 3 for vowel length.

128.1   Summarize the use of the variable vowel in the present system as learned to date. (Cf. 20, 111)

131-132.1   How could accent help identify a compound verb form?

135.I   Aids to exercise I, Lesson XI.

1.   ἠκούομεν τῆς φωνῆς αὐτοῦ ἐν ἐκείναις ταῖς ἡμέραις, νῦν δὲ οὐκέτι ἀκούομεν αὐτῆς.

   a.   Contrast the two verbs.
   Removing their endings and variable vowels, locate the tense stems: _____ and _____. (20.1).
   b.   The tense stem of ἠκούομεν is then ἠκού-. (1) From this point several options present themselves. The word could be:

      1.   P.A.I., 1 pl., of verb ἠκούω.
      2.   Impf. A. I., 1 pl., of verb ἀκούω.
      3.   Impf. A. I., 1 pl., of verb ἑκούω.

   With _no_ prior knowledge of the vocabulary the reader would be unable to decide without reference to a lexicon. Choice No. 1 assumes an "unaltered" present stem. Choices 2 and 3 assume lengthening of an initial vowel as an _____(126).

   (2) Consultation of a lexicon would show that neither ἠκούω nor ἑκούω exist. (3) Prior knowledge of ἀκούω would make it the most likely choice from the start. Vocabulary learning is an irreplaceable aid to identification.
   c.   τῆς φωνῆς αὐτῆς: why genitive (119)?
   d.   αὐτῆς: antecedent? Why so (97.3)?

2.   ὁ δὲ μαθητὴς τοῦ κυρίου ἔλεγε παραβολὴω τοῖς ἀδελφοῖς αὐτοῦ.

   a.   "Dissect" ἔλεγε:
   -ε = _____(123, 128)
   ἔ- = _____(125)
   λεγ = _____(123.3, 4)
   Full identification of this verb:

68

  b. Why imperfect and not aorist or some other secondary tense
     (123.3, 4)?
  c. What type of action occuring when (122.2)? Reflected in
     translation?
  d. All other words accurately identified and function discovered?

3. ἀπέκτεινον οἱ δοῦλοι τὰ τέκνα σὺν τοῖς μαθηταῖς.

   a. ἀπέκτεινον: could be second declension masculine noun, but
      if so, where is the verb?
   b. Primary or secondary verb endings (127.2)?
   c. What is the epsilon in ἀπε - (131-132)?
   d. ἀποκτειν- How do you identify it as present stem?
   e. Secondary ending, augment, present stem: make identification
      certain as _____(123.4).

4. τότε μὲν κατέβαινον εἰς τὸν οἶκον, νῦν δὲ οὐκέτι καταβαίνω.

   a. καταβαίνω and κατέβαινον are both built on what verb
      stem _____?
      What identifies the former as a primary verb form and the
      latter as secondary (127.2).
      What signals past tense on κατέβαινον (124.1)?
      How does parallel καταβαίνω clarify κατέβαινον (130)?
   b. Why not "went down" (122.2)?
   c. οὐκέτι = οὐκ ("not") + ἔτι ("yet").
   d. μέν . . . δέ spotted (121)?

5. παρελαμβάνετε τὸν ἄρτον παρὰ τῶν δούλων καὶ ἠσθίετε αὐτόν.

   a. παρελαμβάνετε: what one feature distinguishes the form from
      P.A.I., 2 pl? (124.1; 131-132) ?
   b. ἠσθίετε could be either
      P.A.I. of _____ or
      Imf.A.I. of _____ or _____(126).
      Which is it? How do you know (121)? Trouble? See 1b above.
   c. παρά- with the genitive = _____.

6. διὰ τὴν ἀλήθειαν ἀπέθνησκον οἱ μαθηταὶ ἐν ταῖς ἡμέραις ἐκείναις.

   a. ἀπέθνησκον: to what word in the vocabulary do you relate this?
      -ον = (127.2) _____indicating _____(20.2-3).

69

b. Why ἀποθν - to ἀπεθν - (131)?

c. Identification (123.4)? Meaning (122.2)?

d. ἐκείναις goes with what noun?

e. διά: plus the accusative tells what: cause or agent?

7. συνῆγεν οὗτος ὁ ἀπόστολος εἰς τὴν ἐκκλησίαν τοὺς μαθητὰς τοῦ κυρίου ἡμῶν.

a. συνῆγεν: why suspect the augment of a compound verb (132)? Could either be συνεγ - or συναγ - plus secondary endings (126)? Vocabulary knowledge suggests <u>which one</u>?

b. Why the final -ν (129)?

c. How can you be sure of its identification as imperfect (123.4)?

8. νῦν μὲν διδασκόμεθα ὑπὸ τῶν ἀποστόλων, τότε δὲ ἐδιδάσκομεν ἡμεῖς τὴν ἐκκλησίαν.

a. διδασκόμεθα. "dissect." (110-112.5). Active or middle-passive? How do you know (110-112.1)? Present or Aorist? How do you know (20.1)? Present or imperfect? How do you know (123.4)? Full identification:

b. ἐδιδάσκομεν Augment on present stem = _____ tense (123.4). Indicative or subjunctive (123.3; 20.3)? Why not "we taught" (122.2)?

c. μέν. . . δέ reflects the contrast carried also by _____ . . . _____.

9. ὁ κύριος ἡμῶν ἦρε τὰς ἁμαρτίας ἡμῶν.

a. ἦρε: if it is verbal, what one personal ending can -ε be (123)? The variable vowel stands without an ending (= zero morpheme) and thus becomes itself the person and number indicator (127.2).

b. ἦρε: η - would have to be lengthened form of either αι or ει (126). Which is it here? Present stem, unaugmented = _____ (121).

10. τότε μὲν ἀνέβαινον εἰς τὸ ἱερόν, νῦν δὲ οὐκέτι ἀναβαίνουσιν.

a. ἀναβ - /ἀνεβ -: what is the difference (131.2)?

70

b. Contrast and compare the verbal endings (127.2).
Both are _____, _____, and _____,
but -ον = _____; -ουσι = _____.
How does parallel structure assist the identifications (130)?

c. μέν . . . δέ (121)?

11. πονηροὶ ἦτε, ἀγαθοὶ δὲ ἐστέ.

a. Compare and contrast ἦτε and ἐστέ (133, 98).
b. Why the adjectives in nominative case (99)?

12. ὑμεῖς μέν ἐστε ἀγαθοί, ἡμεῖς δέ ἐσμεν πονηροί

Why the personal pronoun subjects (97.(4b))? Note μέν . . .
δέ in this connection.

13. τότε ἤμην ἐν τῷ ἱερῷ καὶ ἐδίδασκέ με ὁ κύριος.

a. ἤμην: full identification (133)?
b. ἐδίδασκε: knowing διδάσκω the initial ε- has to be an
_____ (126).
Present tense stem with augment must be what tense _____
(123.4)? What confirms this (127.2)?
c. Accent of ἐδίδασκέ με (93.1-2)?

14. λέγομεν ὑμῖν ὅτι ἐν τῷ οἴκῳ ἡμῶν ἦμεν.

a. ὅτι introduces the content of the "saying." In this case the
whole "ὅτι - clause" is the direct object of λέγομεν.
b. ὑμῖν: why dative (34)? Not means, why (114-115.1-2)?
c. Diagram.

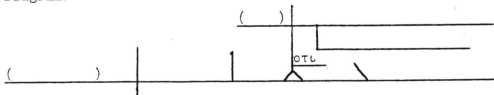

15. ἐξέβαλλες αὐτοὺς ἐκ τοῦ ἱεροῦ.

a. ἐξέβαλλες
-ες = secondary or primary ending (127.2)?
Why ἐξέβ - not ἐκβ - (131)?
What tense stem?   With what significance (123.1)?

b. Note ἐξέβαλλες . . . ἐκ . . .

16. ἀπέστελλον οἱ ἄνθρωποι τοὺς δούλους αὐτῶν πρός με.

    a. ἀπέστελλον: Impf. A. I., 3 pl. How do you know?
    b. αὐτῶν: antecedent?
    c. Why not πρὸς ἐμέ (97.(6))?

17. ὁ κύριος ἀπέστελλεν ἀγγέλους πρὸς ἡμᾶς.

Compare and contrast the verbs of No. 16 and 17. See also (129).

18. ἐν τῷ κόσμῳ ἦν καὶ ὁ κόσμος οὐκ ἔβλεπεν αὐτόν.

    a. ἦν: identify fully (133).
    b. ἔβλεπεν: good example of <u>repeated</u> <u>action</u> <u>in</u> <u>past</u> time for the imperfect (122.2).
    c. αὐτόν: antecedent?

19. δοῦλος ἦς τοῦ πονηροῦ, ἀλλὰ νῦν οὐκέτι εἶ δοῦλος.

    a. Subject (133)?
    b. Why nominative δοῦλος (99)? Anarthrous (99.3)?
    c. τοῦ πονηροῦ: what use of the adjective (70, 71, 75)?
    d. Compare and contrast the verbs (98, 133).

20. τοῦτό ἐστι τὸ δῶρον τοῦ ἀνθρώπου, καλὸν δὲ οὐκ ἔστιν.

    a. καλόν: why neuter, nominative sg.?
       Is "the man" or "the gift" not good? How do you know?
    b. Why no movable <u>nu</u> on ἐστι (44)?

135.II NEW TESTAMENT GREEK READING, John 1.1-13

Review all the <u>finite</u> verb forms (i.e., verbs which designate person and number) in Jn. 1.1-12. Convert all forms which are not imperfect verbs into imperfect indicative forms of the same person, number and voice as the form in John. For the imperfect middle-passive forms use paras. 138 and 143.

Notice that it is the tense stem alone which distinguishes the second aorist forms in John from these imperfects you have formed.

Translate 1.13

οἵ	"Who." M.N. pl. relative pronoun, introducing a clause which further describes αὐτοῖς, 1.12. See para. 395.
οὐκ. . . οὐδέ . . . οὐδέ. . . ἀλλ'	"Not . . . neither . . . neither . . . but . . ." See para. 136.
αἱμάτων	Look up αἷμα and see the third declension neuter noun paradigm in para. 222.
θελήματος	Look up θέλημα and see para. 222.
σαρκός	F. G. sg. of σάρξ. See paras. 210-211.
ἀνδρός	M. G. sg. of ἀνήρ. See para. 565.
ἐγεννήθησαν	"Were begotten." Aorist passive indicative, 3 pl., of γεννάω, "I beget." See para. 201 on form.
	All the preceding prepositional phrases in 1.13 modify this verb whose subject is the pronoun, οἵ, "who."

136.1   With what words in the vocabulary do you relate the following:

"Erg": unit of measure
   of work in physics
   perimeter   a compound with _____
   hypercritical   _____ + _____
                              Why hy- (1.2)?

136.2   In addition to the obvious verbal compounds notice οὐδέ: ____ + ____.

138,
143.1   Dissect the parts of the imperfect middle-passive indicative.

   ἐ   -   λυ   -   ό   -   μην

   augment   present stem   variable   secondary middle
                            vowel   ending

138.2   Again, present stems, found with augment and secondary endings must
        be imperfect, in all voices (123.5).

139.1   With the mastery of the secondary middle endings in this chapter the
        student has learned the majority of the verb endings to be found on
Greek indicative verbs. Be able to recognize and accurately identify all of
these endings on sight in any context.

	Primary Active			Primary Middle	
Sg.		Pl.	Sg.		Pl.
1. - ω	1. - μεν		1. - μαι	1. - μεθα	
2. - εις	2. - τε		2. - η (-σαι)	2. - σθε	
3. - ει	3. - ουσι(ν)		3. - ται	3. - νται	

	Secondary Active			Secondary Middle	
Sg.		Pl.	Sg.		Pl.
1. - ν	1. - μεν		1. - μην	1. - μεθα	
2. - ς	2. - τε		2. - ου (-σο)	2. - σθε	
3. - #	3. - ν (σαν)		3. - το	3. - ντο	

139.2   Compare -το, -ντο. As in -ται, -νται, the sign of the plural in the
        third person middle endings is the _____. Where have you seen -μην
for 1 sg. (133)?

139.3   -ου stands in the Impf. middle passive indicative, 2 sg., as result
        of a contraction of the variable vowel and the personal ending vowel
after the loss of intervocalic sigma: - εϕο - εο - ου. Learn both - ου
and - σο, in that order. Cf. 110-112.3.

144.1   The unity of the present system is seen in the patterns exhibited
        by the deponent verb. How? Cf. 123.1.

74

145.1   How does the neuter plural subject sometimes function outside the
        pattern of subject-verb agreement hitherto expected (29)?

146-
148.1   Contrast the emphatic and the correlative uses of both καί and οὐδέ.
        Make certain you understand the illustrations.

149.I. Aids to exercise I, Lesson XII.

   1.   ἐγράφοντο οὗτοι οἱ λόγοι ἐν βιβλίῳ.

        a. ἐγράφοντο: what tense stem? Indicates what type of action
            (123.3)?
            Active or middle-passive (139.1)?
            Present or past (126)?
        b. Full identification of the verb in context?
        c. Would the middle make sense (109)?

   2.   ἐδιδασκόμην ὑπ' αὐτοῦ ἐκ τῶν βιβλίων τῶν προφητῶν.

        a. ἐδιδασκόμην: dissect (138.1).
        b. Agent here is _____ (114).
        c. Gender of προφητῶν (78-79)?
        d. Are you sure the verb means continuing action? What would
            indicate that (122.1)?

   3.   ἐν ἐκείναις ταῖς ἡμέραις καὶ ἐδιδασκόμεθα ὑπ' αὐτοῦ καὶ ἐδιδάσκομεν
        τοὺς ἄλλους, ἀλλὰ νῦν οὐδὲ διδασκόμεθα οὐδὲ διδάσκομεν.

        a. ἐδιδασκόμην καὶ ἐδιδάσκομεν
            Compare and contrast their tense stem, personal ending, augment,
            and from this their tense, mood, voice, person, number.
            How do they differ? How alike?
        b. Do the same with διδασκόμεθα and διδάσκομεν.
        c. How do the verbs in the two clauses differ (110-112.1)?
        d. καί . . . καί and οὐδέ . . . οὐδέ as correlatives mean what
            (148)? What do they connect in these clauses?

   4.   ἀπήρχοντο οἱ ἁμαρτωλοὶ πρὸς τὴν θάλασσαν.

        a. ἀπήρχοντο: analyze all parts (138.1).
            -ντο secondary or primary (139.1)? Active or middle-passive
            (139.1)?

b. Secondary endings lead one to suspect ἀπη - has what signal
    (123.3 and 131.2)?
c. The vocabulary form (P.M-P.I. dep. 1 sg.) is _____.

5. ἐξεπορεύετο πρὸς αὐτὸν ἡ ἐκκλησία, ἀλλὰ νῦν οὐκέτε ἐκπορεύεται.

   a. ἐξεπορεύετο
      Secondary middle or secondary active endings (139.1)?
      Verb stem is _____. Remember para. 116.
   b. How does knowledge of the vocabulary help you avoid taking
      the initial epsilon as an augment?
      Where is the augment (131 and 136)?
   c. How do the two verbs differ (139.1)? How are they alike?

6. οὔπω βλέπομεν τὸν κύριον ἐν τῇ δόξῃ αὐτοῦ, ἀλλὰ ἐδιδασκόμεθα
   ὑπ᾽ αὐτοῦ καὶ ἐν ταῖς ἡμέραις ταῖς κακαῖς.

   a. ἐδιδασκόμεθα
      Why past (123.3)?
      Why passive (20.2; 139.1)?
      Why indicative (20.3)?
   b. Agent here expressed by _____(114-115.2)?
   c. καί used how? Can it be a simple connective, "and"? What
      sense then? Check 146.

7. ἐλέγετο ἐν τῷ ἱερῷ καλὸς λόγος περὶ τούτου τοῦ ἀποστόλου.

   a. Verb is present or imperfect? active or passive?
      How do you know (123.4; 139.1)?
   b. Don't mind the word order. Pay attention to the case endings
      to tell you the function of each unit in the sentence.
      What is the subject?
   c. περί - with-the-genitive = _____.

8. περὶ αὐτὸν ἐβλέπετο ἡ δόξα αὐτοῦ.

   a. ἐβλέπετο
      Imperfect, not present; why (139.1)? Imperfect, not aorist;
      why (139.1)?
      What indicates past time (123.3)?
      What indicates continuing action (123.3)?
   b. περί: contrast with περί in last sentence.
      Notice that with the accusative περί means "around" in the con-
      crete sense of around a person or object; with the genitive
      case it is abstract, "around" in the sense of "conceptionally
      around" or "concerning."

9. ἐφέρετο τὰ δῶρα καὶ πρὸς τοὺς πονηρούς.

a. ἐφέρετο: dissection (138.1) and identification should be
relatively easy by now. Full identification of all items
continues to be necessary.
b. Can there be a direct object with the passive verb (113.2;
114-115.1)? Then what case and function is the neuter
τὰ δῶρα (34)?
Remember para. 145.

10. ἐδέχου τὰ βιβλία ἀπὸ τῶν προφητῶν.

a. ἐδέχου: -ου can only be one of two morphemes--a genitive
singular noun ending or _____(139.1). In
some contexts you would have to try both; here only one
makes sense.
b. What is δεχ - (20.1 and 138.2)?
What lexical form did you learn? What does this tell you
about the nature of the verb (116)?

11. συνήρχοντο οἱ μαθηταὶ πρὸς τοῦτον.

a. συνήρχοντο
Personal ending identified (139.1) _____?
Why the eta (123.3, 126, and 131)?
Lexical form: _____
b. What use of the demonstrative (104.5)?

12. τὰ ἔργα τοῦ πονηροῦ πονηρά ἐστιν.

a. Note τὰ ἔργα and ἐστίν. Identify and remember 145.
b. πονηρά: feminine or neuter adjective? Why? (66; 99.1-2).

13. οὐδὲ αὐτὸς πονηρὸς οὐδὲ τὰ ἔργα πονηρά.

a. The two statements are αὐτὸς πονηρός and τὰ ἔργα πονηρά.
What use of the adjectives (71)? How would αὐτος ὁ
πονηρός change the sense (99.3)?
b. αὐτός is either intensive or pronominal (as subject). Why
so (105.2-3)? Which makes most sense?
c. What use of οὐδέ. . .οὐδέ (148)?

14. ὑπὲρ τῆς ἐκκλησίας αὐτοῦ ἀπέθνησκεν ὁ κύριος.

    a. ἀπέθνησκεν: can - εν be a secondary personal ending (127 and 128)?
       What is the <u>nu</u> (129)?
    b. Where is the augment? Why there (131)?
       Can the α- be the augment (126)?

15. οὐκ ἔστιν μαθητὴς ὑπὲρ τὸν διδάσκαλον αὐτοῦ οὐδὲ δοῦλος ὑπὲρ τὸν κύριον αὐτοῦ.

    a. Contrast ὑπέρ here with its use in the last sentence. Notice again the preposition with the accusative has more concrete meaning. Cf. 8.b. above.
    b. What is the subject of ἔστιν? the predicate?
    c. What is assumed as understood in clause two?

16. ἐν τῷ πλοίῳ ἤγου πρὸς τὸν κύριον διὰ τῆς θαλάσσης.

    a. Do you need to look up the nominative singular of πλοίῳ in order to see the syntax or even to translate, provided you remember the meaning of this noun?
    b. ἤγου. What is -ου (139.1)?
    c. What are the four sense units in the sentence?

17. ἐξήρχεσθε ἐκ τῶν οἴκων ὑμῶν.

    a. ἐξήρχεσθε: what item distinguishes this from a present tense verb (124)?
       Where is it (131)?
    b. What are key indications of the imperfect (123.4; 138.2)?
    c. Type of action must be _____(122.1-2)?

18. ταῦτα τὰ δαιμόνια ἐξήρχετο διὰ τοῦ λόγου αὐτοῦ.

    a. Full identifications made? ἐξηρ = ἐξερ- or ἐξαρ- ?
    b. Remember para. 116 and 145.

19. ἠκούοντο καὶ ἤκουον· ἀκούονται καὶ ἀκούουσιν.

    a. Study these verb sets carefully. Each clause has instructive similarities and contrasts in its verbs. What are they?

b. Why is it best to take the second verb as third person plural? Cf. 135.I.4 and its parallel verbs.

20. ἠρχόμην πρὸς τὸν κύριον, ἦγον δὲ καὶ τοὺς ἄλλους.

   a. ἠρχόμην: Formally it could be either one of what two present stems (see 125-126)?
      1. _____meaning_____
      2. _____meaning_____
      (Sense demands which choice here?)
   b. Why take ἦγον as first person singular when -ν can be 3rd plural as well (see 19.b above).
   c. On καί see 146.

149.II NEW TESTAMENT GREEK READING, John 1.14

Translate

σάρξ	See note above on 1.13 and look through Ch. XVII. Note para. 219.
ἐγένετο	Can this be imperfect of γίνομαι? Why not (138.2 and identifications in preceding verses)?
ἐσκήνωσεν	"(It) tented, dwelt." Aorist active indicative, 3 sg., of σκηνόω.
ἐθεασάμεθα	Aorist middle indicative deponent form of θεάομαι. Look up meaning. Remember 116.
ὡς	"As"
μονογενοῦς	"Of an only begotten one." M. G. sg. of a third declension adjective, μονογενής, -ές. See 360 on form.
πατρός	M. G. sg. of πατήρ. See 565.
πλήρης	"Full." Another third declension adjective like μονογενής. See para. 360 again.
χάριτος	F. G. sg. of χάρις. See para. 347. -ος as genitive sg. should signal third declension by now. What other similar forms have you seen in these verses (1.7, 8, 13, 14)?
	Why genitive? No possession here. Signals content. Full of what? See 45.I.17c and CEG, p. 28.

Read back over 1.1-5 now.

150.1   From now on, whenever more than one form of a verb is given in the vocabulary list, learn them all, e.g., ἀναβλέπω, ἀναβλέψω.

In addition, relate new forms of old words carefully to those words previously learned, e.g., relate γνώσομαι to γινώσκω.

150.2   Note the following Greek roots which can help in tying varying word forms together.

βαίνω, βήσομαι	βα	go
γίνομαι, γενήσομαι	γεν	become
γινώσκω, γηώσομαι	γνο	know
διδάσκω, διδάξω	διδάχ	teach
ἐλεύσομαι	ἐλθ	come
ἔχω, ἕξω	(σ) εχ	have
λαμβάνω, λήμφομαι	λαβ	receive

Notice that many present stems will be formed with the spelling - σκω attached somehow to the root. See Lexical Aids, pp. 44-46.

Present verbs spelled - σσω/-σσομαι have roots with κ, γ, χ, instead of the -σσ -.

150.3   English derivatives: The Kerygma, κήρυγμα, related to κηρύσσω.

151.1   The student has learned the indicative of the present verb system, with six full verb conjugations built on the present stem. Each voice of a tense is considered a separate conjugation.

Review the six conjugations of the present system by listing them here (123.1; cf. para. 589). Do it!

1.   4.

2.   5.

3.   6.

151.2   The future verb system is built on the future tense stem and includes two conjugation:
        1.

        2.   (not passive; 153)

151.3   The present active indicative, first person singular, is the "first principal part" of the Greek verb system. From it one may extract the present stem, the foundation of the presents (active, middle and passive) and the imperfects (active, middle and passive).

151.4   The future active indicative is the "second principal part" of the Greek verb (there can be six in all). From it one may readily discover the future tense stem, the foundation of the future active and middle.

151.5   Deponent verbs have middle or passive principal parts in those verb systems in which they are deponent. The first two principal parts of "to know," (1) γινώσκω and (2) γνώσομαι, for example, show that the verb is deponent in the future system (2) but not in the present system (1). Cf. para. 163.

151.6   The principal parts of a verb are the foundational forms which allow one to use the various tenses of that verb accurately in a language. The student is already familiar with the principal parts of English verbs. Thus, English has

           "regular" verbs: love, love<u>d</u>, love<u>d</u>
                                         hate, hate<u>d</u>, hate<u>d</u>

     and

           "irregular" verbs: eat, ate, eaten
                                         freeze, froze, frozen
                                         go, went, gone

It is a person's knowledge of these principal parts which keep one from conjugating

           regular verbs irregularly: love, lave, laven

           irregular verbs regularly: eat, eat<u>ed</u>, eat<u>ed</u>
                                         freeze, <u>freezed</u>, freeze<u>d</u>

So also in Greek, the student's mastery of the principal parts, γινώσκω, γνώσομαι, or ἔρχομαι, ἐλεύσομαι is the basis of accurate recognition of these verbs in varying tenses.

151.7   Mixed verb sets. ἐλεύσομαι (root -ελ) has become the future of ἔρχομαι. But it was obviously not originally a part of that verb set, judging from the drastically varying forms of the two verbs. Other principal parts used in the New Testament tense forms of ἔρχομαι were also related to the root ἐλ- rather than ἔρχομαι (ἦλθον, = augmented ἐλ-, for example).

Such "mixed verb sets" are familiar to the student from Egnlish verbs such as "go," "went," "gone." "Go" and "gone" are apparently related to each other (from Anglo-saxon g<u>a</u>n). "Went" is from an entirely different word with a related meaning, "to w<u>e</u>nd" (Anglo-saxon, <u>wendan</u>; cf. German <u>wenden</u>). In the minds of English speakers they are a unit, whose different origin and varying form have no effect on their regular use. Verbs like ἔρχομαι, ἐλεύσομαι, and like λέγω, ἐρῶ, εἶπον functioned the same say.

151.8   In most lexicons the first verb form given is the first principal part,
          followed by the second and third principal parts, and so on. See
in the vocabulary, p. 262, as an example. When a verb does not occur in
the New Testament in a given principal part, a space will often be left showing
the omission. In Machen's list such principal parts are in parenthesis (p. 255).

152.1   The primary personal endings appear on "non-past" tenses or on tenses
          in non-temporal reference (that is, outside the indicative mood).
Secondary personal endings appear on the past tenses. Present, future and perfect are primary tenses then. Imperfect, aorist, and pluperfect (see p. 21. n. 1)
are secondary tenses.

153.1   Why will a future verb like λύσομαι never be identified as the future
          "middle-passive" indicative, even without a context?

154-5.1 Study the conjugation of the future active and future middle indica-
          tive of λύω.

          What endings do you recognize (139.1 and 152)?
          Why are secondary endings not found on the future (127.1)?
          What variable vowels are used (cf. 20, 111, and 152)?
          What is the sign of the future tense (151, 152)?

154.2   Be able to "dissect" the future verbs just as you have the verbs of
          the present system (Cf. 20.4; 110-112.5; 123.2 and 138.1).

tense stem (verb stem & tense suffix)	variable vowel	primary ending	
λυσ (λυ-σ)	- ο -	μεν	λύσομεν
διωξ (διωκ - σ)	- ε -	τε	διώξετε

156.1   The consonant changes produced by the addition of sigma to each
          of the three main classes of consonants are in most cases exactly
what one would expect.

	Verb stem ends in			tense suffix		resultant consonant
labial	π	β	φ			ψ
palatal	κ	γ	χ	+ σ	=	ξ
dental	τ	δ,ζ	θ			σ

156.2   Knowledge of these phonetic "equations" will greatly simplify the task
          of verb identification. One simply must know that behind a verb ending
in psi (ψ) there will probably be either final π, β, or φ plus sigma and behind
final xi (ξ) a combination of κ, γ or χ and sigma.

157.1   The distinction the author draws between the tense stems and the basic verb stem upon which the tense stems are each built is important.

From a very regular verb like λύω, one might incorrectly suppose that the future λύσω was formed by simply adding the tense suffix to the present stem (λυ-σ). This is not so. This incorrect diagram would be:

λυ	+	σ	=	λυσ(ω)
Present stem	+	Tense suf.	=	Future stem

This confusion is possible only because in λύω the present stem and the verb stem happen to coincide.

157.2   Actually, the principal parts are each formed separately from a single verb stem which is basic to all of them or from additional verb stems in sets where two different verbs have come together to form a single verb system.

The situation can more accurately be diagramed as follows:

Present stem   Future stem

γινώσκω   γνώσομαι

-σκω forms   tense suffix
many presents   + σ

γνο-
Verb stem
(basic to both)

163.1   How are compound verbs listed in the lexicon in NTGFB?

165.1   Translation techniques again! Precise identifications will always be necessary. Make sure you know precisely what each form in the text is and how it functions in the sentence (i.e., what does the form indicate). In most cases this will be second nature to you now, but never minimize the importance of this discipline.

Maintain a healthy independence in your translation. Do not allow yourself in any case to be dependent upon the translations provided in the answer sheets, if you are using them. It will be increasingly obvious to you that several English phrasings would correctly render the sentences. Do not slavishly follow the "answers."

165.I   Aids to exercise I, Lesson XIII.

   1. ἄξει ὁ κύριος τοὺς μαθητὰς αὐτοῦ εἰς τὴν βασιλείαν.

XIII
165.I.2

a. ἄξει: primary active ending, so it can only be future or present.
If it is present, the lexical form is _____.
If it is future, it could either be from ἄγω, ἄκω, or ἄχω.
Why? Don't go on unless you can explain it (156 and 156.1).

b. Gender of μαθητάς (78-79)?

2. γνωσόμεθα καὶ τοὺς ἀγαθοὺς καὶ τοὺς πονηρούς.

    a. γνωσόμεθα: dissect: /   /   /
       Identify, always relating it to the <u>first</u> principal part.
    b. <u>Sigma</u> indicates what (151)?
    c. This is not a "middle-passive." Why (153.1)?
    d. καί. . .καί (148)?

3. λήμψεσθε τὰ πλοῖα ἐκ τῆς θαλάσσης.

    a. λήμψεσθε: ending and variable vowel removed?
       Review the roots (150.2).
       Whence the ψ (156)?
       What significance for verb identification (151)?
    b. Why not passive (116)?

4. λύσεις τοὺς δούλους.

    a. Verb fully identified?
    b. Why not present? Why not middle? Passive?

5. ἕξουσιν οἱ πονηροὶ οὐδὲ χαρὰν οὐδὲ εἰρήνην.

    a. ἕξουσιν: primary active ending can only signal what two
       tenses (see 1a)?
    b. ἕξ - could have been formed from what (156)?
       Vocabulary knowledge narrows to _____.
    c. οὐδέ...οὐδέ (148)?

6. ἐν ἐκείνῃ τῇ ὥρᾳ ἐλεύσεται ὁ υἱὸς τοῦ ἀνθρώπου σὺν τοῖς ἀγγέλοις
αὐτοῦ.

    a. ἐλεύσεται: if this is present tense, what is the lexical form?
    b. If it is not, what would make you identify it as future (151)?
       indicative (20.3)?   as a middle (139.1)?

7. ἁμαρτωλοί ἐστε, γενήσεσθε δὲ μαθηταὶ τοῦ κυρίου.

    a. Compare and contrast the verbs in as many ways as possible (99: 139.1).
    b. What is the difference in meaning between the two verbs (108.1)?

8. διώκουσιν οἱ πονηροὶ τοὺς προφήτας, ἀλλ' ἐν ταῖς ἡμέραις τοῦ υἱοῦ τοῦ ἀνθρώπου οὐκέτι διώξουσιν αὐτούς.

    a. What distinguishes the future from the present in the two verbs (151).
    b. οἱ πονηροί: what use of the adjective?
       If you cannot name the use and explain it, read para. 75 and 75.1-3 until you can. Then ask the instructor, if it is still not clear.

9. προσεύξῃ τῷ θεῷ σου καὶ δοξάσεις αὐτόν.

    a. προσεύξῃ. -ῃ = what ending (139.1)?
    b. Explain the ξ on προσεύξ -(156)?
    c. δοξάσεις, if present tense, what is the lexical form?
       If it is future, what consonant stems could lie behind this form (156)?

10. τότε γνώσεσθε ὅτι αὐτός ἐστιν ὁ κύριος.

    a. γνώσεσθε: notice the lengthened root vowel ο to ω before the tense suffix. Sigma indicates what here (151)?
    b. αὐτός: use (105.2)?
    c. The ὅτι clause supplies what information here? What is the object of γνώσεσθε.
       How can a verb with -εσθε have an object (116)?

11. ταῦτα γνώσομαι οὐδὲ ἐγώ.

οὐδε ἐγώ would be roughly equivalent to οὐ καὶ ἐγώ "not even I," but is used instead of it (147).

12. ἄλλους διδάξει ὁ δοῦλος, ἀλλ' ἐμὲ διδάξει ὁ διδάσκαλος ὁ πιστός.

    a. διδάξει: explain the origin of the ξ (150.2 and 156) and its significance (151.2).
       Why primary endings (127.1 and NTGFB, p. 21 n. 1)?

85

XIII
165.I.13.

b. Why use ἐμέ rather than με (94).

13. ἐκεῖνα λήμψονται οἱ ἀπόστολοι, ταῦτα δὲ καὶ οἱ ἀδελφοί.

   a. λήμψονται: ending = _____ (139.1).
       Variable vowel = _____ (151).
       Explain the origin of the ψ (150.2 and 156) and its signifi-
       cance (151-2).
   b. λημψ - from the root λαβ. Notice the <u>mu</u> inserted before the
       beta (λημβ + σ). The same development occurs in the present
       λαμβ(άνω). Notice also that - ανω(or -αινω) is frequently
       used to form present stems from a word root.
   c. δέ connects the two clauses. not καί. What is the function
       of καί (146)?

14. διὰ τοῦ λόγου τοῦ κυρίου ἀναβλέψουσιν οἱ τυφλοὶ οὗτοι.

   a. ἀναβλέψουσιν: has primary endings, no augment.
       Why not present tense (151-2, and 156.1)?
   b. Full identifications continue to be necessary, either done
       automatically, or step by step, if there is any hesitation.

15. ὁ προφήτης αὐτὸς γράψει ταῦτα ἐν ταῖς γραφαῖς.

   a. αὐτός: what use (105.2)?
       What would ὁ αὐτὸς προφήτης be?
   b. γράψει: explain the form and the basis of your identification
       (156).
   c. ταῖς γραφαῖς: "the Scriptures" are a particular set of
       writings, specified by the article.

16. ἐλεύσονται κακαὶ ἡμέραι.

ἐλεύσονται has become the future of ἔρχομαι but was obviously
not originally part of the ἔρχομαι verbs. See 151.7.

17. ἀπελεύσῃ καὶ σὺ εἰς τὰς ὁδοὺς τῶν πονηρῶν καὶ διδάξεις οὕτως
     τοὺς ἀνθρώπους.

   a. ἀπελεύσῃ: what would lead you to identify it as a future
       even if you had not learned ἐλεύσομαι as the second principal
       part of ἔρχομαι (139.1; 151)?

b. ἀπελευσ- why <u>not</u> take the first <u>epsilon</u> as an augment (123.3)?
c. There are two καί-s, but they do not work here as the καί...καί construction (148). How is the first one used (146)?

18. κηρύξουσιν καὶ αὐτοὶ τὸ εὐαγγέλιον ἐν τούτῳ τῷ κόσμῳ τῷ κακῷ.

a. What distinguishes κηρύξουσιν from the present form (156)?
b. Remember that αὐτός is rarely used simply as a subject.

19. ἐλεύσεται καὶ αὕτη πρὸς αὐτόν, καὶ αὐτὸς διδάξει αὐτήν.

a. αὕτη: not an intensive use of αὐτός. What is it (102)?
b. Probably not καί...καί since καὶ ἐλεύσεται... καὶ διδάξει would make sense here, but not καὶ αὕτη ... καὶ αὐτός(146-48).

20. ἐκηρύσσετο τὸ εὐαγγέλιον ἐν ταῖς ἡμέραις ταῖς κακαῖς, κηρύσσεται δὲ καὶ νῦν, ἀλλ' ἐν ἐκείνῃ τῇ ἡμέρᾳ ἐλεύσεται ὁ κύριος αὐτός.

165.II NEW TESTAMENT GREEK READING, John 1.15

μαρτυρεῖ	P. A. I., 3 sg., of μαρτυρέω. Note irregular verb accent here (13). It has resulted from a contraction of the verb stem's final vowel and the vowel of the personal ending (μαρτυρε + ει = μαρτυρεῖ). If you are interested in an explanation now, see Ch. XXIII.
	Note the use of the present tense here to narrate a <u>past</u> event with vividness; called the "historic present" in Greek (see CEG. p. 53 and DM, p. 185). Colloquial English has a similar use.
κέκραγεν λέγων	"Cried, saying." Perfect (426, 451 ff.) active indicative, 3 sg., of κραζω, followed by the present active participle of λέγω (226).
ὃν εἶπον	"Whom I said." Relative clause (395ff.). Function as predicate noun for οὗτος ἦν (133).
	εἶπον is second (i.e., irregular) aorist active indicative, 1 sg., of λέγω (193).

ὁ (ὀπίσω μου) ἐρχόμενος   "The one who (after me) comes." P. M-P. ptc., deponent of ἔρχομαι. On form see para. 230; on use see para. 235, but don't linger.

ἔμπροσθέν μου γέγονεν   "He became/has come to be ahead of me." On ἔμπροσθεν, see AG, p. 256 (2 d. under the word). "Ahead" in what respect?

γέγονεν   "Is become/has become/has come to be." Perfect active indicative, 3 sg., of γίνομαι. Note γεγ - and κεκ - on the perfects in this verse and see again paras. 430 and 436, then 426.

Review this verse now and read back over 1.6-10.

Lesson XIV

166.1   Notice the English derivatives to aid in memorization of the vocabulary and to increase your understanding of English.

apostrophe _____ + _____ "a turning away"
thaumaturge (a wonder worker) _____
therapeutic _____

166.2   The aorist active indicative, first person singular, will be the third principal part of a Greek verb (middle for deponent verbs) and so will be the third word listed in the vocabulary. Learn all of the principal parts for each new entry.

167.1   The difference between the so-called first aorist and the second aorist is strictly in form. Both are aorists with aorist meaning. First aorists are regular verbs, second aorists are irregular verbs. That is all.

168.1   How is the aorist like the imperfect?

168.2   How do the aorist and the imperfect differ?

168.3   To say the aorist denotes "simple action" is actually to describe the way a writer/speaker refers to the act, not necessarily the nature of the act itself. It is better to talk of a "simple reference" to an act (whether present, past or future). The context will often have to show whether the act was completed, or was continuing (i.e., the nature of the act).

For example, one may say that "Niagara Falls flowed," using a simple reference to the act (aorist in Greek). Or one may say "Niagara Falls was flowing," a reference specifying continued action in the past (Greek imperfect). Both are simply ways of referring to an action which by its very nature is continuing, whether the reference indicates it or not.

168.4   Aorist means unspecified, ὁρίζειν, "to mark out," ἀορίζειν, "not to mark out."

170.1   Why does Machen suggest adopting the English preterit (a simple reference to a past act) as the standard translation of the aorist in the exercises?

171-
80.1   Study the aorist active and aorist middle conjugations in view of your knowledge of the secondary active and middle endings (139.1).
What personal endings are used (173)? Why (127.1)?
With what modifications (174)?

171-
80.2   What in these aorist conjugations indicates past time (124.1)?
The aorist tense stem does not indicate past time: it simply indicates:
   1. an aoristic (simple) reference to the act
   2. the act itself (whether "seeing" or "walking")

171-
80.3   It is preferable to regard <u>sigma</u> as the aorist tense suffix and
       <u>alpha</u> as the connecting vowel, even though - σα together are sure
       indications of the first aorist (cf. 175 and 182).

       Be able to dissect the aorists and label the verb parts.

       ελυσαμεν: ε - λυ - σ - α - μεν

       ελυσαμεθα: ε - λυ - σ - α - μεθα

       _____   _____   _____   _____   _____   (Fill in).

171-
80.4   Why, as in the future, will an aorist deponent verb never be identi-
       fied as aorist "middle-passive" even without a context (cf. 153.1)?

171-
80.5   Compare para. 176 and 129.

181.1 By now the student is accustomed to the irregularity in the second
       person singular middle endings caused by the loss of intervocalic <u>sigma</u>
between the variable vowel and the vowel of the personal ending.

       present   λυεϕαι   >   λυεαι   >   λυῃ
       future   λυσεϕαι   >   λυσεαι   >   λυσῃ
       imperfect   ελυεϕο   >   ελυεο   >   ελυου
       first aorist   ελυσαϕο   >   ελυσαο   >   ελυσω

183.1 Review the consonant changes learned in Chapter XIII in connection
       with the addition of the <u>sigma</u> future tense suffix, para. 156. Be
able to write the equations in 156.1!

183.2 How are the consonant changes in 156 relevant here?

185.I Aids to exercise I, Lesson XIV

       1. ἀπέλυσεν ὁ κύριος τὸν δοῦλον αὐτοῦ, ὁ δὲ δοῦλος οὐκ ἀπέλυσε
           τὸν ἄλλον.

           a. What is the formal difference between the two verb forms (176)?
           b. -ε (ν) is what personal ending (139.1: 173)?
           c. The <u>sigma</u> here cannot be the <u>future</u> tense suffix. Why?
               What personal endings must follow the future tense suffix (152.1)?
           d. What three items cause you to identify the verbs as first
               aorist (171-80.3)?

2. ἤδη ἐπέστρεφαν οὗτοι πρὸς τὸν κύριον, ἐκεῖνοι δὲ ἐπιστρέφουσιν ἐν ταῖς ἡμέραις ταῖς κακαῖς.

    a. ἐπέστρεφαν cannot be future. Why (154.5.1; 171-80.3)?
What signs indicate aorist (171-80.3)?

    b. ἐπιστρέφουσιν: Why not aorist (171-80.1-2)?

    c. οὗτοι and ἐκεῖνοι. Remember 104.5.

3. ἐπιστεύσαμεν εἰς τὸν κύριον καὶ σώσει ἡμᾶς.

    a. —σα— with augmented verb stems can only be the first aorist indicative. Never miss it (175 and 171-80.3)!

    b. σώσει: Sigma suffix with primary endings must be _____
(152.1 and 154.2).
Tense stems ending in sigma probably conceal original consonants _____, _____, _____ or _____ (156.1).

    c. Action continuous or not in ἐπιστεύσαμεν? Can you tell by the aorist (168.3)?

4. καὶ ἐπίστευσας εἰς αὐτὸν καὶ πιστεύσεις.

    a. καί...καί (148).

    b. Compare and contrast the verbs and endings (138.1), variable vowel (154-5.1; 171-80.1) and augment (172). The identifications should be obvious.

5. ὑπέστρεψας πρὸς τὸν κύριον καὶ ἐδέξατό σε εἰς τὴν ἐκκλησίαν αὐτοῦ.

    a. ὑπέστρεψας: augment is where (131-32)?

    b. Explain the psi (156.1 and 183).

    c. ἐδέξατό σε: make a full and precise identification.
Explain the accent (93.1-2).

    d. Explain the xi (156.1 and 183).

6. ἐν ἐκείναις ταῖς ἡμέραις ἐπορεύεσθε ἐν ταῖς ὁδοῖς ταῖς κακαῖς.

    a. ἐπορεύεσθε: What tense stem (remove ending, variable vowel, and augment)?
Any tense suffixes?

    b. Augmented present stem can only be _____ (123.5).

    c. How translated different if it were aorist (123.3 and 168.3)?

7. ἐπεστρέψατε πρὸς τὸν κύριον καὶ ἐθεράπευσεν ὑμᾶς.

    a. ἐπεστρέψατε: what indications of aorist are here (173-177)?
       Identification and lexical form?
    b. Remember 176.

8. ἐκεῖνοι πονηροί, ἀλλ' ἡμεῖς ἐπείσαμεν αὐτούς.

    a. Why is ἡμεῖς used (97(4b))?
    b. ἐπείσαμεν: explain the consonant changes (156.1).
       What could the sigma have replaced?

9. ἡτοίμασα ὑμῖν τόπον ἐν τῷ οὐρανῷ.

    a. ἡτοίμασα. η- as augment is lengthened from either _____
       or _____ (126).
    b. Sigma replaced what final consonant (156.1 and 183)?
    c. Does the statement talk of the specific place prepared
       or of the sort of thing prepared (99.3)?

10. ἐδεξάμην σε εἰς τὸν οἶκόν μου, ἀλλ' οὗτοι οἱ πονηροι οὐκ ἐδέξαντο.

    a. -μην and -ντο are what endings (secondary/primary? 139.1)?
       Therefore, preceded here by alpha, their verbs must be what
       tense (171-80.1-2)?
    b. What part of the sentence is omitted in the second clause?

11. ἀνέβλεφαν οἱ τυφλοί.

    a. ἀνέβλεφαν: compound verb with preposition ἀνά. This pre-
       position means "up" as in ἀναβαίνω, "to go up;" it also fre-
       quently means "again," when it is in compound. So here, "to
       see again."
       What signs of the aorist are here (172-174)?
    b. Why can it not be future with psi (154-5.1)?

12. ἔσωσα ὑμᾶς ἐγώ, ὑμεῖς δὲ ἐμὲ οὐκ ἐδέξασθε εἰς τοὺς οἴκους ὑμῶν.

    a. ἔσωσα: identify fully. Remember 156.1 and 183.
       Why no -ν on this first person singular verb (174)?

b. Contrast ἔσωσα and σώσω in form and meaning.

c. ἐδέξασθε: <u>alpha</u> connecting vowel with probable <u>sigma</u> in
    -ξ- certainly indicates what (175 and 171-80.3)?
    Middle or middle-passive (171-80.4)?

13. πονηροὶ ἦσαν αὐτοί, πονηροὺς δὲ ἔπεμψαν εἰς τὴν ἐκκλησίαν.

a. ἦσαν. ε-root plus -σαν ending. Review para. 133 and 127.

b. Does πονηροί have to be definite to be substantive use (75)?

c. ἔπεμψαν: identify all parts. Do you see the <u>sigma-alpha</u>?
    Where (156.1; 183)? What significance (175; 171-80.3)?

14. ἐδίδαξάς με ἐν τῷ ἱερῷ.

a. ἐδίδαξάς με: if it is a verb, -ς can only be what person
    and number (139.1)?
    What signs of first aorist (171-80.1)?

b. How would you change the form to make it future (154-5.1)?

c. Explain the enclitic accent (93.1-2).

15. τότε ἠκούσαμεν ταύτας τὰς ἐντολάς, ἄλλας δὲ ἀκούσομεν ἐν τῇ
     ἐκκλησίᾳ.

a. Contrast the two verbs. What differentiates the aorist from
    the future (154-5.1 and 171-80.1)?

b. Why cannot ἠκούσαμεν be imperfect with its augment and
    secondary endings (123.5)?

16. ἐν ἐκείνῃ τῇ ὥρᾳ ἐξελεύσονται ἐκ τοῦ κόσμου, τότε δὲ ἐδέξαντο
     ἡμᾶς.

a. ἐξεκεύσονται: <u>sigma</u> tense suffix, primary endings; can
    the ἐξε - include an augment (124.1; 154-5.1)?
    Identify fully and explain the middle ending (116).

b. ἐδέξαντο: contrast with ἐδέξασθε in No. 12.
    What is the sign of the plural (139.2)?
    Why not "were receiving" (cf. 122.2; 168.1-2)?

17. ἤκουσαν αὐτοῦ καὶ ἐθαύμασαν

a. Why the genitive on αὐτοῦ (119)?

b. <u>Sigma</u> tense suffix standing alone will either indicate a verb stem ending in a vowel (ἀκου-) or ending in ____, ____, ____, or ____ (156.1).

18. ἐδέξω σὺ τὸ εὐαγγέλιον, οὗτοι δὲ οὐ δέξονται αὐτό.

    a. ἐδέξω: this ending is easily confused (-ω). Knowing δέχομαι, the initial <u>epsilon</u> must be an _____ (125)? Thus -ω cannot be a primary ending. Review 181 and 181.1.

    b. Why the independent σύ (97(4b))? Cf. the pronouns in No. 8 and especially No. 12.

19. οὐδὲ ἠκούσαμεν τὸν κύριον οὐδὲ ἐπιστεύσαμεν εἰς αὐτόν.

    a. Why does <u>sigma-alpha</u> stand unaltered in these aorists? Can the verbs be anything but first aorist (171-80.3)?

    b. Review 184 and recall οὐδέ. . .οὐδέ (148).

185.II NEW TESTAMENT GREEK READING, John 1.16-17

    Translate 1.16

πληρώματος	Look up πλήρωμα and see para. 222. Review the nouns in 1.13 also (135.II). Note that this noun is built on the same root as the adjective πλήρης. See <u>Lexical Aids</u>, pp. 66-67.
ἡμεῖς	Unfamiliar? Review paras. 94-95 now!
πάντες	Paras. 365-369 on form and use. Review verses 3 and 7.
ἐλάβομεν	"We received." Second (i.e., irregular) aorist active indicative of λαμβάνω (193). Cannot be imperfect in spite of the augment and secondary endings. Why (123.5)?
χάριν. . . χάριτος	See paras. 347-348.
ἐδόθη	Aorist passive indicative, 3 sg., of the <u>mi</u>-verb, δίδωμι. Review again paras. 482-485, 490 and then 201.
ἐγένετο	Second (i.e., irregular) aorist middle indicative, 3 sg., deponent, of γίνομαι. Cannot be imperfect in spite of augment and secondary middle ending. Why (123.5)?

Review John 1.11-13.

186.1   Some English derivatives may not be obvious in the vocabulary.

εἶδον   root is ιδ-, with the older Greek digamma, pronounced
            "wid;" thus video through Latin.
ὄψομαι   root is οπ- "see;" hence "optics."

187.1   Do the first and second aorist differ in meaning? How do they differ?

189.1   To ascertain the tense of any verb one must identify the tense stem.
        Some tense stems are formed with tense suffixes (first aorist, future),
some are not (present, second aorist). How can you distinguish a second aorist
form from an imperfect form which may be very similar?

189.2   The second aorist stems are very often similar to, if not the same as,
        the basic verb stem and in many cases as the word root itself from
which several other related words are formed.   Study the second aorists in
the vocabulary noting their tense stems and where possible their roots.[1]

	root	
ἔβαλον	βαλ	throw
ἐγενόμην	γεν	become; compare γενήσομαι
εἶδον	ἰδ	see
ἔλαβον	λαβ	take
ἤγαγον	ἀγ	lead (2A = doubled verb stem)
ἦλθον	ἐλ	come; cf. ἐλεύσομαι fut.
ἔλιπον	λιπ	leave
ὄψομαι (fut.)	ὀπ	see

189.3   Very often the consonants will carry the essential meaning through
        several varying verb forms with change of vowel or vowel position.
Notice γ-ν in γίνομαι, γενήσομαι, ἐγενόμην, γέγονα, and ἐγενήθην or the β-λ
in βάλλω, βαλῶ, ἔβαλον, βέβληκα, βέβλημαι and ἐβλήθην.

190.1   The third principal part of any verb, whether it has first aorist or
        second aorist, is the basis for what two verb conjugations?
        1.

        2.

190.2   The future passive and aorist passive are both formed on the sixth
        principal part.

191.1   What indicates past time in the second aorist? (171-80.2; 124.1)

191.2   What does the second aorist stem itself indicate: (20.1; 171-80.2)?
        1.

        2.

192-
194.1   Be able to "dissect" any second aorist form.

---

[1]Recall the root lists in Lexical Aids, pp. 41, 49-72.

ἔλιπον : ἔ - λιπ - ο - ν

ἐβάλομεν: ἐ - βάλ - ο - μεν

      <u>augment</u>   tense   variable   personal
                <u>stem</u>   <u>vowel</u>   <u>ending</u>

195.1 Exercises: Preliminary

Remember the function of the study questions. The student need not write an answer to every question asked, but he <u>must</u> be able to answer it. Unless the answer comes quickly, the student should consider it an assignment to look up the reference and find the answer. The repeated reading of information allows the student to continue an informal review of the important items of the grammar.

195.I Aids to exercise I. Lesson XV.

1. καὶ εἴδομεν τὸν κύριον καὶ ἠκούσαμεν τοὺς λόγους αὐτοῦ.

    a. Since first person plural endings are the same for primary and secondary verbs (139.1), one must look elsewhere for clues to the tense. What do you see (172-176 and 191)?

    b. The identification of the tense stem is always the answer to the question of a verb's tense, regardless of the voice or mood. How do you know εἴδομεν is second aorist and ἠκούσαμεν is first aorist? Because εἰδ - and ἠκουσ - are (augmented) <u>aorist stems.</u>

2. οὐδὲ γὰρ εἰσῆλθες εἰς τοὺς οἴκους αὐτῶν οὐδὲ εἶπες αὐτοῖς παραβολήν.

    a. εἰσῆλθες: person and number (139.1)?
        Has to be either imperfect or aorist; why (152.1)?

    b. If it is imperfect, what is its first principal part (123.5)? If it is aorist, it must be second aorist; why (171-80.3 and 175)? Second aorists are irregular, so that one would either have to look up ἦλθον or know it as the third principal part of _____ (186).

    c. Remember the augment position (131-32).

    d. εἶπον: the third principal part of _____ (186). What indications of indicative mood (20.3)? Of past time (124.1)?

3. ἐν ἐκείνῃ τῇ ὥρᾳ ἐγένοντο μαθηταὶ τοῦ κυρίου.

    a. ἐγένοντο: what is the root (189.2)? _____?
        Same in the future, but future is impossible here. Why (154-5.1)?

    b. Why nominative in μαθηταὶ (109 and 99)? Remember 99.3.

c. The verb is deponent. How do you know (151.5)?
If the deponent verb is still confusing to you, review carefully paragraph 116, and state the concept in your own words.

4. οὗτοι μὲν ἐγένοντο μαθηταὶ ἀγαθοί, ἐκεῖνοι δὲ ἔτι ἦσαν πονηροί.

    a. Compare and contrast ἐγένοντο and ἦσαν (127, 133, 116, 108.1, 168.3).
    b. Remember the predicate nominatives (99, 108).
    c. It can't be "these good disciples;" why (104.4)?

5. προσέφερον αὐτῷ τοὺς τυφλούς.

    a. προσέφερον: secondary active ending (139.1), augment (131-32); why not aorist (123.5)?
    b. What would the aorist form be (186)?
    c. The imperfect could here well indicate an action repeated often in the past, even perhaps a customary action, and so continuous.

6. ἔπεσον ἐκ τοῦ οὐρανοῦ οἱ ἄγγελοι οἱ πονηροί.

    a. ἔπεσον: <u>sigma</u> here cannot indicate future. Why (152.1)? <u>Sigma-omicron</u> cannot indicate first aorist. Why (171-80.3)? That must be <u>sigma-</u> _____ (175).
    b. Full identification. Notice the value of knowing the principal parts as part of the vocabulary when it comes to identifying second aorists (186).

7. τὰ μὲν δαιμόνια ἐξεβάλετε, τὰ δὲ τέκνα ἐθεραπεύσατε.

    a. ἐξεβάλετε: why not imperfect? What clearly distinguishes it (123.5)? In this word the two tenses are identical except for this feature. Where is the augment (131-32)?
    b. How do the two verbs differ (187.1 and 167.1; 175)?
    c. μέν . .δέ (121): notice how the word order indicates contrast along with these conjunctions.

8. τοὺς μὲν πονηροὺς συνηγάγετε ὑμεῖς εἰς τοὺς οἴκους ὑμῶν, τοὺς δὲ ἀγαθοὺς ἡμεῖς.

    a. συνηγάγετε: differs from the imperfect how (123.5; 189.2)?
    b. -ετε tells you what (139.1: 20.2-3)?
    c. What part of the sentence is omitted in the second clause, to be supplied on the basis of parallel structure?
    d. Review 97(4b) on the independent personal pronouns.

9. οὐκ ἐκύρυξας τὸ εὐαγγέλιον ἐν τῇ ἐκκλησίᾳ, οὐδὲ γὰρ ἐγένου μαθητής.

    a. ἐκήρυξας: -ς personal ending (139.1), augment, and <u>alpha</u>
          connecting vowel can only mean what (173-175)?
          <u>Xi</u> therefore conceals what (156.1 and 183)?

    b. ἐγένου: -ου is what secondary ending (139.1)?
          γεν - root (here also tense stem) signals what word (189.2)?
          Cannot be imperfect, why (123.5)? What has tense stem to
          do with the answer (189.1)?

    c. μαθητής: is identity or characterization the point? Review 99.3!

10. νῦν μὲν λέγετε λόγους ἀγαθούς, εἶπον δὲ οὗτοι τοὺς αὐτοὺς λόγους
    καὶ ἐν ταῖς ἡμέραις ἐκειναις.

    a. εἶπον is <u>unambiguous</u> in this context; (why 139)?
          Active or passive? How do you know (20.2)?

    b. αὐτός in attributive position must mean _____ (105.2).

    c. καί makes no sense here as coordinator, "and." How used (146)?

11. ἐπιστεύσαμεν εἰς τὸν κύριον, οἱ γὰρ μαθηταὶ ἤγαγον ἡμᾶς πρὸς
    αὐτόν.

    a. γάρ clauses give what information? time? place? reason?
          result?
          Compare ὅτι clauses. Why does γάρ follow οἱ (186, 91)?

    b. ἤγαγον: full identification. Was the action continuous (168.3)?

12. ταῦτα μὲν εἶπον ὑμῖν ἐν τῷ ἱερῷ, ἐκεῖνα δὲ οὔπω λέγω.

    a. Why identify εἶπον as first person singular (33.4)?

    b. The demonstratives are used how (104.5)?
          What is to be supplied, judging by the gender?

13. τότε μὲν εἰσήλθετε εἰς τὴν ἐκκλησίαν, ἐν ἐκείνῃ δὲ τῇ ἡμέρᾳ
    εἰσελεύσεσθε εἰς τὸν οὐρανόν.

    a. εἰσήλθετε: compound verbs of this sort are best recognized
          when the principal parts of the base verb are known: ἔρχομαι,
          ἐλεύσομαι, ἦλθον. So also the verb in the second clause.

    b. Whence the <u>eta</u> in ἦλθετε (24.1; cf. the root, 189.2)?

    c. Remember εἰσέρχομαι . . . εἰς.

    d. εἰσελεύσεσθε: why middle (151.5)? Why not middle-passive (151.2)?

14. τότε ὀψόμεθα τὸν κύριον ἐν τῇ δόξῃ αὐτοῦ· ἐπιστεύσαμεν γὰρ εἰς
    αὐτόν.

a. ὀψόμεθα: what might be a clue to the future tense (156.1)?
Remember the root (189.2) _____. This is the second principal
part of _____ (186).
b. Second clause is causal. How do you know (186)?
c. ἐπιστεύσαμεν: what sure signs of the first aorist (171-80.1,3)?
"were believing" or "believed"? (168 and 168.3).

15. ὁ μὲν κύριος ἐξῆλθε τότε ἐκ τοῦ κόσμου, οἱ δὲ μαθηταὶ αὐτοῦ ἔτι
μένουσιν ἐν αὐτῷ.

a. ἐξῆλθε: verb with short ultima and accent only on penult should
indicate what (131-32)?
b. Personal ending -# with variable vowel -ε alone can only be
what person and number of what major set of endings (139.1)?

16. ταύτας τὰς ἐντολάς ἔλαβον ἀπὸ τοῦ κυρίου, ἤμην γὰρ μαθητὴς αὐτοῦ.

a. λαβ root means what (189.2)?
Here it coincides with the second aorist stem.
b. Contrast the form of ἔλαβον with the corresponding imperfect
(123.5). Why identify as first person singular (cf. No. 12)?
c. ἤμην = root ἐ- plus what ending (180)? See 133.
d. Anarthrous μαθητής: does it state identity or character (99.3)?

17. τότε μὲν παρελάβετε τὴν ἐπαγγελίαν παρὰ τοῦ κυρίου, νῦν δὲ καὶ
κηρύσσετε αὐτὴν ἐν τῷ κόσμῳ.

a. παρελάβετε: is the tense stem present or aorist (186 and 189.2)?
b. κηρύσσετε: tense stems ending in double sigma usually have
verb stem ending in _____ (150.2)?
c. What elements point to contrast in the two clauses?
d. αὐτήν: why feminine singular (97.3)?

18. ἤλθετε πρὸς τὸν κύριον καὶ παρελάβετε παρ' αὐτοῦ ταῦτα.

19 συνήγαγεν ἡμᾶς αὐτὸς εἰς τὴν ἐκκλησίαν αὐτοῦ.

a. συνήγαγεν: what is the final nu here (176)?
Reduplicated stem αγ-signals what tense stem here (186)?
b. αὐτός: probably not just a subject, so how is it functioning
(105.2)?

20. εἶδον οἱ ἄνθρωποι τὸν υἱὸν τοῦ θεοῦ· ἐγένετο γὰρ αὐτὸς ἄνθρωπος
καὶ ἔμενεν ἐν τούτῳ τῷ κόσμῳ.

a. εἶδον: what principal part of βλέπω? Must be learned for it is too irregular to be logically deduced from βλέπω.

b. ἐγένετο: imperfect or aorist? How do you know (123.5 and 189.2).

c. Of what specifically does the γάρ clause give the reason? Anarthrous ἄνθρωπος tells what? Para. 99.3 again.

d. οἱ ἄνθρωποι: the article specifies a certain group of beings, men in particular. The corresponding English class designation lacks the article, "men."

195.II   NEW TESTAMENT GREEK READING, John 1.18

Review John 1.1-17. Find the second aorist verb forms and identify them more accurately now in view of your study in chapter XV.

Translate.

οὐδείς	"No one." οὐ + δέ + εἷς, "Not + even + one." See para. 371.
ἑώρακεν	"Has seen." Perfect active indicative, 3 sg., of ὁράω (serves also for βλέπω).

Note the lack of reduplication on this perfect form. See again paras. 430, 435-436, and 452ff.

μονογενής	See para. 360 again on this third declension adjective. Review 1.14 above (149.II).
μονογενὴς θεός	Compare several translations with the American Bible Society Greek text of 1966 and

1968, edited by Kurt Aland and others. Look carefully at the note no. 18 in the critical apparatus of that text and see the four main readings that have arisen in the course of the transmission of this verse in John's Gospel.

List the readings and translate them.

1.   1.

2.   2.

3.   3.

4.   4.

Read the introduction to the ABS text, pp. x-xiv and locate some of the manuscripts listed in note no. 18 as evidence for the readings.

ὁ ὤν	"Who is (in the bosom)." Present participle construction of εἰμί (580), used adjectivally

(234) to describe μονογενὴς θεός.

ἐξηγήσατο	-σατο has to signal aorist middle indicative, 3 sg. Look up ἐξηγέομαι. Remember 116.

196.1   Study the vocabulary, recognizing as many verb roots as you can from para. 189.2. This can be done best after learning para. 204.

197.1   Review the principal parts of the Greek verb learned thus far by filling in completely the following summary including information from this chapter. Compare para. 589. Do it! Now!

  I. Principal Part λύω

conjugations derived	tense suffix	varible vowel	personal endings
1. Present active			Primary active
2. _____	N	_____	_____
3. _____		_____	_____
4. _____	O	_____	_____
5. _____	N	_____	_____
6. _____	E	_____	_____

 II. Principal part _____

1. _____	_____	_____	_____
2. _____	_____	_____	_____

 III. Principal part _____

1. _____	_____	_____	_____
2. _____	_____	_____	_____

 IV. Principal part _____

1. _____	_____	_____	_____
2. _____	_____	_____	_____

198.1   θε- is for all practical purposes the tense suffix of the aorist passive although it may be analyzed as tense suffix (θ) and connecting vowel (ε), lengthened to η in the indicative.

199.1   What indicates past time on the aorist passive (124.1)?

199.2   What personal endings are used (139.1)? Be careful!
Where have you used -σαν before as 3 pl. secondary ending (133)?

200.1   The future passive tense stem is simply formed by adding the regular future tense suffix (σ) to the aorist passive tense stem and variable vowel: λυθη + σ = λυθησ- (the future passive tense stem).

200.2   What variable vowels appear on the future passive?

200.3   Future passive uses what personal endings (cf. 139.1)? Why (20.2; 152)?
Why no augment (124.1)?

201-
2.1   Be able to dissect the aorist passive verbs.

ἐλύθην: ε   -   λυθ   -   η   -   ν

     augment   aorist passive   connecting   secondary
               tense stem   vowel   active endings
              (verb stem +
              suffix)

201-2.2   Be able to dissect any future passive verb form.

λυθησομαι: λυθησ   -   ο   -   μαι

     future passive   variable
     tense stem   vowel   middle endings
     (Aor. Pass. and
     tense suffix)

204.1   Review the three major sets of consonants presented in 156, labials, palatals and dentals. The addition of the θ tense suffix to verb stems with final consonants occasions phonetic changes similar to those encountered in the 2nd and 3rd principal parts.

204.2   Analyze the consonant changes presented in 204. Observe that in the labials and palatals the addition of the fricative (or spirant) theta has the effect of spirantizing the final consonant or turning it into the corresponding fricative. That is, the preceding consonant assimilates to (becomes like) the theta.

		verb stem ends			tense suffix		resultant consonant
labial	π	β					φ
palatal	κ	γ		+	θ	=	χ
dental	τ	δ	θ				σ
	voiceless	voiced	fricative				

204.3   Return now to a study of the vocabulary. In each instance of the aorist passives given, explain the consonantal change occasioned by adding theta to the verb stem. See para. 189.2 for some roots which are often close to the verb stem.

206.1   Notice again that "second aorist" simply means irregular. In this case, what is the irregularity?
The eta connecting vowels and secondary active endings on an augmented stem are still pretty clear signs of the aorist passive.

209.I   Aids to exercises I, Lesson XVI.

    1. ἐπιστεύσαμεν εἰς τὸν κύριον καὶ ἐγνώσθημεν ὑπ' αὐτοῦ.

        a. -σαμεν must be what tense, voice, person and number (173, 175)? There should be no question of this with the sigma-alpha.

What is the first person singular of ἐπιστεύσαμεν (i.e., the third principal part)?

b. ἐγνώσθημεν: <u>theta</u> tense suffix, <u>eta</u> connecting vowel with secondary ending can only be _____ (200). Don't be confused by the active ending when the -θη - is so obvious (199). Note the prominence of the root γνο- in the future and present (150.2).

c. Give the corresponding future passive forms (200, 202). Do it!

2. ταῦτα ἐγράφη ἐν τοῖς βιβλίοις.

a. ἐγράφη: review 206 and 206.1. <u>Eta</u> connecting vowel by itself can only be what (201)? Compare the similar -ε in the aorist and imperfect active, 129 and 176.

b. On ταῦτα with the singular verb, review 145.

c. ὑπ᾽ αὐτοῦ gives what information (114)?

d. Give the corresponding future passive.

3. ἐδιδάξατε τὰ τέκνα, ἐδιδάχθητε δὲ καὶ αὐτοὶ ὑπὸ τοῦ κυρίου.

a. Compare and contrast ἐδιδάξατε and ἐδιδάχθητε carefully. Knowing διδάσκω, don't make these more difficult than they are. Explain the -ξα (156.1 and 183; 175).
   -θη - can only be what tense and voice (200)?

b. What indicates past time on these aorists (171-80.2)?

c. καὶ αὐτοί: review 146 and 105.2 if this gives you trouble. αὐτοί cannot be the subject. Why?

d. Give the corresponding future forms of both verbs.

4. ἐλήμφθησαν οἱ πιστοὶ εἰς τὸν οὐρανόν, ἐξεβλήθησαν δὲ ἐξ αὐτοῦ οἱ ἄγγελοι οἱ πονηροί.

a. ἐλήμφθησαν: dissect: ending (199; 139.1), tense suffix and connecting vowel (199), augment.
   It is probably just as easy here to simply learn this as the sixth principal part of λαμβάνω. But, knowing the root λαβ, the present λαμβ, and future λημφ, the form λημφ is understandable (β + θ = φθ, 204.2).

b. ἐξεβλήθησαν: remember -σαν as an alternate <u>secondary</u> (active) ending, third person plural (127).
   β-λ is prominent in what verbal idea (189.3)?
   Here with θη- it must be what tense and voice (200)?

c. Give the corresponding future passives.

5. ἐγερθήσονται οἱ νεκροὶ τῷ λόγῳ τοῦ κυρίου.

a. ἐγερθήσονται: primary endings (139.1 and 200), <u>sigma</u> future suffix, and absence of augment, lead to future passive identification. Identify fully.
b. Why the dative on τῷ λόγῳ (115)?
c. Note the substantive adjective (75).
d. Give the corresponding aorist passive.

6. οὗτοι οἱ τυφλοὶ συνήχθησαν εἰς τὴν ἐκκλησίαν.

    a. συνήχθησαν: secondary ending, plus <u>theta-eta</u> tense suffix and connecting vowel; must be _____ (200).
    b. -χθ - could arise from what, considering the consonant change before <u>theta</u> (204.2)?
    Explain the change from συναγ- to συνηχ- (204.2; 126).
    c. The corresponding future passive would be _____.

7. ἐξεβλήθη τὰ δαιμόνια· ὁ γὰρ κύριος ἐξέβαλεν αὐτά.

    a. ἐξεβλήθη: contrast with the second verb in No. 4 (201).
    b. Where is the augment (131-32)?
    c. Why plural subject and singular verb (145)?
    d. ἐξέβαλεν: second aorist or imperfect (123.5; 189.2)? How do you know?

8. πέμπονται μὲν καὶ νῦν οἱ μαθηταί, ἐπέμφθησαν δὲ τότε οἱ ἀπόστολοι καὶ πεμφθήσονται ἐν ἐκείνῃ τῇ ἡμέρᾳ καὶ οἱ ἄγγελοι.

    a. Compare πέμπονται and ἐπέμφθησαν.
    Both are _____, _____, and _____. πεμπ- is the _____ stem (20.1), πεμφθ- is the _____ stem (202.1). Explain the -φθ - (204.2).
    b. Analyze the sentence clause by clause (there are three).
    c. πεμφθήσονται: what signs of the future passive do you see (200)?

9. εἰσῆλθες εἰς τὴν ἐκκλησίαν καὶ ἐβαπτίσθης.

    a. εἰσηλθες: why not imperfect (123.5)?
    εισελθ - is what tense stem (186)?
    b. ἐβαπτίσθης: you know it is from βαπτίζω without even looking it up.
    -ς secondary ending is what person and number (139.1)?
    Explain the -σθ - (204.2).
    c. Give the corresponding future passive.

10. ἐπιστεύθη ἐν κόσμῳ, ἀνελήμφθη ἐν δόξῃ.

    a. ἐπιστεύθη: full identification.
       Corresponding future passive?
       "Was believed" or "was being believed" (168.2)?
    b. ἀνελήμφθη: cf. the first verb in No. 4.

11. οἱ ἁμαρτωλοὶ ἐσώθησαν ἐν ἐκείνῃ τῇ ὥρᾳ καὶ ἐγενήθησαν μαθηταὶ τοῦ κυρίου.

    a. ἐγενήθησαν: γεν- is the root of what verb (189.2)?
    b. Why the nominative, μαθηταί (108)?
    c. Corresponding aorist middle is _____ (186, 194).

12. ἐπορεύθημεν εἰς ἕτερον τόπον· οὐ γὰρ δέξονται ἡμᾶς οὗτοι.

    a. ἐπορεύθημεν: is this really passive (207)?
    b. δεχ- to δεξ- (156.1)?
    c. γάρ clause tells what?

13. ἐδοξάσθη ὁ θεὸς ὑπὸ τοῦ υἱοῦ, ἐδόξασε δὲ αὐτόν.

    a. Contrast the verbs. Full identifications?
    b. Explain the -σθ - and the -σε from δοξαζ- (204.2 and 183).

14. τὸ εὐαγγέλιον ἐκηρύχθη ἐν ταῖς ἡμέραις ἐκείναις, κηρυχθήσεται δὲ καὶ νῦν.

    a. ἐκηρύχθη: verb root of κηρύσσω apparently has what kind of
       final consonant, judging from κηρύξω and ἐκήρυξα (156.1)?
       Explain the -χθ- then (204.2).
    b. κηρυχθήσεται: primary middle ending, <u>sigma</u> tense suffix on
       the aorist passive stem, can only be <u>what</u> tense and voice (200)?

15. ἑτοιμασθήσεται ἡμῖν τόπος ἐν οὐρανῷ κατὰ τὴν ἐπαγγελίαν τοῦ κυρίου.

    a. Why not <u>ἡ</u>τοιμασθησ<u>ο</u>- (126; 199.1)?
    b. "Was prepared" would have been _____ in Greek.

16. τὰ τέκνα προσηνέχθησαν τῷ κυρίῳ.

a. προσηνέχθησαν: explain the form, recalling the second aorist, ἤνεγκα of φέρω (186 and 204.2).
b. One might expect a directional preposition more than the indirect object, but recall the vocabulary note in 186.

17. εἶδον οὗτοι τὸ πρόσωπον τοῦ κυρίου καὶ ἤκουσαν τῆς φωνῆς αὐτοῦ.

a. εἶδον: what form of βλέπω (186)? Identification?
b. Why the genitive τῆς φωνῆς (119)?

18. ἐν τῷ μικρῷ οἴκῳ ἀκουσθήσεται ἡ φωνὴ τοῦ ἀποστόλου.

19. πρῶτός εἰμι τῶν ἁμαρτωλῶν, ἐσώθην δὲ καὶ ἐγώ.

20. ὀψόμεθα μὲν τοὺς ἀγγέλους, ὀφθησόμεθα δὲ καὶ ὑπ' αὐτῶν.

a. ὀψόμεθα must be either middle or deponent. Why (151.2)?
b. ὀφθησόμεθα: a real passive. The agent phrase (ὑπό) helps here. Full identification?
How would this be augmented for an aorist passive (196, 129)?
c. Use of καί? Not a co-ordinator here (146).

209.II NEW TESTAMENT GREEK READING, John 1.19-20

Review John 1.1-18. Find the aorist passive forms encountered and identify them again in light of your study of chapter XVI.

Translate

1.19 αὕτη — Review para. 102. Why F. N. sg. here (98-99)?

ὅτε — "When." Adverb.

ἀπέστειλαν — Aorist active indicative, 3 sg., of ἀποστέλλω. What is missing (175)?
See paras. 326 and 333 on this "liquid" verb form.

ἱερεῖς — "Priests." M. A. pl. One of an important type of third declension masculine nouns.
See paras. 355 and 345.2.

ἵνα ἐρωτήσωσιν — "In order that they might ask." ἵνα with the subjunctive expressing the purpose of the sending. See 274 and also 277 on this form of ἐρωτάω.

Σὺ τίς εἶ — See paras. 385, 98 and 7.

1.20

ὡμολόγησεν   Identify. Note augment, o > ω.
ὁμολογέω, "I confess."

ἠρνήσατο   -σατο again (cf. ἐξηγήσατο in 1.18,
para. 195.II above). Could be from

ερν- or αρν-; which is it?   Remember 116 and 171-80.4.

Ἐγώ   Note the emphasis. Wouldn't εἰμί be
sufficient?

210.1 Reinforce your memorization of the vocabulary by relating the following English words to Greek words from which they are derived. If you don't know the English word, look it up.

hagiographa _____ + _____

hematology _____ + _____

arch (bishop) _____

nocturnal _____ (by way of Latin loan word nox, noct- and then nocturnalis)

onomasticon _____

pneumatic _____

psychosomatic _____ + _____

sarcophagus _____ + φαγεῖν "to eat" via Latin.

211.1 Machen's paradigms here give three representative sets of third declension nouns. The pattern of ἄρχων, ἄρχοντος is of particular importance for the mastery of Greek participle forms.

1. Nouns with dental stems: ἐλπιδ -, ἐλπίς, ἐλπίδος
2. Nouns with velar (palatal) stems: σαρκ -, σάρξ, σαρκός
   νυκτ -, νύξ, νυκτός
3. Nouns with nasal stems: αἰων - , αἰών, αἰῶνος
   ἄρχοντ -, ἄρχων, ἄρχοντος

211.2 The paradigms of third declension nouns do not follow gender distinctions. Rather, as seen in 211.1, the stem formation is the basis of the slightly varying paradigms of the third declension. Compare para. 218.

212.1 Compare these endings with previously learned noun endings. What are the similarities and differences?

213.1 Why is it necessary to learn both the nominative and the genitive singular in third declension nouns?

213.2 Patterns outlined in 211.1 remove much of the mystery in relating the nominative and genitive singular forms.

217.1 Study the paradigms of ἐλπίς, νύξ and ἄρχων in light of the endings in para. 212. What consonant changes do you see?

218-
19.1 Why is it advisable to learn third declension nouns in an "article-nom.-gen.sg." unit: ἡ σάρξ, σαρκός?

221.1 Comment on the accent change: νύξ, νυκτός.

221.2 Explain the accent position of ἐλπίς, ἐλπίδος (para. 14).

222.1 "Nouns in -μα" are one of the most easily recognized sets of third declension nouns. What significant "all" statement is found here?

222.2 How are these nouns like other neuter nouns you have encountered?

222.3 These are dental stems ending in <u>tau</u>: - ματ.
compare their formation with ἐλπίς, ἐλπίδος.

224.I. Aids to exercises I. Lesson XVII.

1. ἐλπίδα οὐκ ἔχουσιν οὐδὲ τὸ πνεῦμα τὸ ἅγιον.

a. What is the nominative and genitive singular of ἐλπίδα?
Why accusative (212) here?
b. οὐκ and οὐδέ are not paralled in a correlative relationship
(148). οὐκ negates what word?
c. Why do you relate τὸ ἅγιον to τὸ πνεῦμα (66.3)?
Why attributively (70)?

2. διὰ τὴν ἐλπίδα τὴν καλὴν ἤνεγκαν ταῦτα οἱ μαθηταὶ τοῦ κυρίου.

a. What is the case ending and what is the noun stem of ἐλπίδα (211
and 212)?
b. ἤνεγκαν: if this is a verb -αν can only be what, with <u>alpha</u>
connecting vowel and secondary active ending (173-175)? Review
186 or look up ἤνεγκα in the vocabulary.
c. Why not "these disciples" (66)? What function then for ταῦτα?
d. Logically, the διά phrase gives what information? Review 120.1.A.

3. ταῦτά ἐστιν τὰ ῥήματα τοῦ ἁγίου πνεύματος.

a. ταῦτα agrees with τὰ ῥήματα: why (99)? Why singular verb and
plural subject (145)?
b. Why identify πνεύματος as neuter genitive singular, and not
masculine nominative singular (222 and 212)?
c. Compare τοῦ ἁγίου πνεύματος with its equivalent in sentence 1,
and review 70.3.

4. ἐγράφη τὰ ὀνόματα ὑμῶν ὑπὸ τοῦ θεοῦ ἐν τῷ βιβλίῳ τῆς ζωῆς.

a. τὰ ὀνόματα: N. sg. of all nouns like this will end how (222)?
b. ἐγράφη: why not ἐγράφθη (206)? Identify fully (201).
Why the singular verb with plural subject (145)?
c. τῆς ζωῆς: what would you say is the function of the genitive
case here (45.I.17c.)?

5. τῷ λόγῳ τοῦ κυρίου ἔσωσεν ἡμᾶς ὁ θεός.

a. τῷ λόγῳ: why not a construction with ὑπό (114-115)?
b. ἔσωσεν: movable <u>nu</u> (176, -ε secondary ending (139.1) and <u>sigma</u> tense suffix (175) can only indicate what identification? Why translate as past tense here (171-80.2)?
c. What would you say was being emphasized by word order?

6. οἱ ἄρχοντες οἱ πονηροὶ οὐκ ἐπίστευσαν εἰς τὸ ὄνομα τοῦ κυρίου.

a. οἱ ἄρχοντες: -ες on a noun can only be one of two things: _____ or _____ (212). Identification?
b. How would you expect the nominative singular of a word ending -οντες to be spelled (217)?
c. ἐπίστευσαν: what sure signs of first aorist (171-176)?
d. ὄνομα: corresponding plural would be _____ (222).

7. ταῦτα εἶπον ἐκεῖνοι τοῖς ἄρχουσιν τούτου τοῦ αἰῶνος.

a. ταῦτα out of context could be subject or object (nom. or acc.). Why accusative here (33.4)?
b. εἶπον: obviously either an Impf. A.I. or 2A.A.I. 3 pl. or 1 sg. Without knowledge of the vocabulary you couldn't tell (186).
c. τοῖς ἄρχουσιν: context (here the article) usually prevents confusion of this third declension dative plural form with verbs having the primary active 3rd. pl. ending -ουσιν.

8. ὄψεσθε ὑμεῖς τὸ πρόσωπον τοῦ κυρίου εἰς τὸν αἰῶνα, ἀλλ᾽ οὐκ ὄψονται αὐτὸ οἱ πονηροί, ὅτι οὐκ ἐπίστευσαν εἰς τὸ ὄνομα αὐτοῦ.

a. ὄψεσθε and ὄψονται: primary middle verb endings. Must be either _____ or _____ tense (152.1). Where is the sign of the future here (156.1)?
b. αἰῶνα: identify. The nominative singular is _____. The corresponding plural form is _____.
c. What is the antecedent of neuter singular αὐτό?
d. How does the ἀλλ᾽ clause relate to the preceding statement? What is the logical function of the ὅτι clause?

9. οὐκέτι κατὰ σάρκα γινώσκομεν τὸν κύριον.

a. κατά- with the accusative = _____. Often used to give a frame to reference, a viewpoint (cf. I Cor. 3:3).
b. σάρκα: the corresponding plural is _____. Nom. and gen. sg.?

10. ἐν τῇ σαρκί ὑμῶν εἴδετε τὸν θάνατον, ἀλλὰ διὰ τοῦ ἁγίου πνεύματος ἔχετε ἐλπίδα καλήν.

    a. σαρκί: what indicates dative (212)?

    b. εἴδετε: 2A of what verb (186)?
       Unaugmented tense stem would be _____ (189.2).

    c. Why relate καλήν to ἐλπίδα (66)? Remember it is <u>grammatical</u> agreement, not similarity of appearance that is crucial.

    d. διά phrase gives what information here (114-115.2)?

    e. πνεύματος: corresponding plural is _____.

11. τὸ μὲν γράμμα ἀποκτείνει, ἐν τῷ δὲ πνεύματι ἔχετε ζωήν.

    a. What sort of "location" is noted by ἐν τῷ πνεύματι (DM, p. 81)?

    b. Would you say the <u>identity</u> or the <u>character</u> of the thing possessed "in the Spirit" is more prominent here (cf. 100.I.9d and 107.I.6b)? See again paragraph 99.3.

12. βλέπομεν τὸ πρόσωπον τοῦ κυρίου καὶ ἐν νυκτί καὶ ἐν ἡμέρᾳ.

    a. Note the footnote on ἐν νυκτί and ἐν ἡμέρᾳ. The point of such temporal phrases is usually characterization, and hence they are anarthrous. If a specific night or day were important as the time of an event, the article would be present (99.3).

    b. Note again how the dative case locates, here in a <u>time</u>, in sentence 11 in a <u>sphere</u> (ἐν τῷ πνεύματι).

13. ἐδίδαξαν οἱ μαθηταὶ καὶ τοὺς ἄρχοντας καὶ τοὺς δούλους.

    a. ἄρχοντας: -ας is familiar by now as an accusative plural indicator. What is the nominative and genitive sg. form? Corresponding singular form?

    b. Review all the signs of aorist, of active, of indicative, of past time in ἐδίδαξαν (172-177).

14. ἐν ἐκείνῃ τῇ νυκτί εἴδετε τὸν ἄρχοντα τὸν πονηρόν.

    a. Why is νυκτί articular? Compare 12a above and para. 104.4.

    b. How νυκτ- from νύξ (217.1-3)?

    c. Is the adjective attributive or substantive or predicate (70, 75, 71)? An equivalent expression would be _____.

15. μετὰ τῶν ἀρχόντων ἤμην ἐν ἐκείνῳ τῷ οἴκῳ.

    a. τῶν αρχόντων: why genitive (85)?
        Corresponding singular would be _____.
    b. ἤμην: augmented ε- verb stem plus secondary middle ending is
        the irregular _____ of _____(133).

16. μετὰ δὲ ἐκείνην τὴν νύκτα ἦλθεν οὗτος ἐν τῷ πνεύματι εἰς τὴν ἔρημον.

    a. How do you know to relate the feminine modifiers ἐκείνην and
        τήν to νύκτα (218 and 66.3)?
    b. οὗτος used how here (104.5)?
        Functions as what part of the sentence (34)?
    c. ἔρημον: gender (60)?

17. ταῦτά ἐστιν ῥήματα ἐλπίδος καὶ ζωῆς.

    a. How are ἐλπίδος and ζωῆς alike?
        _____, _____ and _____.
        How different? _____
    b. Note again the use of the genitive and the absence of the article
        in a statement <u>characterizing</u> ῥήματα (rather than specifying
        which words). Cf. 45.I.17c and 4c above and see 99.3.

18. ἤγαγεν αὐτὸν τὸ ἅγιον πνεῦμα εἰς τὸ ἱερόν.

    a. ἤγαγεν: 2A of what verb (186)? _____
        Why -ν (176)? Why ἠγαγ- not ἀγαγ- (125)?
        Tells what (191.1)?
    b. How do ἅγιον and πνεῦμα agree (166; 66.3)?
    c. Why not translate, "the Holy Spirit Himself?"

19. ταῦτα τὰ ῥήματα ἐκηρύχθη ἐν ἐκείνῃ τῇ νυκτὶ τοῖς δούλοις τοῦ
    ἄρχοντος.

    a. ἐκηρύχθη: verb stem ending in ϑ- is sure sign of what tense
        and voice (198.1; 201-2.1)? -ϑη what person and number (201)?
        How is it similar to other secondary active endings, 3 sg. (139.1)?
    b. Singular verb, plural subject. Why (145)?

20. ἠγέρϑησαν τὰ σώματα τῶν ἁγίων.

    a. -ϑησαν has to indicate what tense, voice, person and number (201)?
    b. τῶν ἁγίων used how (75; 45.I.17c)?

224.II NEW TESTAMENT GREEK READING, John 1.21

Review John 1.1-20. Locate the third declension nouns and identify them again in the light of your study in chapter XVII.

Read para. 99.3 again. Now go back over Jn. 1.1-20 a second time. Look for articular and anarthrous nouns and adjectives. Note how the writer specifies (articular) and characterizes (anarthrous). Note also important examples of emphasis signaled by prominent word position.

For example, in 1.4: note anarthrous ζωή, describing the kind of quality found in the Word, "life" as opposed to some other <u>kind</u> of quality like "death." Then comes articular ἡ ζωή. The <u>particular life</u> just referred to is now specified as being also "<u>the</u> light" of mankind. The life is not described, characterized as light (anarthrous φῶς), but is rather identified as being a particular light, namely <u>the</u> light which illumines men.

Translate 1.21

ἠρώτησαν	Paras. 321 and 384. Identify.
οὖν	"Therefore." Conjunction.
τί	See para. 385. Why not τίς?
ὁ προφήτης	Don't overlook the article. See para. 99.3 again.
ἀπεκρίθη	-θη must indicate what on this verb (200)? Deponent?

225.1   Compare the declension of the present participle of εἰμί in para. 580
         with the present participle forms of λύω in para. 226. What parts of
the regular present active participle declension serve as the forms of the
εἰμί participle?

228.1   Study the forms of the present participle, active (226) and middle-
         passive (230) and learn them immediately. A preview of the Greek
participle forms in para. 589 will reveal how important these basic endings
are to their formation. To what forms already learned can you relate the
masculine and neuter forms? λύων, λύοντος and λῦον, λύοντος (211)?

228.2   What is the difference between the M.N. sg. and the N.N. sg.? Watch
         this means of differentiating the two, for it will appear again in
participles of other tenses.

231.1   Notice that the <u>tense</u> of the <u>participle</u> is <u>discerned</u> in the same way the
         tense of any verbal form is discovered, namely <u>by</u> the <u>identification</u> of
the <u>tense stem</u> (review 20.1; 151.2; 189.1-2).

         How then are all the forms in paras. 226 and 230 readily identified as
present participles?

231.2   Be able to dissect the participles as follows:

(present)	tense stem		connecting vowel		Participle ending
λύων	λυ	-	ω	-	ν
λύοντος	λυ	-	ο	-	ντος
λύουσα	λυ	-	ου	-	σα
λυούσης	λυ	-	ου	-	σης
λυόμενος	λυ	-	ο	-	μενος

232.1   In what ways do participles function and form like adjectives? Find
         illustrations in the examples in Machen's discussion.

         In what ways are the verbal qualities of the participle seen? Find
illustrations in the examples.

232.2   Translate every one of Machen's examples (1) - (4) for yourself. Under-
         stand the <u>point</u> of the illustration. If any question remains after
study, ask the instructor for clarification.

232.3   <u>Participle agreement</u>. All participles agree in gender, number and case
         with the person or thing doing the act of the participle. As Machen
states (p. 104) participles do not have subjects whose only function in the
sentence is to be the subject of the participle. (Note 232(2): the doer of the
participle act is the direct object of the sentence, in 232(3) and (4), the
indirect object.)

         Nevertheless it is appropriate to refer to the doer of the participle action
as its subject. <u>In that sense the participle agrees in gender, number and case
with its subject.</u>

232.4 How, then, may one tell who/what is doing the act of the participle?

232.5 <u>The Adverbial Participle</u>. Study Machen's first example.

ὁ ἀπόστολος   λέγων ταῦτα ἐν τῷ ἱερῷ   βλέπει τὸν κύριον.

"The apostle, saying these things in the temple, sees the Lord."
or one could translate, "Saying these things in the temple, the apostle sees
the Lord."

It is obvious from the translations that this use of the Greek participle
is, at least in some ways, similar to the use of the English adverbial participle
("saying" is such a participle in the English sentences).

232.6 Since this use of the Greek participle corresponds to the English usage,
many times one could translate the Greek participle directly into the
corresponding English participle as Machen has done it first.

In many instances, however, such "direct" translations will produce
ambiguous sentences in English, if not actual distortion of the Greek sentence.
Hence, one must abandon a simply direct participle translation of many adverbial
participles and <u>translate by</u> a full, <u>equivalent adverbial clause</u> in English.

232.7 Adverbial participles in Greek (as in English) express a full range of
adverbial ideas, supplying information as to how, when, why, and under
what circumstances the main act of the sentence was done.

For <u>now</u>, as Machen has suggested, the student may assume that all adverbial participles in the exercises are <u>temporal</u> adverbial participles, giving
the time when the main act was one. Review Machen's examples, pp. 104-105, and
see this again.

232.8 The adverbial participle is <u>anarthrous</u> (lacks the article). Participles
with the article are <u>not</u> adverbial.

232.9 The adverbial participle's main function is to modify a verb. The adverbial participle agrees with the noun naming its subject, but does
not actually modify that noun. Rather it gives information (here we are assuming
temporal information) that qualifies the verb of the sentence. Review Machen's
examples.

233.1 The tense of the participle is conveyed by the tense stem.

The tense of the participle indicates:
(1) The <u>relative time</u> of the action.
(2) The <u>nature</u> of the <u>reference</u> to the action. See 168.3 and 233.5.

Both of these important items are conveyed by the tense of the participle.

233.2 <u>Tense and time</u>. In the study of the imperfect (123.1, 3) and the aorist
(168.3; 171-80.2) the student has already learned to separate tense from
time. Outside of the indicative mood, tense has either no temporal reference or
only relative temporal reference as in the case of the participle.

233.3 In light of 233.1-2 notice that the present participle is "present with reference to the time of the leading verb," or "present relative to the time of the leading verb." The tense of all participles has a similar relative reference to time.

233.4 Why then is it appropriate for Machen to suggest that temporal, adverbial participles be translated with English clauses introduced by "While . . ?"

233.5 Tense and kind of Act. You have already learned to associate the present tense with continuing action. Reference to the act as continuing (or repeated) is a very prominent part of the meaning of the present participle. Cf. 17.1 and 122.1. See 233.1(2) above.

234.1 The adjectival participle functions just like the attributive adjectives already studied (para. 70 and 75). That is, just as one may modify an expressed or unexpressed noun directly by an attributive adjective, so one may modify an expressed or unexpressed noun directly with the adjectival participle.

234.2 Study the following syntactic parallels.

(1) ὁ ἀγαθὸς ἀπόστολος   "The good apostle"
(2) ὁ ἀπόστολος ὁ ἀγαθός   "The apostle, the good one,"
                                i.e., "The good apostle."
(3) ὁ διδάσκων ἀπόστολος   "The teaching apostle."
(4) ὁ ἀπόστολος ὁ διδάσκων   "The apostle, the teaching one."

Both (3) and (4) would better be translated, "The apostle who teaches" (a relative clause). Example (4) is the usual order for the adjectival participle.

234.3 In most cases the Greek adjectival participle will be best translated by an English _____ _____. See (3) and (4) above and illustrate from Machen's examples.

234.4 Observe carefully that with a definite noun, the adjectival participle regularly stands with the article, either between the article and its noun or after the noun, following a repeated article. In this regard the attributive adjective and the attributive participle are parallel.

Notice also that with indefinite nouns, context must determine whether the participle is adjectival or adverbial.

235.1 The substantival participle is an extension of the attributive (adjectival) participle, just as the substantive adjective is an extension of the attributive adjective. In both cases the modifier (here the participle, there the adjective) qualifies an unexpressed noun. If there is any confusion in your mind with regard to the substantive use of the adjective, review para. 75 now.

235.2 Compare the following substantival expressions.

(1) ὁ ἀγαθός   "The good man (one, person)."
(2) ὁ διδάσκων   "The teaching man (one, person)," or
                      better, "The man/the one/the person who teaches."

116

235.3 From what word, expressed or unexpressed, does the adjectival participle derive its gender, number and case (232)? _____

240.I Aids to Exercise I, Lesson XVIII.

    1. διωκόμενοι ὑπὸ τοῦ ἄρχοντος προσευχόμεθα τῷ θεῷ.

        a. The participle is _____.
            Full identification: tense, voice, ptc. gender, number, case, and lexical form. Get every item, every time! Do it! -μενος, -η, -ον endings on participle all indicate either _____ or _____ voice (230).
            These participles are among the easiest to spot.
        b. What in the context points to passive ptc. identification (114)?
        c. Why insist it is a present participle (231.1)? What does that mean for the time of the participle's action (233)?
        d. Why probably an adverbial participle (232.8, but see also 234.4)?
        e. What is the main verb? Middle-passive endings in this case do not indicate middle-passive meaning. Why not (116)?
        f. How does διωκόμενοι modify προσευχόμεθα adverbially? What information does it give (232.7)?

    2. ὁ σὲ δεχόμενος δέχεται καὶ τὸν κύριον.

        a. What do you learn about the participles of deponent verbs in this sentence?
        b. Even though the personal pronoun separates the participle and its article, the article is still considered to be with the participle.
            The σέ functions as what part of the participle construction (232)? ὁ δεχόμενος: what kind of participle: adverbial, attributive, substantive (234.4)?
        c. The participle phrase itself, being the equivalent of a noun in the nominative case, is functioning as what part of the larger sentence?

    3. ταῦτα λέγομεν τοῖς πορευομένοις εἰς τὸν οἶκον περὶ τοῦ ἐγείροντος τοὺς νεκρούς.

        a. Articular participles modifying unexpressed nouns are used how (235.1)?
            List the participles so used here: _____
        b. τοῖς πορευομένοις: why dative? Note its function in the sentence (36).
            τοῦ ἐγείροντος: why genitive (136)?

c. εἰς τὸν οἶκον modifies what and how (232)? _____.
τοὺς νεκρούς is the direct object of _____.

4. ἐξερχομένοις ἐκ τῆς ἐκκλησίας λέγει ἡμῖν ταῦτα.

    a. ἐξερχομένοις: anarthrous participle would usually be adjectival/ adverbial (232.8)?
    b. M.D.pl. declensional ending shows "us" to be the doer of the "going out." How do you know (232.3)?
    c. Full identification of the participle? Why middle-passive endings (116)?
    d. The prepositional phrase modifies what?
    e. When is the "going out" taking place? How do you know (233.1-3)?

5. αἱ ἐκκλησίαι αἱ διωκόμεναι ὑπὸ τῶν ἀρχόντων πιστεύουσιν εἰς τὸν κύριον.

    a. Would the order αἱ διωκόμεναι ἐκκλησίαι alter the meaning significantly (234(4) and 234.1-2; cf. 70.3)?
    b. Of what act are "the rulers" the agents (114)?
    c. Why is the participle F.N.pl. (235.3)?

6. οἱ πιστεύοντες εἰς τὸν κύριον σώζονται.

    a. οἱ πιστεύοντες: can this be adverbial? Why or why not (232.8)? How is it used then (235)?
    b. Why is the participle in the nominative case (235.3)? Shows what sentence function (34)?
    c. The prepositional phrase modifies what (232)?

7. γινώσκει ὁ θεὸς τὰ γραφόμενα ἐν τῷ βιβλίῳ τῆς ζωῆς.

    a. τὰ γραφόμενα: identification? Actual passive, or deponent (116)?
    b. Articular participle modifying an unexpressed noun is used how (235)?
    c. Accusative signals what sentence function for the whole participle construction? Can you diagram it?
    d. What all would you include in the participle construction (232)?

8. ἐξήλθομεν πρὸς αὐτοὺς ἄγοντες τὰ τέκνα.

    a. ἄγοντες: full identification. Why present ptc. (231.1)? Why active (226)?
    b. Why see the "we" as subject of the participle as well as the main verb (232.3)?

    c. Why probably adverbial (232.8)?
    d. Why translate "while we <u>were</u> leading . . ." instead of "while we lead/are leading . . ." (233.1,3)?

9. εἴδομεν τοὺς λαμβάνοντας τὰ δῶρα ἀπὸ τῶν τέκνων.

    a. τοὺς λαμβάνοντας: articular participle modifying unexpressed noun, must be what kind of participle (235)?
    b. Why is the participle act <u>past</u> even though the participle is present form (233.1-3)?
    c. Accusative case signals what use in the sentence for the entire participle construction (234)?
    d. εἴδομεν: full identification. Any hesitation? Review forms and vocabulary in Lesson XV.

10. οὗτός ἐστιν ὁ ἄρχων ὁ δεχόμενός με εἰς τὸν οἶκον αὐτοῦ.

    a. ὁ δεχόμενος modifies what word? How do you know (235.3)?
    b. Accent connects με closely with what word (93)?
    c. How do you know δεχόμενος is a present participle, not aorist (231.1)?

11. ἅγιοί εἰσιν οἱ πιστεύοντες εἰς τὸν κύριον καὶ σωζόμενοι ὑπ' αὐτοῦ.

    a. οἱ πιστεύοντες: articular ptc., modifying unexpressed noun. This use should be obvious to you by now. If not, review carefully 235. Functions how here (34)?
    b. The single article binds <u>both</u> participles into a closely knit substantive expression. The expression should be analyzed as: οἱ πιστεύοντες...καὶ σωζόμενοι. The construction means that <u>one group</u> of people are characterized as both believers and "being-saved-ones." οἱ πιστεύοντες...καὶ οἱ σωζόμενοι would imply two groups of people not necessarily the same or related. Cf. BD, ff. 144-145.
    c. Nominative case in the participles signals what function for the participle construction as a whole?
    Why is ἅγιοι nominative (99)?
    d. Does the statement give the <u>character</u> or the <u>identity</u> of the believers? Note anarthrous ἅγιοι (cf. 107.I.6c and see 99.3).

12. τοῦτό ἐστι τὸ πνεῦμα τὸ σῶζον ἡμᾶς.

    a. τὸ πνεῦμα τὸ σῶζον: is this the usual word order for an attributive ptc. (234(2))?
    b. τοῦτό ἐστι : why N.N.S. (99)? Why accented ultima (93)?
    c. What is the meaning of the tense of the ptc. here (233.1 and 5)?

The student will observe that the present ptc. often means continuing action in the sense of going on at the time of the
leading verb. But the present ptc. also often means continuing
action in the sense of habitual, or customary, or generally
continuing action. So perhaps here. Deciding is the interpreter'
task.

13. ἦσαν ἐν τῷ οἴκῳ τῷ λυομένῳ ὑπὸ τοῦ ἄρχοντος.

 a. The participle modifies τῷ οἴκῳ. Can you be certain (232)?
 b. ἦσαν. Augmented ε- verb root; secondary ending, must be
 what (133)?

14. ἦσαν ἐν τῷ οἴκῳ λυομένῳ ὑπὸ τοῦ ἄρχοντος.

Contrast the use of the participles in sentences No. 13 and 14.
 a. Presence and absence of article signals what (232.8; 234.4)?
 b. "Subject" of the ptc. in both cases is _____ (232.9; 235.3
 c. The first participle in No. 13 modifies _____; the
 participle in No. 14 modifies _____.
 How do you know (232.9; 234.1)?

15. αὕτη ἐστὶν ἡ ἐκκλησία ἡ πιστεύουσα εἰς τὸν κύριον.

 a. Is the church believing or being believed with regard to the
 Lord (226, 230)? What is the difference grammatically?
 b. αὕτη, not αὐτή (102, 96).

16. διδασκόμενοι ὑπὸ τοῦ κυρίου ἐπορεύεσθε ἐν τῇ ὁδῷ τῇ ἀναβαινούσῃ
 εἰς τὴν ἔρημον.

 a. διδασκόμενοι: full identification. Probably adverbial, why
 (232.8)?
 b. Justify identification of "you (pl.)" as the subject of the ptc.
 (232.9).
 c. Logically, what information is supplied by the participle clause
 (232.7)?
 d. τῇ ἀναβαινούσῃ: why F.D. sg.?
 Study the meaning of this participle's present tense (233.1-5).
 What is the real point, action contemporary with the leading
 verb or customary or regular action in the case of ἡ ὁδός?
 Cf. 12.c above.

17. ἐκηρύχθη ὑπ' αὐτῶν τὸ εὐαγγέλιον τὸ σῷζον τοὺς ἁμαρτωλούς.

a. ἐκηρύχθη: augmented verb stem, θ - tense suffix, -η - vowel without formal ending? Must be what tense, mood, voice, person and number (198-199, 201)?

b. τὸ σῷζον: how is this participle functioning (234)?

c. Again study its tense and compare the meaning of the tense here and in sentences 6, 12 and 16 with the tense meaning of the participles in sentences 1, 5, 13 and 14. Do it!

18. τοῦτό ἐστιν τὸ εὐαγγέλιον τὸ κηρυσσόμενον ἐν τῷ κόσμῳ καὶ σῷζον τοὺς ἀνθρώπους.

a. Compare the compound participle construction in No. 11. The single article with the two participles allows you to infer what?

b. The participles are presents. How do you know (231.1)?

19. ἦλθον πρὸς αὐτὸν βαπτίζοντα τοὺς μαθητάς.

a. ἦλθον: -θον cannot be aorist passive indicative; why (198.1)? Augmented ε-, on secondary endings, o connecting vowel must either be _____ tense, if built on the present stem (123.3-5) or _____ tense if built on an irregular aorist (167.1; 191).

b. βαπτίζοντα: identification (226)? Probably adverbial; why (232.8)? Ptc. subject is αὐτόν. How do you know (232.9)?

c. Why "was baptizing . . ." and not "is baptizing . . ." (233.3)? Why "was baptizing" instead of "had baptized" (233.3)? Why "was baptizing" instead of "was baptized" (226. and 230)?

20. ἔτι ὄντα ἐν τῷ ἱερῷ εἴδομεν αὐτόν.

a. ὄντα: remember 225.1. Probably adverbial; why (232.8)?

b. Subject of the participle can only be _____. Why (232.9)?

c. Participle clause gives logically what adverbial information (232.7)?

240.II NEW TESTAMENT GREEK READING, John 1.22

Review Jn. 1.1-21. Study the participles encountered in 1.6, 9, 12, 15, 18, identifying their function as far as possible in each context.

Note especially 1.9. The form of ἐρχόμενον can be identified as either (230)
    1.
    2.
    or 3.

As an adverbial ptc., it would modify the verb, _____, and would have the noun, _____, as its subject (232.3).
    Translate:

As an adjectival ptc., it would modify the noun, _____ (234).
Translate:

The ptc. can also be associated with the opening verb, ἦν, in the "periphrastic" construction, ἦν . . .ερχόμενον, "(The light) was . . . coming."

Translate Jn. 1.22

εἶπαν   Para. 521. Recall NTGFB, p. 87, n.1.

ἵνα. . . δῶμεν   "In order that. . . we may give." ἵνα
                              with the subjunctive mood expresses here
          the purpose of "They said" (286,269.5).

δῶμεν   Aorist active subjunctive, 1 pl. of mi-
                              verb, δίδωμι. Review again chapter XXXI
          and para. 509. Keep working on the mi-verbs.

ἀπόκρισιν   F.A. sg., of third declension ἀπόκρισις.
                              See paras. 348-350 on third declension
          accusative in -ν.

τοῖς πέμψασιν   "To those who sent." Substantive ptc.
                              (235) of the verb, πέμπω. Judging by
          the sigma alpha in ψα-, what would you expect the tense of
          this ptc. to be (156.1; 175)?

τίς, τί   Paras. 385, 387, and 389. What does the
                              accent tell you?

σεαυτοῦ   Para. 338.

241.1 ἀπέθανον. 2A of ἀποθνήσκω, "I died." The root, θαν, obvious in the
noun, θάνατος, somewhat concealed in the present, ἀποθνήσκω, is plain
here again in the second aorist. Recall para. 189.2 about the frequent appearance
of basic forms in the second aorist.

ἀπεκρίθην. Review 207.

241.2 After a study of paras. 249-253 return to an analysis of the 2A participle
forms here: ἀγαγών, εἰπών, ἐλθών, ἰδών, ἐνεγκών.

How do you know they are (second) aorists (231.1)?

242.1 Compare and contrast the aorist active participle forms here with the
forms of the present active participle in 226.
1. How are the A. A. ptc. and the P. A. ptc. forms alike?
   Go on to 243 if you can't see the main items.
2. How are they different?

242.2 Notice again the long connecting vowel in the aorist active, M. N. S.
λύσας and the short connecting vowel in the corresponding N. N. S.
λῦσαν. Review 228.2 and 11, rules 3b and 4.

244.1 <u>Tense and tense stem</u>. As in any verb form the tense is determined by
the tense stem or systematic modifications of it. Thus, all present tense
verbs--whether present indicative, subjunctive, optative, imperative, infinitive
or participle--are built on the present tense stem, and from it they may be
clearly identified as presents.

244.2 So the aorist active and middle participles, along with all other aorist
active and middle verb forms (indicative, subjunctive, optative, imperative and infinitive) are all built on the aorist tense stem (third principal part).
From it they may be clearly identified as aorists.

244.3 In the aorist active and middle participle, as in other aorist verb forms,
what is the aorist tense suffix? _____
What remains the regular aorist connecting vowel (cf. 171-80.3)?

244.4 <u>Tense stem and kind of act</u>. In the aorist participle, as elsewhere, the
<u>aorist tense stem</u> indicates an "aoristic reference" to the action. The
aorist indicates the occurrence of the act <u>without</u> specifying its nature as
continuing, or repeated, or completed. Compare 168.3 and also the present tense's
reference to the act as continuing, 17.1 and 233.5.

245.1 <u>Aorist tense and time</u>. The student has already learned to separate "aorist
tense" from "past time." (Review 168.3 and 171-80.2). The augment itself
indicated past time on the aorist indicative and imperfect indicative verbs.

Outside of the indicative mood such absolute temporal reference disappears,
so that the aorist outside of the indicative mood is either without temporal reference (as in aorist subjunctives and infinitives) or is relative as in the aorist
participle. Thus, the augment does not appear on the aorist participle forms (or
on other aorists outside of the indicative). (See 251.)

246.1 Compare the middle ptc. endings -μενος, -η, -ον with the present
middle-passive forms (230). Why are these aorist participles, built
on the third participle part, only aorist middle (not passive)? Remember
(153.1 and 179). Review 197.1 thoroughly if this is not fresh in your mind.

246.2 -μενος, -μενη, -μενον is the characteristic middle-passive participle
set of endings. All middle participles have these endings. Where the
middle and passive coincide these endings also appear.

247.1 Use the learning of these middle ptc. endings here as an occasion to
review the first and second declension endings (61 and 568). Why is
that possible?

248.1 Be able to "dissect" the aorist active and middle participles:

Aorist stem includes tense suffix			connecting vowel		particle endings
λύσας	λυσ	-	α	-	ς
λύσαντος	λυσ	-	α	-	ντος
λυσάμενος	λυσ	-	α	-	μενος
κηρύξαντος	κηρυξ	-	α	-	ντος
πεμφαμενος	πεμφ	-	α	-	μενος

249.1 Compare these _second_ aorist active participle forms with the present
active participle forms in 226. See also 253 on the second aorist middle
ptc. The 2A.A.Ptc. forms differ from the P.A.Ptc. in what two ways?

1. _____ 2. _____

249.2 How is the discussion of tense in 244.1-4, 245.1 relevant to the second
aorist? What, again, is the _only_ difference between a first aorist verb
and a second aorist (167.1)?

250.1 Second aorist active and middle participles differ from present active
and middle-passive participles forms in:
1. tense stem and
2. non-recessive accent.
This is particularly well illustrated in verbs whose present and second aorist
forms are very similar.
Identify the following participles:
βάλλοντες
βαλόντες
What distinguishes them?
1.
2.

250.2 Observe that the entire second aorist system uses the same connecting
vowels as in the present system, here o/ου/ω.

251.1 After reading 251 and reviewing 245.1, study the 2A ptc. forms in 241.

251.2   What is peculiar about the spelling of εἰπ- (εἶπον)?

254.1   Review 233.1-3. In so far as the aorist participle denotes time (cf. 244.4
it denotes an event that is "past with respect to the leading verb."

254.2   If a direct translation of the present participle was λύων, "loosing,"
or διδάσκων, "teaching," what is a direct, literal translation of the
aorist participle out of context:

λύσας   = _____   _____

διδάξας = _____   _____

Sometimes such translations are acceptable (cf. 232.5-6).

254.3   Aorist Adverbial participle. Continuing the assumption (232.7) that all
the adverbial participles to be encountered will be temporal participles,
the aorist adverbial participle (of time) will be translated by English temporal
clauses beginning with "when" or "after" such as "when he had _____ . . . "
or "after he had _____ . . . "
What specifically is the point of the comparison Machen asks for in
254(1) referring to 232(1)?

255.1   Aorist adjectival participle. The basic syntactic features of the
adjectival participle learned in 234-235 are unaltered here. Only the
different relative time denoted by the aorist must be taken into account.

255.2   Be sure you can express any adjectival participle with the sort of wooden,
literal translations given by Machen in the examples, such as "the having-
heard-these-things-in-the-temple disciple" (255(1)). The next (and usually
indispensible) step then is translation into the English Equivalent, the relative clause.

256.1   What is the difference in the uses of the negatives μή and οὐ?

257.1   Exercises, Lesson XIX.

General suggestions. Full identifications are important for mastery of
the participles. Any identification of a participle should include: tense,
voice, participle recognition, gender, case, number, lexical form.

Thus, εἰπών: second aorist active ptc., masculine, nominative singular of λέγω
(2A. A. ptc. M. N.).

257.I   Aids to exercise I, Lesson XIX.

1. λαβόντες ταῦτα παρα τῶν πιστευόντων εἰς τον κύριον ἐξήλθομεν εἰς την
    ἔρημον.

    a. λαβόντες: full identification before anything else (249, 257.1).
        Non-recessive accent (250) on endings otherwise like present,
        points to identification clinched by the λαβ-tense stem (189.2).

Anarthrous ptc. is probably used _____ -ly (232.8).
Here gives what logical information (254.3)?_____

Nominative case, ptc. subject almost certainly to be sought in
the subject of the sentence; why (232.3)?

b. Did the action of λαβόντες occur at the same time as (233.3)
or prior to (254.1) the leading verb?

c. τῶν πιστευόντων: full identification. Built on what tense stem?
Articular ptc. modifying an unexpressed noun is what use of the
ptc. (235)?
Why genitive case (85)?
How is the whole ptc. expression functioning here?

d. ἐξήλθομεν: don't be fooled by the theta (-θομεν) in this common
form of ἔρχομαι.
Aorist passive would have to have what connecting vowel (certainly
not -ο-) (198)?
What is the form of this irregular verb which you will look up
in the lexicon if you do not know the verb (cf. 252)?

2. πισταί εἰσιν αἱ δεξάμεναι τοὺς διωκομένους ὑπὸ τοῦ ἄρχοντος.

a. αἱ δεξάμεναι: case signals function either as _____
(34) or as _____ (99)?
Full identification (246). What about the middle form here (116)?
What are the marks of the regular aorist (171-80.3)?

b. τοὺς διωκομένους: substantive ptc. in accusative, functions as
what part of the sentence?

c. Of what act is ὑπὸ τοῦ ἄρχοντος the agent (114)?

3. εἴδομεν αὐτοὺς καὶ μένοντας ἐν τῷ οἴκῳ καὶ ἐξελθόντας ἐξ αὐτοῦ.

a. Isolate, identify and translate the main verb, εἴδομεν.
ο- connecting vowel, augmented ιδ verb stem? (192-194.1).

b. Note the two anarthrous participles. Both are probably used
how (232.7-8; 254.3)? Full identifications (225 and 249).

c. What sentence elements are linked correlatively by καί. . .καί
(148)?

d. What two items help differentiate the tense of the two adverbial
ptc. (250.1)?

4. οἱ ἰδόντες τὸν κύριον ἦλθον πρὸς τοὺς ἀγαγόντας τὸν μαθητὴω ἐκ
τοῦ ἱεροῦ.

a. οἱ ἰδόντες: substantive ptc. in nominative case. Almost
certainly is functioning as the _____ of the sentence
(34). You see why these are called "noun clauses;" they perform noun jobs.
Full identification (249). Note the non-recessive accent (250).

b. Why not "those who <u>were</u> seeing" (233.3 and 254.1-2)?

c. ἀγαγόντας: identify and contrast fully with the corresponding present form (226; 249, 250 and 250.1). Why accusative?

d. ἦλθον: compare the form of the final ptc. in No. 3. What is the obvious difference in the tense stem (245.1)?

5. ταῦτα εἴπομεν περὶ τοῦ σώσαντος ἡμᾶς.

    a. εἴπομεν: should be familiar by now! Full identification (186, 193).

    b. τοῦ σώσαντος: full identification is a must (257.1). Signs of the first aorist (171-80.3) _____. Why not adverbial (232.8)? Used how, then (235)?

6. οὗτοί εἰσιν οἱ κηρύξαντες τὸ εὐαγγέλιον, ἀλλ' ἐκεῖνοί εἰσιν οἱ διώξαντες τοὺς πιστεύοντας.

    a. εἰσιν: review the forms in 98.

    b. οἱ κηρύξαντες: -ξα- conceals what (156, 171-80.3)? Full identification (242). τὸ εὐαγγέλιον = direct object of what (232)?

    c. Would "the believers" be acceptable for the final participle? Compare ὁ σπείρων, "the sower."

    d. Remember para. 99 for these two clauses.

7. προσενεγκόντες τῷ κυρίῳ τὸν διωκόμενον ὑπὸ τοῦ ἄρχοντος τοῦ πονηροῦ ἀπήλθετε εἰς ἄλλον τόπον.

    a. προσενεγκόντες: non-recessive accent on endings otherwise like the present system (150.1)? What fixes the tense as 2A (244.1; 249)?

    b. Main verb is _____. Identify (193). See why προσενεγκόντες is M. N. Pl. (232.3).

    c. τὸν διωκόμενον: _____ (235) ptc. here functions as the direct object (34) of what?

    d. Anarthrous προσενεγκόντες probably to be construed how (232.8; 254.3)? Why not translate "while . . ." (254.3)?

8. προσῆλθον τῷ κυρίῳ ἐλθόντι εἰς τὸ ἱερόν.

    a. Why associate the ptc. with the indirect object (232.3 and 249)?

    b. Ptc. is adjectival or adverbial (232.8)?

9. ἐπίστευσας εἰς αὐτὸν εἰπόντα ταῦτα.

a. Main verb is _____. Full identification (171).
Augment signals what (124.1)? Aorist tense stem indicates
what (168.3)?

b. Why link the ptc. to (εἰς) αὐτόν (232.3)?

c. Why εἰπ- and not ἰπ- (251)?

10. ταῦτα εἶπον ἐξελθὼν ἐκ τῆς ἐκκλησίας.

a. ἐξελθών: full identification (249).
What establishes the tense (244.1-2)?

b. How does the participle help determine the number of the
verb's subject, removing the I/they ambiguity of εἶπον?

11. ὁ μὴ ἰδὼν τὸν κύριον οὐκ ἐπίστευσεν εἰς αὐτόν.

a. ὁ μὴ ἰδών: nominative substantive ptc. would be expected to
function as what part of the sentence (34)?
Would you expect a sg. or pl. verb after this ptc.?

b. ἐπίστευσεν: <u>sigma</u> tense suffix, ε-vowel with zero morpheme and
movable <u>nu</u>, augmented verb stem all lead to what identification
(171)? If this was not clear to you at sight review 171-180
and learn the aorists now.

c. Why μή and then οὐκ (256)?

12. ταῦτα εἶπεν ὁ κύριος ἔτι ὢν ἐν τῇ ὁδῷ τοῖς ἐξελθοῦσιν ἐκ τοῦ οἴκου
καὶ πορευομένοις μετ' αὐτοῦ.

a. ὤν: the participle ending by itself serves as the participle
of what verb (225)? Identify fully (580).
Adverbial or adjectival here (232.8)?

b. τοῖς ἐξελθοῦσιν: -ουσι (ν) is found regularly in four places.
What are they?
1. (20.2) _____ 3. (226) _____
2. (211) _____ 4. (249) _____
Full identification (249).
This substantive ptc. is related to what verb? How (36)?

c. πορευομένοις: can one connect this second participle with the
article τοῖς (cf. 240.I.11b.)?
What is implied in such a construction?

d. How does the time element change with πορευομένοις (233.3)?

e. καὶ πορευομένοις could be adverbial, with emphatic καί (146)?
How translated then (232.7)?

13. ἀκούσαντες τὰ λεγόμενα ὑπὸ τοῦ κυρίου ἐπίστευσαν εἰς αὐτόν.

a. ἀκούσαντες: what word in the sentence does this ptc. modify
(232.9)? What syntactic clue is there to this usage (232.8)?
Full identification (257.1).

b. Why not ἠκούσαντες (245.1-2)?

c. τὰ λεγόμενα: why "the things being said. . ."?
What participle use is this, adverbial or adjectival (234/235)?

d. Reconsider the adverbial meaning of ἀκούσαντες and review 232.7 and 254.3. The assumed temporal meaning is entirely possible here (so on the answer sheet). It could just as well be an "adverbial participle of cause," (casual ptc.), giving the reason why "they believed." It would then be translated "Because they had heard. . .(they believed)." The matter could not be solved without a context, and so we will continue with the assumption that adverbial participles in the exercise are giving time information. Nevertheless, the student can see the interpretive alternatives presented by the adverbial participle since the form itself does not tell which adverbial question is being answered by a given adverbial ptc.

14. εἴδομεν τοὺς γενομένους μαθητὰς τοῦ κυρίου καὶ ἔτι μένοντας ἐν τῇ ἐλπίδι αὐτῶν τῇ πρώτῃ.

a. Were the men already disciples when "we saw them" or were they then in the process of becoming disciples? How do you know from τοὺς γενομένους (233.3; 254.1)?
Full identification, including the use in this construction (257.1; 255.1). Remember 171-80.4.

b. μαθητάς is a predicate noun with γίνομαι (99)? Here in accusative to agree with the understood noun with the ptc.

c. καὶ (ἔτι): may function either as a co-ordinator, or emphatically (146). How would each use be translated here?

d. Why link μένοντας with "those who had become" (232.9)?

15. τὰ τέκνα τὰ λαβόντα ταῦτα ἀπὸ τῶν ἀκουσάντων τοῦ κυρίου εἶδον αὐτὸν ἔτι ὄντα ἐν τῷ οἴκῳ.

a. τὰ λαβόντα: full identification on forms with λαβ - should not be a problem (249 and 189.2). What use of the ptc. (255)?

b. ἀπὸ τῶν ἀκουσάντων: what use of the ptc. (255)?
Why the genitive case (85)?
Such substantive expressions function just like nouns.

c. ὄντα: anarthrous; probably used how (232.8)?
Is the state here spoken of contemporary with the governing verb? Why (233.2-3)? Why relate to (εἶδον) αὐτόν (232.9)?

16. ἰδοῦσαι αὗται τὸν κηρύξαντα τὸ εὐαγγέλιον ἐκεῖνο ἦλθον πρὸς αὐτον ἐρχόμενον εἰς τὸν οἶκον.

a. Identify and translate the main verb.
What word is the subject of the sentence?

b. The subject is <u>not</u> "these women who had seen. . ." Why (104.4)? In that case, how would it read?
c. Thus, ἰδοῦσαι is used how (254.3)?
d. τὸν κηρύξαντα: signs of first aorist (175)? Of active ptc. (242)?
e. ἐρχόμενον: adjectival or adverbial (232.8)?

17. οἱ ἄγγελοι οἱ πεσόντες ἐκ τοῦ οὐρανοῦ πονηροὶ ἦσαν.

   a. οἱ πεσόντες: full identification (257.1)? What is the tense stem here (189.2)? Why so accented (250)?
   b. This participle answers what question for the sentence?

18. ἰδόντες τοὺς ἔτι ὄντας ἐν τῷ ἱερῷ ἐκήρυξαν αὐτοῖς τὴν βασιλείαν τοῦ θεοῦ.

   a. τοὺς ἔτι ὄντας: the adjectival ptc. may be separated from its article by words in the ptc. construction itself, governed by the ptc.
   b. ἰδόντες: one should start immediately with "when. . ." on a ptc. of this sort (254.3).

19. ταῦτα ἀπεκρίθη τοῖς προσενεγκοῦσιν αὐτῷ τὰ τέκνα.

20. ἀπήλθομεν μὴ ἰδόντες τὸν διδάξαντα ἡμᾶς.

257.II NEW TESTAMENT GREEK READING

Translate Jn. 1.23-26

1.23	ἔφη	2A.A.I., 3 sg. of φημί, "I say." See para. 600 and 601 on -mi verb forms.
	ἐγὼ φωνή	Why is φωνή nominative (99)? What is understood?
	βοῶντος	From βοάω, "I call, cry out." Another contract verb; βοα + οντος. See 321

again and 316 (or 316.2) if you want an explanation now. How is this participle used (235.1)? Why genitive?

εὐθύνατε

A.A. imperative, 2 pl. of εὐθύνω, I make straight." Compare ἀπέστειλαν (209.II on Jn. 1.19) and consult paras. 326 and 333 again.

On the aorist imperative see paras. 411 and 420.

1.24 ἀπεσταλμένοι

Perfect passive ptc., of ἀποστέλλω probably used substantively: "Ones sent" or "men sent." If substantive, how is it used in the clause (99)?

Note absence of perfect tense suffix (κ), on the passive ptc. form of the perfect.

1.25 ἠρώτησαν

Paras. 321, 384, and 317.1.

εἰ σὺ οὐκ εἶ

What kind of condition here (288.2 and 98)? Exegetical translation (288.4)? Why σύ (97(4))?

1.26 ἀπεκρίθη. . . λέγων

Para. 402.1.

ὕδατι

ὕδωρ, ὕδατος, τό, "water." Cf. para. 222.

μέσος

Adjective, used with genitive case as a preposition, "In the midst of" (AG, 509, 3b).

ἕστηκεν

Pf.A.I., 3 sg., of ἵστημι, "I stand." Cf. para. 600 and review again the -mi verb endings there.

ὅν

"Whom." Relative pronoun (395), M. A. sg.

οἴδατε

Para. 603 and 549. Whole relative clause functions as subject of _____ (397.4).

Lesson XX

258.1   γραφείς: 2A.P.Pct. of γράφω. Why not γραφθείς? Review 206.

   ἡ συναγωγή. σύν + word built on what root? _____

See Metzger, Lexical Aids, p. 49.

258.2   το παιδίον. -ιον the second declension neuter nouns formed this way
   (with iota before the stem vowel -ιον, -ιου, -ιῳ, -ιον, etc.) are
diminutive nouns. Thus "little child." Compare τέκνον, "child," but τεκνίον,
"little child" (cf. I Jn. 2:1). Cf. French and English "-ette."

ὁ στρατιώτης. First declension masculine nouns in -της are "occupation" nouns.
What others do you know which illustrate this (79.2)? _____ _____ _____

259.1   Analyze the aorist passive participle endings carefully, comparing them
   with all previous participles learned. Note similarities and differences.

259.2   Aorist passive tense suffix is _____ (198).
   Connecting vowels in the aorist passive ptc. are _____ and _____.

259.3   Note again the differentiation of the M.N.sg. and N.N.sg. in the length
   of the connecting vowel (228.2; 242.2).

260.1   New information to be learned, as far as the form of the aorist passive
   participle is concerned, should be mostly confined to the altered
connecting vowels and the recognition of the aorist passive tense stems in a
new set of words. Why is this so?

261.1   Be sure to review para. 201.

262.1   What is the reason for the drop of the augment on the A.P.ptc. (245.1)?

263.1   How can accent help in the identification of A.P.ptc. forms?

264.1   Does the temporal significance of the aorist passive participle differ
   from the time information conveyed by other aorist participles?

264.2   Review: What time information is conveyed by aorist participles (254.1-2)?

264.3   Make sure that in each of the examples given here by Machen you
   1) understand the literal translation, and then
   2) understand the less literal, English equivalent translation.

265.1   In a context, what type of participle construction would the participles
   in section I be (232, 254)?

265.2   What use of the participle is illustrated by the summary in section II?

266.1   All genitive absolute participles are adverbial participles (survey
   Machen's examples).

266.2   The subject of the genitive absolute participles has no direct function
        in the sentence core. That is, the subject of the genitive absolute
ptc. can not also function as subject, object, indirect object, predicate noun
or object of a preposition. How does Machen describe this relationship to the
sentence?

266.3   What is the point of the comparisons called for in 266(2) and (3)?

266.4   In view of the "absolute" relationship of the participle and its subject
        to the rest of the sentence, one will not look for a further meaning in
the genitive case itself. Here the genitive, for example, has no possessive or
descriptive force.

266.5   The genitive absolute ptc. still gets its gender, number and case from
        what word (232.9)? _____

267.1   General suggestions for the exercises.

        A. Continue complete identification of all forms.
        B. Break the sentence up into its major units. You may not be able to
            do it automatically; but as the sentence unfolds to you, consciously
            mark off its main parts. A major unit may be an entire construction,
            not just a word or two, as when a substantive participle construction
            functions as subject or object (see 267.I.12). See it as a whole.
        C. Be sure you can give both a literal and an equivalent translation
            for any item where both are possible (cf. 264.3).

267.I   Aids to exercise I, Lesson XX.

    1. πορευθέντος τοῦ ἄρχοντος πρὸς τὸν κύριον οἱ δοῦλοι εἶπον ταῦτα
        τοῖς μαθηταῖς.

        a. Identify and translate the core of the sentence.
        b. πορευθέντος: identify fully (259 and 116). What enables you
            to identify τοῦ ἄρχοντος as the subject of the ptc. (232.3,9)?
        c. Does τοῦ ἄρχοντος appear to modify any other word in the
            sentence in a genitive relationship? Then why in the genitive
            case with the ptc. (266 and 266.4)?
        d. Is the ptc. adverbial or adjectival (232.7; 266.1)?
        e. Tense of the ptc. means what here (264)?

    2. πορευθεὶς πρὸς αὐτοὺς ὁ ἄρχων ἐπίστευσεν εἰς τὸν κύριον.

        a. πορευθεὶς: identify fully (259; 116)? Why would you expect
            the subject of the sentence itself to be the subject of this
            ptc. (232.9)?
        b. Did the "going" precede or follow the "believing?"
            How can you tell (254.1; 264)?

c. ἐπίστευσεν: identification of this should be automatic by now. If not, review ch. XIV.

3. πιστευσάντων ὑμῶν εἰς τὸν κύριον εὐθὺς ἐπίστευσε καὶ ὁ ἄρχων.

a. πιστευσάντων ὑμῶν: adverbial ptc. in the genitive case. Without apparent reasons related to a genitive relationship, one suspects what ptc. construction (266)?

b. Who is the subject of the sentence core? _____ Note 146. What is the subject of the ptc. (232.9)? Any direct relation to the sentence core (266.4)?

c. Why not translate "while you were believing..." (233.3; 254.1; 264)?

4. εἰσελθόντος εἰς τὴν οἰκίαν τοῦ ἐγερθέντος ὑπὸ τοῦ κυρίου οἱ μαθηταὶ ἐθαύμασαν.

a. Identify the brief sentence core and translate.

b. Opening adverbial ptc. in genitive case raises what suspicion (266.4)? Identify εἰσελθόντος fully (249).

c. τοῦ ἐγερθέντος: full identification (259). Is it adverbial (232.8)? What then (235; 264)? One might translate as genitive of possession modifying τ. οἰκίαν. If so, then where is the subject of εἰσελθόντος?

d. Logically what information does the ptc. construction give (232.7)?

5. ἐκβληθέντος αὐτοῦ ἐκ τῆς συναγωγῆς συνήχθησαν οἱ ἄρχοντες.

a. ἐκβληθέντος αὐτοῦ: full identification made (259).

b. Is αὐτοῦ in a genitive relationship with some noun in the sentence? Why in the genitive then (266.4)?

c. συνήχθησαν: -θησαν has to be what verb form (201)? Label the parts above (201-2.1). ἠχθ- augmented verb stem with phonetic change from γ + θ (204.2). Identify fully. If the identification eluded you, what would the uncompounded (no συν) sixth principal part be (A.P.I.1 sg)? Look this up in the lexicon.

6. ἐκβληθέντα ἐκ τῆς συναγωγῆς ἐδίδαξεν αὐτὸν ὁ κύριος.

a. ἐκβληθέντα: adverbial ptc. in (M) accusative sg. One expects to link a participle of this case with what part of the sentence as its subject (34)? Full identification (259).

b. Identify the core sentence and translate.

c. Did the teaching precede the expulsion? How do you know (254.1; 264)?

7. εἰπόντος ταῦτα τοῦ πνεύματος τοῦ ἁγίου οἱ μαθηταὶ ἐκήρυξαν τὸν λόγον τοῦ θεοῦ.

a. Core sentence identified and translated?
b. ἐκήρυξαν: augmented verb stem with sigma-alpha (175; 156) before secondary ending (172; 139.1) must be what tense (ch. XIV)?
c. εἰπόντος: what leads to 2A identification (250.1)?
   The doer of this act will be in what gender, number, and case (232.3)?
d. Why not link εἰπόντος with τ. θεοῦ as subject?

8. τοῖς θεραπευθεῖσιν ὑπ' αὐτοῦ εἴπετε ῥήματα ἐλπίδος καὶ ζωῆς.

a. τοῖς θεραπευθεῖσιν: full identification.
   How, will this noun clause (cf. 235) function in the sentence (36)?
b. What use of the genitive case do you see in ἐλπίδος and ζωῆς? It isn't possession (45.I.17c). Translate the expressions in such a way as to show the meaning of the genitives here (an ("exegetical translation").

9. ἐλθόντος τούτου εἰς τὴν οἰκίαν αὐτοῦ εὐθέως εἴπομεν τοῖς ἄλλοις τὰ ῥήματα τὰ παραλημφθέντα ἀπὸ τοῦ κυρίου.

a. ἐλθόντος: what are the clear marks of second aorist ptc. (250.1)?
   Full identification? What use of the adverbial ptc. (266)?
   Why in the genitive case (266.4)?
b. τὰ παραλημφθέντα: -θέντα? Should clinch general identification as an A.P.Ptc. Full identification (259)?
   What question does this ptc. construction answer in the sentence?
   Therefore, what is the participle use (255.1)?
   How do you know (234.4)?

10. βληθέντες εἰς φυλακὴν διὰ τὸ εὐαγγέλιον τὸ κηρυχθὲν αὐτοῖς ὑπὸ τοῦ ἀποστόλου ἐδόξασαν ἐκεῖ τὸν σώσαντα αὐτούς.

a. βληθέντες: adverbial or adjectival (232.8; 234.4)?
   Gender, number, and cases leads one to look where for the grammatical subject of the ptc. (232.3)?
b. The διά phrase modifies what word? with what information?
c. τὸ κηρυχθέν: full identification (259)?
   Articular ptc. must either be attributive or substantive use. Which here (234-5)?
d. How far does the first ptc. construction reach?
   βληθέντες . . . _____.
   How far does the second ptc. construction reach?
   τὸ κηρυχθέν . . . _____.
e. ἐδόξασαν: first aorist with sigma tense suffix standing unaltered must either be a verb stem ending in a vowel or one of the _____ consonants (256). Cf. σώσαντα form also.

135

11. ἀναλημφθέντος αὐτοῦ εἰς οὐρανὸν εἰσῆλθον οἱ μαθηταὶ εἰς τὴν οἰκίαν αὐτῶν.

    a. Opening adverbial ptc. with subject in genitive case. Must be what use (266)?

    b. What function does αὐτοῦ have in the sentence other than subject of the ptc. (266.2)?

    c. λημφ - and λημφ - are forms of what verb root (see vocabulary in XIII and XVI)? What adverbial information is the ptc. supplying (254.3)?

12. ἐδέξασθε τοὺς ἐκβληθέντας ἐκ τῆς συναγωγῆς καὶ τὰς δεξαμένας αὐτοὺς εἰς τὰς οἰκίας αὐτῶν.

    a. Identify the ptc. constructions fully.

    b. Are the ptcs. adverbial? Why not (232)? attributive (234; 255)? Why not? Substantive (235, 255)?

    c. These ptc. noun clauses have what function in the sentence (34)?

    d. ἐδέξασθε: full identification (178)? Why -ξασθε (with ξ) (183.1)?

13. αὗταί εἰσιν αἱ διωχθεῖσαι καὶ ἔτι διωκόμεναι ὑπὸ τῶν ἀρχόντων.

    a. One group or two groups of women persecuted? How do you know (240.I.11b)?

    b. What is the main contrast between the two ptcs. (233.3 and 254.1)?

14. αὕτη ἐστιν ἡ ἐλπὶς ἡ κηρυχθεῖσα ἐν τῷ κόσμῳ ὑπο τῶν ἰδόντων τον κύριον.

    a. ἡ κηρυχθεῖσα: modifies what word? How? How do you know (232.3)? How far does the ptc. construction reach (cf. examples in 264)?

    b. τῶν ἰδόντων: why genitive (85)?

15. τῶν στρατιωτῶν διωξάντων ἡμᾶς εἰς τὴν οἰκίαν ἐδέξαντο οἱ ὄντες ἐκεῖ.

    a. Can διωξάντων be adjectival (234.4)?

    b. ἐδέξαντο: what are the clear signs of aorist (172-175)? Built on what principal part (197.1)?

    c. οἱ ὄντες ἐκεῖ, literal translation (265)? "the - _____ - _____ - _____."

16. διωχθέντας ἡμᾶς ὑπὸ τῶν στρατιωτῶν ἐδέξαντο οἱ ὄντες ἐν τῇ οἰκιᾳ.

    a. ἡμᾶς: what function in the sentence <u>core</u> (34)?

    b. ὑπὸ τ. στρατιωτῶν: modifies what verb and how (114)?

   c. What is the main verb of the sentence? Full identification? What construction serves as its subject? How do you know (34)?

   d. The subject of διωχθέντας is ἡμᾶς. How do you know (232.3)? But the participle modifies the main verb. How do you know?

17. εἰσερχομένῳ σοι εἰς τὴν οἰκίαν προσῆλθον οἱ ἄρχοντες, εἰσελθόντα δὲ ἐξέβαλον.

   a. First locate the main verb and subject in the opening clause. Where are they?

   b. σοι: identify. Case indicates what function (95; 36)?

   c. εἰσερχομένῳ: adverbial or adjectival? Who is doing the "entering" (232.3)?

   d. How do the participles in the two clauses compare and contrast? They are alike in _____, but different in _____ and _____.

   e. Figure out the elision in clause two by parallel structure. Judging by the gender, number, case of the participle, its subject (here missing) has what function in the clause (34; 232.3)?

   f. Parallel structure also indicates person and number of ἐξέβαλον.

18. ταῦτα μὲν εἶπον αὐτοῖς προσφέρουσι τὰ παιδία τῷ κυρίῳ, ἐκεῖνα δὲ προσενεγκοῦσιν.

   a. προσφέρουσι: could be P.A.I. 3 pl., but would that make sense? What is it (226)? How used (32)? Related to what noun or pronoun (232.9)?

   b. Second main clause has object and adverbial ptc. What is assumed from clause one?

   c. How do the two ptcs. contrast (249, 254.1)?

19. πορευομένου μὲν τοῦ κυρίου μετὰ τῶν μαθητῶν αὐτοῦ ἔλεγον οἱ ἀπόστολοι ταῦτα, ἐλθόντος δὲ εἰς τὴν οἰκίαν ἐκεῖνα.

20. ταῦτα εἶπον ὑμῖν ἔτι οὖσιν μετ' ἐμοῦ.

267.II NEW TESTAMENT GREEK READING

Translate Jn. 1.27-28, 35-37.
Review Jn. 1.26 to recall context.

1.27   ὁ . . . ἐρχόμενος   Cf. Jn. 1.15 (165.II). Modifies what unit in 1.26?

οὗ   "Of whom." M.G. sg. relative pronoun (395). Read para. 397. To whom does this relative refer?

ἵνα λύσω   See paras. 274 and 283 on verb form and meaning. Not a purpose clause here, but an explanation of ἄξιος.

ἱμάντα   ἱμάς, ἱμάντος, ὁ. "Strap."

ὑποδήματος   Remember para. 222.

1.28   ἐγένετο   Paras. 552-553.

1.35   τῇ ἐπαύριον   "On the next day." Cf. para. 471; AG, p. 283.

εἱστήκει   Pluperfect active indicative (i.e., the perfect tense set in past time), 3 sg., of ἵστημι. See para. 589 under the fourth principal part. Note augment and -ει- connecting vowel on the perfect tense stem to form the plpf. "He stood."

ἔμβλεψας   ἐμβλέπω (ἐν + βλέπω), "I look at/upon." (Takes the dative). What construction (242)? How used (254.3)?

περιπατοῦντι   περιπατε + οντι (321 and 316.2.4). See 424.1 on the participle used as object (here indirect object) complement.

ἴδε   2A.A. imperative of βλέπω (εἶδον). Para. 416. Note lack of augment (245.1). Used as interjection, "Look!" not as a transitive verb, so has no object here.

1.37   αὐτοῦ   Not possessive! Relate to ἀκούω (119).

λαλοῦντος   See 424.1 again. Why genitive (232.3)?

268.1

ἁμαρτάνω Relate to nouns _____(108) and _____
_____(101). The verb root is
ἁμαρτ-; compare this with other verbs you know whose
present stem is built with -ανω or -αινω:
_____, _____. See Lexical Aids, p. 45.

ἐάν = εἰ (if) + ἄν (ever), indefinite particle

εὐαγγελίζομαι Relate to the Greek noun _____
and to the English verb _____.(Cf. 101.2)

μηδέ and μηκέτι Parallel to _____ and _____
with subjunctives. (121) with indicative verbs.

268.2

ἡ δικαιοσύνη First declension nouns ending in -σύνη
(-σύνης, -σύνῃ, -σύνην) are abstract
nouns. Cf. δίκαιος, "righteous," but δικαιοσύνη,
"righteousness." Cf. Lexical Aids, p. 43.

269.1 The subjunctive is a tense, a mood, a voice (circle one).

269.2 The subjunctive occurs mainly in what tenses?
    1.
    2.

269.3 Study paragraphs 270, 271, 274, 275, and 279, analyzing the personal
endings.
What personal endings are used on the subjunctive (139.1)?
What modification indicates subjunctive mood (269 and 20.3)?

269.4 Be able to "dissect" all subjunctive forms.

Tense stem		Variable Vowel		Primary Person Ending	
λυ	–	ω	–	μεν	λύωμεν
λυ	–	η	–	ται	λύηται
λυσ	–	ω	–	μεν	λύσωμεν
λυσ	–	η	–	τε	λύσητε
λυθ	–	η	–	τε	λύθητε

Of course some forms have contracted variable vowel (λύω, λύῃς).

269.5 The meaning of the subjunctive mood. The indicative mood is the mood of
fact (17.3), of what either is or is not the case. The subjunctive mood
is the mood of contingency, of what could be, should be, might be; of what is
intended, is probable or possible. See how the subjunctive's meaning explains
its use in the constructions introduced in this chapter.

272.1 Variable vowel and Mood. Review 20.3. The most conspicuous indicator of
the subjunctive mood is the _____ variable vowel. Indicative
has a short variable vowel.

276.1   Tense and tense stem. Review 270, 271, 274, 275, and 279 again and observe the tense stems, λυ- for the present subjunctives, λυσ- for the aorist subjunctives, and λυθ- for the aorist passive subjunctives. Just as in all other verb forms, the tense of the subjunctive mood verbs is discerned by identifying the tense stem (244.1-2).

276.2   On aorist tense stems the presence of primary endings is a sure indication of subjunctive mood. Why (173)?

277.1   Why is there no augment on aorist subjunctives? Review 245.1 and, if necessary, 168.3 and 171-80.2.

277.2   Relate this to 281.

280.1   In what sense is the aorist passive subjunctive accent irregular? Illustrate.

280.2   Why the "irregularity"?

282.1   How are the present subjunctives of εἰμί (602) like the present participles of that being verb (225.1)?

283.1   Tense and time of action in subordinate moods (non-indicative). Review 245.1. In the subjunctive mood tense has _____ reference to time. Have you related this to para. 277 and 245.1?

283.2   Tense and kind of action. Review 17.1 and 168.3-4. In the subjunctive mood, the present tense refers to the act as _____, the aorist tense refers to the act _____.

283.3   Make "exegetical" (interpretive, periphrastic) translations which as far as possible do convey the actual force of the tense. These "exegetical" translations will not be suitable final translations, perhaps, but are valuable nonetheless.

286.1   A purpose clause naturally takes the subjunctive mood, since it is a statement of what the writer or speaker intends, not necessarily of what is now the case.

286.2   Learn the set syntactic construction, "ἵνα-with-the-subjunctive-for-purpose."

286.3   Purpose clauses are adverbial. Make sure you see precisely what verb it is in the main sentence of which a given ἵνα clause is stating the purpose. Draw lines and circle verbs if it will help.

286.4   If the main verb is a present, translate the purpose clause with "may;" if the main verb is a past tense verb, translate the purpose clause with "might." See the illustrations.

288.1 <u>Conditional clauses</u>. "A complete conditional sentence. . . sets forth
a supposed condition (called the <u>condition,</u> or <u>protasis</u>) upon the basis
of which a given conclusion (called the <u>conclusion,</u> or <u>apodosis</u>) is to be expected."[1]

288.2 <u>Conditions of Fact</u>. A conditional statement whose "if clause" (the
supposition, condition, or protasis) states something which either is
or is not now the case, or was or was not the case, is a condition of fact.
εἰ opens these conditions, and the indicative mood understandably follows in
such statements of fact (17.3).

Learn "εἰ-with-the-indicative-for-conditions-of-fact" as a set syntactic construction. See 288(1), second illustration.

Compare examples in 291.I,4,15, and 291.II.4,5,9, and 10. See Machen's bracketed
translation in 289: "If that is now a fact."

288.3 <u>Conditions of contingency (or future conditions)</u>.
A conditional statement whose "if clause" (protasis) states a condition
in any way contingent--something which should be, could be, might be--or a
generalization is called a <u>condition of contingency</u>.

Such conditions are stated with ἐάν, "if (ever)," and understandably use the
subjunctive, the mood of probability, possibility (not fact).

Learn "ἐάν-with-the-subjunctive-for-conditions-of-contingency" as a set syntactic
construction. In this class of conditions one may distinguish present general
conditions (generalizations) and future conditions. See NTGFB, p. 132, n 1.
See the examples in 291.I.1,2,3,8.16, 291.II.2,3,6,7,11, and 13.

288.4 Give "exegetical" translations of the conditional clauses. "If (as a
matter of fact) we are studying" = 288.2; "If we (ever, should) study"
= 288.3.

288.5 Conditional clauses are adverbial clauses. Make sure you see clearly
which verb supplies the apodosis (conclusion) for the "if clause"
(protasis). Draw arrows and circle verbs if it will help.

291.I Aids to exercise I, Lesson XXI.

1. Fill in the diagram with the Greek sentence.

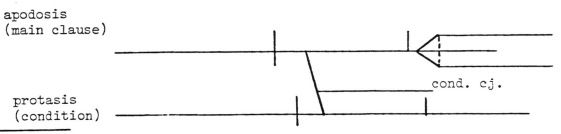

apodosis
(main clause)

cond. cj.

protasis
(condition)

_____
[1]Stephen W. Paine, <u>Beginning Greek: A Functional Approach</u> (New York:
Oxford University Press, 1961), p. 286. See also pp. 286-291.

    a. Diagram the sentence to make clause relations clear.
Review meaning of apodosis and protasis (288.1).

    b. Go first to the main clause, identify and translate. The "if-
clause" will be dependent upon this verb.
λήμφεσθε. Primary middle endings, sigma tense suffix (φ),
indicates what identification (ch. XIII, and 154-5.1)?

    c. ἐάν: you would expect the verb of this clause to be in what
mood (288)? Why (288.3; 269.5)?
Does this deal with what might be or could be or with what
actually is or is not the case (288.1-3)?

    d. εὐαγγελισώμεθα.
Why not P.M.-P.S. (170-80.3)?
Why not F.M.I. (272.1)?
Why not A. or M.I. (272.1 and 170-80.3)?
What is the meaning of this verb's tense (269.5; 283.2)?

2. Fill in the diagram with the Greek sentence.

apodosis

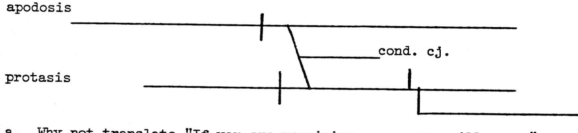

protasis

    a. Why not translate "If you are receiving . . ., you will . . ."
(288 and 288.1-3)? What specifically prohibits such a translation?

    b. Dissect and identify the:
       subj. verb. _____ - _____ - _____
       ind. verb. _____ - _____ -_____

    c. Why μή, but then, οὐ (256)?

3. ἐὰν μὴ ἴδῃ οὗτος τὸν κύριον, οὐ πιστεύσει εἰς αὐτόν.

    a. Identify the sentence core and translate.
In this case the sentence core is called an _____ (288.1).

    b. How is this verb modified (288.5)?
Circle the dependent verb and draw an arrow from it to the main
verb.

    c. ἴδῃ: ἰδ- is what tense stem (189.2)? Remember 276.1.
What indications of subjunctive?
       1. (269) ____ 2. (277) ____ 3. (272) ____

4. Fill in the diagram with the Greek sentence.

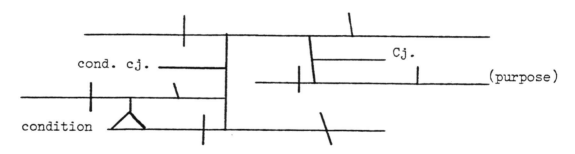

a. Main clause in this case is an exhortation. How can you tell? ὦμεν (285)? καί, remember 146.
b. The ὅτι- clause gives the content of the preaching (287). In this case why is this noun clause the subject of κηρύσσεται (113)?
c. What logical information does the ἵνα clause give (286-287)? Modifies what verb specifically (286.3)? Why subjunctive (269.5; 286.1)?
d. Does the conclusion rest on what is or is not the case, or on what might be or should be (288.1-3)? How do you know?

5. εὐηγγελισάμηω αὐτοὺς ἵνα σωθῶσιν καὶ ἔχωσιν ζωήν.

a. εὐηγγελισάμην: why A.M.I. (272, 269)? Why not F.M.I. (151 and 175)? "Preached them the gospel" preserves the accusative idiom
b. What mood do you expect following ἵνα (286)? Why (269.5 and 286.1)? Both verbs are governed by the ἵνα. How do you know (286.1)?
c. The ἵνα clause gives specifically what information related specifically to what verb (286)?

6. μηκέτι ἁμαρτάνωμεν, ἵνα γενώμεθα μαθηταὶ πιστοί.

a. Is this an exhortation not to practice sin (continuing action) or never to commit a sin? How do you know (283 and 283.2)?
b. Why not οὐκέτι (268)?
c. Of what does ἵνα γενώμεθα give the purpose (286.3)?
d. Can one tell from the verb whether or not the act of becoming a disciple was instantaneous or continuing (283, but see 168.3-4)?

7. Fill in the diagram with the Greek sentence.

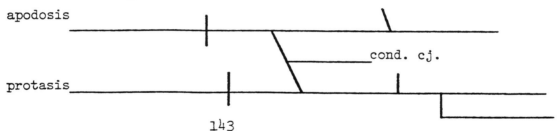

apodosis

cond. cj.

protasis

a. This is probably generalization. Why so (288)?
b. How would the sense change if it were εἰ ἤκουσαν (288.1-3)?

8. ἐὰν εἰσέλθωσιν εἰς ἐκείνην τὴν οἰκίαν οἱ πιστεύοντες εἰς τὸν κύριον, εὐαγγελισόμεθα αὐτοὺς ἐκεῖ.

a. Sentence core? Identify and translate.
b. εὐαγγελισόμεθα: why not A.M.S. (272.1 and 175)?
   Why not P.M-P.I. (156)?
c. Why not "Let us preach the gospel" (285)?
d. εἰσέλθωσιν: distinguish from εἰσελθοῦσιν (A.A. ptc. M.P.pl).
   After ἐάν you expect the _____ mood (269.5 and 288).
   Lack of augment (277), aorist stem (276), primary endings (269)
   with long variable vowel (272)--must be what?

9. ἐκηρύξαμεν τούτῳ τῷ λαῷ τὰ ῥήματα τῆς ζωῆς, ἵνα δέξωνται τὴν ἀλήθειαν καὶ σωθῶσιν.

a. ἐκηρύξαμεν: what sure signs of aorist active indicative
   (175, 156, 172)?
b. τῆς ζωῆς: use of the genitive? Cf. 45.I.17c; 224.I.4c, 17b.
c. ἵνα - clause modifies what verb and how (286.3)?
d. Are the "receiving" and "saving" specifically referred to as
   continuing acts (283)? This is exegesis. Learn to spot such
   matters.
e. σωθ-: what tense and voice with this tense stem of σώζω (279)?

10. προσέλθωμεν τῷ ἰδόντι τὸν κύριον, ἵνα διδάξῃ ἡμᾶς περὶ αὐτοῦ.

a. προσέλθωμεν: what signs of subjunctive (272.1 and 276.2)?
   What use of the subjunctive here (285)?
b. ἵνα-with-the-_____-for-_____." (286; 286.1; 269.5). To what
   other word in the sentence does this clause relate? How (286.3)?
c. Do the verbs in this sentence specify the actions as continuing
   or not (283.2)?

11. ταῦτα εἰπόντων αὐτῶν ἐν τῷ ἱερῷ οἱ ἀκούσαντες ἐδέξαντο τὰ λεγόμενα, ἵνα κηρύξωσιν αὐτὰ καὶ τοῖς λοιποῖς.

a. Any reason for αὐτῶν to be genitive? If not, what do you suspect with adverbial εἰπόντων (266.2,4)?
b. οἱ ἀκούσαντες functions as sentence subject; how do you know (34)?
c. The "receiving" and "saying" are contemporary. How do you
   know (233)?
d. κηρύξωσιν: primary endings (269), long variable vowel (272) must
   indicate what verb form? Here what tense (276.1)? Of what does
   this clause give the purpose (286.3)?

12. πιστεύσωμεν εἰς τὸν ἀποθανόντα ὑπὲρ ἡμῶν, ἵνα γράφῃ τὰ ὀνόματα ἡμῶν εἰς τὸ βιβλίον τῆς ζωῆς.

    a. Contrast πιστεύσωμεν and πιστεύσομεν (Ch. XIII)? and ἐπιστεύσαμεν (Ch. XIV)?
    b. γράφῃ: what sign of aorist (276.1 and 171-80.3)? What sign of subjunctive (272)?
    c. τὸν ἀποθανόντα: what use of the ptc. (255.1)? Full identification?

13. ἐλεύσομαι πρὸς τὸν σώσαντά με, ἵνα μὴ λύω τὰς ἐντολὰς αὐτοῦ μηδὲ πορεύωμαι ἐν ταῖς ὁδοῖς τοῦ θανάτου.

    a. ἐλεύσομαι, -σομαι: <u>sigma</u> tense suffix, short movable vowel, primary endings indicate what identification (151-153-155)?
    b. Why identify λύω as subjunctive (256 and 286.1)? Why link πορεύωμαι with the negative purpose clause ἵνα μὴ λύω (286.1 and 260.1; remember 148)?
    c. The use of the genitives on αὐτοῦ and τοῦ θανάτου? Are they both possession?

14. ταῦτα εἶπον ἐν τῷ ἱερῷ, ἵνα οἱ ἀκούσαντες σωθῶσιν ἀπὸ τῶν ἁμαρτιῶν αὐτῶν καὶ ἔχωσιν τὴν δικαιοσύνην τοῦ θεοῦ.

    a. Full identifications are still a necessity.
    b. Is the "having" seen as a continuing act (283)? How about the "saving" (168.3-4)?

15. εἰ εἴδετε ταῦτα ἐν ταῖς ἡμέραις ταῖς κακαῖς, ὄφεσθε τὰ αὐτὰ καὶ νῦν καὶ εἰς τὸν αἰῶνα.

    a. Identify the sentence core (here the apodosis) and translate.
    b. ὄφεσθε: <u>sigma</u> suffix (ψ), short vowel, primary ending indicate what (151-153)? Remember 105.3 and 148.
    c. Why does εἰ take the indicative (288.2 and 269.5)?

16. ἐὰν μὴ διδαχθῇς ὑπὸ τοῦ κυρίου, οὐ γνώσῃ αὐτὸν εἰς τὸν αἰῶνα.

    a. Why not "If you were not taught" or "If you have not been taught" (288.3)?
    b. οὐ γνώσῃ: the verb is personal ending could be confused with the lengthened primary active ending, 3 sg (-ῃ) for the subjunctive. The negative here warns against that; how (256)? Knowledge of γνώσομαι also helps avoid that error. How (139.1)?

17. ὁ λύων τὰς ἐντολὰς τοῦ θεοῦ οὐκ ἔχει ἐλπίδα, ἐὰν μὴ ἐπιστρέψῃ πρὸς τὸν κύριον.

    a. A continual breaking of the commands is indicated in ὁ λύων. How (283.1 and 233.1(2))?

    b. ἐπιστρέψῃ: full identification. Aorist? How do you know (171-80.3 and 156)? Why no augment (277.1)?

18. ταῦτα παρέλαβεν ἀπὸ τοῦ ἀποθανόντος ὑπὲρ αὐτοῦ, ἵνα παραλαβόντες αὐτὰ οἱ λοιποὶ σωθῶσιν καὶ αὐτοί.

    a. σωθῶσιν: -ωσιν tells what (269)? σωθ- tells what (279)?

    b. σωθῶσιν: modified by what adverbial construction (254.3)?

19. συνελθόντες εἰς τὴν οἰκίαν δεξώμεθα τὴν μαρτυρίαν τοῦ εὐαγγελισαμένου ἡμᾶς.

20. διωξάντων τῶν στρατιωτῶν τοὺς ἁγίους ἵνα μὴ πιστεύσωσιν εἰς τὸν σώσαντα αὐτούς, συνῆλθον οὗτοι εἰς τὴν συναγωγήν.

    a. Adverbial ptc. with noun in genitive case. Suspect what (266)? Temporally qualifies what verb?

    b. Go to the sentence core and translate.

    c. ἵνα...πιστεύσωσιν: qualifies what act with what information (286.3)?

291.II NEW TESTAMENT READING

William S. LaSor's remarks on translation of Hebrew have obvious application to the NT translation now being undertaken by the student.

"There are two ways of translating. (1) Figure out, from the known English version, what the Hebrew ought to be (2) Figure out from what the Hebrew is, what the English ought to be. Obviously, only (2) is worthy of the serious Bible student. For the beginner, however, (1) can be useful if properly used."[1]

Translate I Jn. 1:5-10.

1.5 (1) αὕτη   Most versions take (1) as the subject and
    (2) ἡ ἀγγελία   (2) as predicate noun. "This (it) is the
            message (2)" Cf. εὐαγγέλιον and ἐπαγγελία.

    ἣν ἀκηκόαμεν   "Which we are in the present condition
                 of having heard," i.e., "which we have
        heard." Relative pronoun referring to ἀγγελία plus the
    perfect of ἀκούω (425-426 and 452ff).

---

[1] W. S. LaSor, _Hebrew Handbook_ (The author: Pasadena, California, 1961), I've not yet found it in the new Eerdmans edition.

ὅτι. . . οὐδεμία

ὅτι clause gives the content of ἡ ἀγγελία.

φῶς, σκοτία

Review Jn 1:4-5 vocabulary

ου-δε-μια

"not one bit (of. σκοτία)." οὐδέ plus
μία, F.N. sg. of the number one (371-372).

1.6 ἐὰν εἴπωμεν. . . καὶ
. . . περιπατῶμεν

What kind of condition (288.3)? A more
gentle statement than εἰ + ind. περιπατέω =
"walk (around)," i.e. "to live." What mood in the verbs
(272.1 and 288.3)? What about the kind of action en-
visioned here (282)?

ποιοῦμεν

P.A.I. 1 pl. of ποιέω, "to do." The
connecting diphthong, -ου-, arises from a
contraction (ε-ο): ποιε-ομεν (313-316). What is the
main statement of the verse, and what is the condition
upon which that main assertion rests?

1.7 ἐάν . . . περιπατῶμεν

Para. 288.3 and see 1.6 again. Continued
life "in the light" is in mind here. How
do you know (283)?

ὡς

Particle for comparison, "as." What is
this comparison intended to elucidate?

φωτί

N.D. sg. of φῶς.

μετ' ἀλλήλων

Para. 343. Remember NTGFB p. 49 n.1.

πάσης

F.G.sg. of πᾶς, πᾶσα, πᾶν (265-269).

1.8 ἑαυτούς

"ourselves," 337

πλανῶμεν

P.A.I. 1 pl. of πλανάω, "I lead astray,"
"deceive." Omega connecting vowel is
not lengthened here for subjunctive, but is a contraction
(α + ο =ω): πλανά-ομεν (313-316).

1.9 ἐὰν ὁμολογῶμεν

ὁμολογέω. "I confess." With ἐάν one expects the _____ mood in a condition of
contingency. Note the tense. Is it a life pattern of
confession or a single confession which the author has
in mind (283)?

ἵνα ἀφῇ. . . καθαρίσῃ

ἀφῇ A.A.S. of ἀφίημι "I forgive," (cancel
a debt, see A G, 125). Either the purpose
(286) or the result of πιστὸς καὶ δίκαιος. See A.A.S.
of καθαρίζω, 1.7.

1.10 ὅτι οὐχ ἡμαρτήκαμεν

ὅτι clause gives the content of εἶπον.
ἡμαρτήκαμεν. Pf. A.I. 1 pl of ἁμαρτάνω.
The perfect (426, 452ff) focuses here on a present condition (no sin) resulting from past action (here past
lack of sinful acts).

ψεύστης, -του, -τῃ,
-την

Cf. βαπτίστης, μαθητής (79.2). If ψευδ-
has to do with lying, (cf. ψεύδομαι, 1.6),
the meaning of this word should be obvious.

292.1 Notice the verbs frequently used with infinitival expressions.

δεῖ, ἔξεστιν   almost invariably take a following infinitive

θέλω
κελεύω   frequently takes an infinitive to complete the
μέλλω   verbal expression in Greek just as in English
ὀφείλω
    (from 108) ἄρχομαι

292.2 πάσχω   Compare "paschal" (lamb)
       χριστός   χρίω "to smear," "anoint." "Christos" is "the anointed
                    one," a translation of Hebrew, "Messiah."

293.1 Analyze the forms. Note tense stem, ending, and, where possible,
       connecting vowel (-ειν and -αι are contractions).

294.1 How does one identify the tense of the infinitives?
       Review 276.1 on the subjunctives and 244.1-2 if you do not know.

295.1 Aorist active infinitives can have irregular accent--irregular in what
       way?

296.1 Second Aorist infinitives have the same endings as appear on the present
       infinitives. How then do you tell second aorist infinitives from
presents?
            1.
            2.

296.2 Review 250.1.

299.1 <u>Tense and Kind of Action</u> in the infinitive. Present infinitives refer
       to the act as _____, aorist infinitives make an _____
reference to the act (168.3).

299.2 Why no augment on the aorist infinitives (123.3)?

299.3 Do "exegetical" translations which bring out the infinitive's tense.

300.1 Recall 256 and 268.1.

301.1 What article appears in the articular infinitive construction?

302.1 Note the similarity to the substantive participle which, like the articular
       infinitive, constitutes a noun clause and so is able to function in all
the ways a simple noun can function (subject, object, indirect object, object
of preposition, etc.).

302.2 Do you see how τὸ ἀποθανεῖν functions as the subject of ἐστίν?
       Notice carefully Machen's "exegetical" translations.

303.1 "After (1) the act of loosing, (2) the process of, (3) the fact of, (4) the circumstance of loosing," use these in your own translations to emphasize the noun quality of the articular expressions.

304.1 Make sure you see in Machen's examples the adverbial modifiers which the infinitive, as a real verb form, can take.

304.2 The subject of an infinitive is in the _____ case. Compare English. "I declared him (objective case) to be (infinitive) a prophet."

305.1 You are now learning alternate ways of expressing the same or similar ideas in Greek. Organize them below semantically (according to meaning). Review the constructions presented in 303. They are very important.

305.2 Adverbial clauses of time prior to the leading verb.
   1. _____ participle, _____ tense (254.1-3), "When" "After"
   2. _____ with-the-accusative of the articular infinitive. "After the fact of."

305.3 Clauses of time simultaneous with the leading verb.
   1. _____ participle, _____ tense (232 and 233.3-4), "While"
   2. _____ with-the-dative of the articular infinitive "In the fact of," "During the process of," i.e. "While"

305.4 Adverbial clauses of time subsequent to the leading verb.
   1. _____-with-the-genitive of the articular infinitive, "Before."

305.5 Causal clauses, giving the reason or cause for an act.
   1. With post-positive conjunction _____ (186). "For."
   2. With the conjunction _____ (108). "Because."
   3. _____ with-the-accusative of the articular infinitive, "On account of the fact that" i.e. "Because."

305.6 Purpose clauses, giving the intent of an act.
   1. _____ with-the-subjunctive (286), "In order that," "For the purpose that."
   2. _____ with-the-accusative of the articular infinitive. "Unto the fact of," or "In order to."

306–
307.1 Indirect discourse reports the content of a speech, prayer, thought, wish, vision, etc. without exact quotation. The exact quote reported indirectly in the example of 306 would have been, "He is the prophet."

306–
307.2 Greek expresses indirect discourse in what two ways:
   1.
   2.

308.1 How does Greek indirect discourse differ from English indirect discourse?

309.1 When a proper name has an article in Greek it is not a random appearance of this article. The proper noun is being made specific in some way. Look for the reason for every article's presence.

311.1 With these nouns also the use of the article is usually understandable.
     When the <u>article</u> is present, specification, <u>identity</u> is the point. When
the noun is <u>anarthrous</u>, then <u>characterization</u>, description is usually the point.
Review Jn. 1:1 (with para. 99.3), where anarthrous θεός states the divinity
(character) of the word, not its identity.

312.I Aids to exercise I, Lesson XXII.

1. οὐκ ἔξεστίν σοι ἔχειν αὐτήν.

    a. ἔξεστιν: identify. Takes what case and construction following
       (292).
    b. ἔχειν: full identification (293). Continued action? Why (290)?
    c. αὐτήν = direct object of _____.

2. κελεύσας δὲ τοὺς ὄχλους ἀπολυθῆναι ἐξῆλθεν εἰς τὴν ἔρημον.

    a. κελεύσας: ἐκέλευσας would have been A.A.I. 2sg.
       But what is this (242)? How used (254.3)?
    b. ἀπολυθῆναι: -θῆναι should clinch the identification (293).
    c. τοὺς ὄχλους: why accusative (304)?

3. οὐκ ἔστιν καλὸν λαβεῖν τὸν ἄρτον τῶν τέκνων καὶ ἐκβαλεῖν αὐτόν.

    a. λαβεῖν . . . ἐκβαλεῖν: full identification (296.1).
       Mark off the boundaries of each infinitival clause.
    b. καλόν is predicate adjective (99)? Why is it neuter N. sg. (301)?
    c. What is/are the subject(s) of ἔστίν (302)?

4. ἤρξατο δὲ ὁ Ἰησοῦς λέγειν τοῖς Ἰουδαίοις ὅτι δεῖ αὐτὸν ἀπελθεῖν.

    a. ἤρξατο . . . λέγειν: what form of ἄρχω (178)?
       Full identification of λέγειν (293)?
    b. τοῖς Ἰουδαίοις is indirect object of what verb (304)?
    c. ὅτι clause here gives the content of what verb?
    d. After δεῖ you expect what type of verb (292)?
    e. ἀπελθεῖν: why not ἀπηλθεῖν (299.2)?
       Why not ἀπέλθειν (296.1)? Full identification?

5. μέλλει γὰρ ὁ υἱὸς τοῦ ἀνθρώπου ἔρχεσθαι ἐν δόξῃ μετὰ τῶν ἀγγέλων
   αὐτοῦ.

    a. μέλλει . . . ἔρχεσθαι, (292.1 and 293). Full identifications?
    b. Why - σθαι, not ἔρχειν (116)?

6. εἰ θέλει μετ' ἐμοῦ ἐλθεῖν, δεῖ αὐτὸν ἀποθανεῖν.

    a. θέλει . . . ἐλθεῖν: the infinitive gives the content (object) of the wish. Remember 296.1.

    b. What kind of condition (εἰ + indicative) (288.2)?

    c. Why αὐτόν, not αὐτός (304.2)?

7. καλόν σοί ἐστιν εἰς ζωὴν εἰσελθεῖν.

    Diagram the sentence.

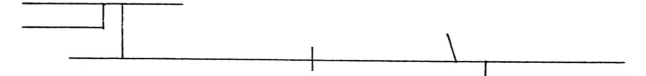

    a. What is the subject of ἐστίν (302)?

    b. εἰς ζωήν: modifies what verb (304)?

    c. καλόν: why neuter, N. Sg. (301)?

8. ἐν δὲ τῷ λέγειν με τοῦτο ἔπεσε τὸ πνεῦμα τὸ ἅγιον ἐπ' αὐτούς.

    a. Identify the main sentence and translate.
       ἔπεσε: see πίπτω.

    b. ἐν τῷ λέγειν με. ἐν with the dative of the articular infinitive expresses what kind of clause (305.3)? με. Why accusative (304)? Would λέγοντός μου be equivalent (305.3 and 266.2)? Why not εἰπόντός μου (254.1-3)?

9. μετὰ δὲ τὸ ἐγερθῆναι τὸν κύριον ἐδίωξαν οἱ Ἰουδαῖοι τοὺς μαθητὰς αὐτοῦ.

    a. μετά with the accusative of the articular infinitive expresses what kind of adverbial clause (305.2)? What would an equivalent expression be?

    b. ἐγερθῆναι: -θῆναι should be easy to spot. Full identification (293)? Who was raised? How do you know (304)?

10. πρὸ δὲ τοῦ βληθῆναι εἰς φυλακὴν τὸν προφήτην ἐβάπτιζον οἱ μαθηταὶ τοῦ Ἰησοῦ τοὺς ἐρχομένους πρὸς αὐτούς.

    a. Go to the main verb, its subject and object, and translate.

    b. τοὺς ἐρχομένους: use of the participle (234) and function in the sentence (34)?

    c. πρό with the genitive of the articular infinitive expresses what kind of adverbial clause (305.4)?
       Which happened first, the baptizing or the casting?
    d. Why relate τὸν προφήτην to βληθῆναι as subject (304)?

11. διὰ δὲ τὸ εἶναι αὐτὸν ἐκεῖ συνῆλθον οἱ Ἰουδαῖοι.

    a. συνῆλθον (193).
    b. The διὰ clause gives what logical information (305.5)?

12. θέλω γὰρ ἰδεῖν ὑμᾶς, ἵνα λάβητε δῶρον ἀγαθόν, εἰς τὸ γενέσθαι ὑμᾶς μαθητὰς πιστούς.

    a. Compare the ἵνα clause (286) and the εἰς + articular infinitive clause (305.6) semantically. What verbs may those clauses modify?
    b. ἰδεῖν, λάβητε, γενέσθαι all have what in common (189.2; 294.1)?
    c. ὑμᾶς is in the accusative. Why (304)?
       Why then accusative μαθητὰς πιστούς (108)?

13. ἀπέθανεν ὑπὲρ αὐτῶν ὁ Ἰησοῦς εἰς τὸ σωθῆναι αὐτούς.

    a. ἀπέθανεν full identification (193)?
    b. εἰς τὸ σωθῆναι αὐτούς: give an alternate Greek expression of the same idea (305.6 and 286).

14. ἔπεμψεν ὁ θεος τὸν Ἰησοῦν, ἵνα ἀποθάνῃ ὑπὲρ ἡμῶν, εἰς τὸ δοξάζειν ἡμᾶς τὸν σώσαντα ἡμᾶς.

    a. ἔπεμψεν: <u>sigma</u> suffix (ψ), -ε with movable <u>nu</u>, augmented verb stem all point to what identification (Ch. XIV)?
    b. ἵνα ἀποθάνῃ (ὑπερ ἡμῶν): give the equivalent infinitival construction (305.6 and 296).
    c. εἰς τὸ δοξάζειν ἡμᾶς (1) τον σώσαντα ἡμᾶς (2).
       What is the nature of the "glorifying" specified here (299)?
       ἡμᾶς (1) functions how (304)?
       ἡμᾶς (2) functions how (232, first para.)?
       Give the equivalent ἵνα construction (286 and 305.6).

15. εἶπεν ὁ τυφλὸς ὅτι βλέπει τοὺς ἀνθρώπους.

    a. What were the blind man's actual words (308)?
    b. How does the ὅτι clause function here?

16. εἶπεν ὁ Ἰησοῦς ὅτι ἐλεύσεται ἐν τῇ βασιλείᾳ αὐτοῦ.

152

a. What were the direct words of Jesus (308.(4))?
b. Remember 309.

17. ταῦτα ἔλεγεν ὁ ἀπόστολος ἔτι ὢν ἐν σαρκί, εἰς τὸ πιστεῦσαι εἰς τὸν Ἰησοῦν τοὺς ἀκούσαντας.

   a. The apostle's speech: continuing or not (122.2)?
   b. ἔτι ὢν ἐν σαρκί: what kind of a clause (232.7-8)?
      Give the infinitival equivalent (305.3).
   c. εἰς τὸ πιστεῦσαι: what kind of a clause (305.6)?
      Give the Greek equivalent expression. Preserve the same sort
      of reference to the act (274).

18. κελεύσας ἡμᾶς ὁ Ἰησοῦς ἐλθεῖν εἰς τὴν κώμην εὐθὺς ἀπέλυσε τὸν ὄχλον.

   a. ἡμᾶς . . . ἐλθεῖν (304).
   b. κελεύσας: what kind of clause (254.1-3)?
      Give the infinitival equivalent (305.2).

19. σωθέντες ὑπὸ τοῦ Ἰησοῦ ὀφείλομεν καὶ πάσχειν διὰ τὸ ὄνομα αὐτοῦ.

   καὶ πάσχειν: remember 146. Full identification.
   Temporary suffering? Why not (299)?

20. ἐν τῷ πάσχειν ἡμᾶς ταῦτα ἔλεγον οἱ ἀδελφοὶ ὅτι βλέπουσι τὸν Ἰησοῦν.

   a. Compare πασχόντων ἡμῶν with the infinitival construction (305.3).
      Why not παθόντων (2A) ἡμῶν (305.2)?
   b. What were the brothers' words?

312.II NEW TESTAMENT READING

   I Jn. 2.1-6

   2.1 τεκνία   Remember 258.2

        ἁμάρτητε   ἁμαρτάνω. ἵνα takes what mood (286)?
        ἁμάρτῃ   Note tense stems ἁμαρτ-.

        τις   "Some one." Indef. pron. See 388-390

        ὁ παράκλητος   "A helper," "intercessor." Read AG, page
                                        623b.

        πατέρα   M.A.sg. of ὁ πατήρ, πατρός (Jn. 1.14).
                                        Did you get the clause connections straight
                              in this verse?

153

2.2 ἡμετέρων   Para. 473.

     μόνον   N.A.sg. of adj., "alone." Used as adv.,
                                "only."

2.3 ἐγνώκαμεν   Pf. A.I., 1 pl. of γινώσκω. Remember the
                                perfect's focus on a present condition
     resulting from past action. What is the tense suffix
     (430)? Do you see the point of the contrast with the
     present?

     τηρῶμεν   P.A.S., 1 pl. of τηρέω. "I keep" a
                                contract verb (τηρε + ωμεν; para. 314-316).
     What is the meaning of the tense here (283)?

2.4 ὁ λέγων . . . μὴ τηρῶν   One person with contradictory life, or
                                two different persons? See 240.I.11b.
                                τηρε + ων (314-316)

     ἔγνωκα   Pf. A.I., 1 sg. γινώσκω.

     ψεύστης   See 1.10.

2.5 ος δ(ε) ἂν τηρῇ   "Whoever keeps."
                                τηρῇ = P.A.S., 3 sg. of τηρέω.
     (τηρε + ῃ).
     ὅς + ἂν See 395 and 400. Similar to a substantive
     ptc. here.

     ἀληθῶς   "Truly" an adverbial -ως. Review 101.3.

     τετελείωται   Pf. P.I. 3 sg. of τελειόω "I am complete,"
                                "I bring to the desired goal." Do you
     see the point of the perfect tense? A focus on present
     situation of love now come to its desired good as
     reflected in past events.

2.6 μένειν/περιπατεῖν   Para. 293. Remember 306 (the accusative
                                is omitted here).

     καθώς   "Just as." Note adverbial -ως again.

313.1   εὐλογέω   εὐ-, a phoneme which adds "positive"
        εὐ-χαριστέω   meaning to words with which it is joined.
                       Cf. τὸ εὐαγγέλιον, "a good message." See Metzger,
Lexical Aids, pp. 47, 62.

313.2   περιπατέω   "I walk (around)"
        προσκυνέω   "I bow the knee to," i.e., "I worship"
        θεωρέω   Compare the derived "theory."
        εὐχαριστέω   Related liturgical term is _____ .

314.1   What is contraction?

314.2   This chapter presents the contraction which regularly occurs in the
         present verb system (321) between 1) the vowel with which certain
present stems end (ε/α/ο) and 2) the variable vowel or vocalic personal ending.

316.1   The descriptive "rules" given by Machen (see NTGFB, p. 143, n.1) may
         be slightly reorganized as follows to emphasize the patterns. You will
need to know para. 3 to make sense of this.

316.2   Rules of contraction. Find illustrations of each rule.
         1. Vowels which can form a diphthong do so (para. 4):
         2. Like or corresponding vowels form their long vowel,
            But: ε + ε = ει and ο + ο = ου.
         3. α with ε/η forms the long of whichever vowel comes first.
         4. "o" vowels (ο/ω) overcome "a" and "e" vowels giving omega (ω).
            But ο + ε/ε + ο = ου
         5. If the second of the two contracting vowels is a dipththong, con-
            traction occurs by the rules above with (a) a remaining iota (ι) be-
            coming a subscript and (b) a remaining upsilon (υ) being lost.
            But: ο + ει/η = οι
         6. A vowel is absorbed into a following diphthong beginning with the
            same vowel.

316.3   How are contracted syllables accented? Work carefully through Machen's
         examples.

317.1   Notice that contraction of contract verbs occurs only throughout the
         present system (123.1; 321.1). Elsewhere contract verbs are highly
regular.

318.1   What are the two exceptions to regular contraction in the present stem
         verbs with final vowel?

320.1   Where and why do you find un-contracted forms of the contract verbs?

321.1   What regularly occurs before the tense suffixes added in the formation
         of principal parts II, III, IV and VI? How does this figure in locating
new forms encountered in reading (322)?

324.I   Aids to exercise I, Lesson XXIII.

1.   οὐκ εὐλογήσει ὁ θεὸς τὸν μὴ περιπατοῦντα κατὰ τὰς ἐντολὰς τοῦ
     Ἰησοῦ.

     a.   εὐλογήσει: primary ending (139.1), sigma tense suffix,
          — what principal part must this be (151.4,2; 154-5)? Why
          - ησ - (321)?
     b.   τὸν περιπατοῦντα: don't panic! - ουντα is obviously an
          active participle form (M.A.sg. judging by the article). Can't
          be aorist (-σαντα or -θεντα). With - ου - connecting "vowel"
          it must be a present ptc. (Why? 317.1) with contraction? Write
          the uncontracted form and explain the contraction (see 316 rules)?
          _____ + _____ = _____

2.   οἱ ἀγαπώμενοι ὑπὸ τοῦ Ἰησοῦ ἀγαπῶσι τὸν ἀγαπῶντα αὐτούς.

     a.   ἀγαπώμενοι
          ἀγαπῶσι
          ἀγαπῶντα
          Write the uncontracted forms and explain the contractions
          (316.2.4-5).
     b.   ἀγαπῶσι could be either indicative or subjunctive in form.
          Why? There is no reason to assume subjunctive here.
     c.   On use of participles memorize para. 265 if there is still
          confusion.

3.   λαλοῦντος τοῦ Ἰησοῦ τοῖς ἀκολουθοῦσιν ἤρξατο ὁ ἄρχων παρακαλεῖν
     αὐτὸν ἀπελθεῖν.

     a.   Opening adverbial participle and its subject is in genitive.
          Probably a _____ (266).
     b.   λαλοῦντας
          ἀκολουθοῦσιν
          παρακαλεῖν
          Write the uncontracted forms and explain the contractions
          (316.2.4 and 6).
     c.   τοῖς ἀκολουθοῦσιν: how related to λαλοῦντος (36)?
          Why not identify ἀκολουθοῦσιν as P.A.I., 3 pl.?
     d.   ἤρξατο . . . παρακαλεῖν (292.1).
     e.   ἀπελθεῖν: why circumflex here (not 316.III as in
          παρακαλεῖν: rather para. 296)? Remember 306.

4.   ἀκολουθήσαντες τῷ λαλήσαντι ταῦτα ζητήσωμεν τὸν οἶκον αὐτοῦ.

     a.   Are the contract verbs irregular here (317.1 and 321)?
     b.   The adverbial participle finds its subject in the subject of
          the main verb. How do you know? If you don't know learn 232.3
          and figure out how it applies here. Ask, if any confusion lingers.

c. First person plural subjunctive probably used how (285)?

5. εἰ ἀγαπῶμεν τὸν θεόν, τηρῶμεν τὰς ἐντολὰς αὐτοῦ καὶ ποιῶμεν τὰ λαλούμενα ἡμῖν ὑπὸ τοῦ Ἰησοῦ.

    a. With εἰ, ἀγαπῶμεν must be in the _____ mood (288.2). Write the uncontracted form and explain the contractions (316.2.5).

    b. τηρῶμεν. . . καὶ ποιῶμεν: must be subjunctive. How can you tell (316.2.4 and note the exception)?

    c. Give exegetical translations (283.3).

6. τοῦτο ποιήσαντος τοῦ Ἰησοῦ ἐλάλει περὶ αὐτοῦ ὁ θεραπευθεὶς τῷ ἀκολουθοῦντι ὄχλῳ.

    a. Genitive absolute should not be a problem now (266.2).

    b. ἐλάλει: with acute accent on penult, the contraction could not have been ἐλαλε + ει (316.III.2 and 11.2).
    Must have been ἐλαλε̄ + ε. Why (316.III and 11.2)?
    Full identification.
    Don't let word order fool you on the subject of this verb (259).

7. ἐθεώρουν οἱ ἀπόστολοι τὰ ἔργα τὰ ποιούμενα ὑπὸ Ἰησοῦ ἐν τῷ περιπατεῖν αὐτοὺς σὺν αὐτῷ.

    a. ου- connecting vowel (ἐθεώρουν and ποιούμενα) most likely is a contraction of what vowels (316.2.2 or 4)?
    Write the uncontracted forms and give clear identifications.

    b. ἐν τῷ περιπατεῖν (316.2.6 and 305.3): what is the equivalent participle expression (305.3)?
    Accent shows that the second contracting element was long (ε + ειν). Otherwise the accent would have rested on πα- and the contraction would not have carried an accent (316.III again if you do not understand).

    c. Why accusative in αὐτούς (304)?

8. μετὰ τὸ βληθῆναι εἰς φυλακὴν τὸν προφήτην οὐκέτι περιεπάτει ὁ Ἰησοῦς ἐν τῇ χώρᾳ ἐκείνῃ.

    a. μετά with articular infinitive (-θῆναι has to indicate what here? para. 293) is equivalent to what participle construction (305.2)?

    b. περιεπάτει: compare ἐλάλει in No. 6 for the contraction. Where is the augment (131-132)?

9. οἱ ἀγαπῶντες τὸν θεὸν ποιοῦσι τὰς ἐντολὰς αὐτοῦ.

    a. ποιοῦσι: of course (it could be P.A. ptc., M.D. pl.
        (ποιέ + οσι), but what would the sentence mean?
        What is the contraction (316.2.5) and the correct identification?
    b. ἀγαπῶντες: explain the contraction (316.2.4) and give full
        identification.

10. ταῦτα ἐποίουν τῷ Ἰησοῦ καὶ οἱ θεραπευθέντες ὑπ' αὐτοῦ.

    a. ἐποίουν: augmented present stem indicates what tense (123.2)?
        Explain the contraction (316.2.2) and give full identification.
    b. καί: doesn't make sense as a coordinating conjunction ("and"),
        so probably used how (146)?

11. ἐζήτουν αὐτὸν οἱ ὄχλοι, ἵνα θεωρῶσι τὰ ποιούμενα ὑπ' αὐτοῦ.

    a. ἐζήτουν
        ποιούμενα
        Write the uncontracted forms and explain the contraction by the
        rules (316).
        How does accent help in the first verb (316.III)?
    b. Of what does the ἵνα clause give the purpose?
        After ἵνα you expect the _____ mood (286). That is all
        θεωρῶσι can be; how do you know (316.2.4)?
    c. Give the infinitival equivalent of the purpose clause (305.6).

12. οὐ φιλοῦσι τὸν Ἰησοῦν οἱ μὴ ποιοῦντες τὰς ἐντολὰς αὐτοῦ.

    a. -ου- connecting vowels arise from what three sources (316.2,
        4 and 5)? Which explains the verbs in this sentence?
    b. Where is the "noun clause" in this sentence (235)?

13. ἀγαπῶμεν τὸν θεὸν ἐν ταῖς καρδίαις ἡμῶν ἀγαπῶντες καὶ τοὺς
    ἀδελφούς.

    a. Is ἀγαπῶμεν indicative or subjunctive? Explain the contraction
        involved in either case (316.2.4). How would you settle the
        question here?
    b. ἀγαπῶντες: explain the contraction (316). If this adverbial
        ptc. were interpreted as a causal ptc., or conditional ptc.,
        how would you translate it? See CEG, pp. 65-66 and para. 257.I.13d.
    c. On καί remember para. 146.

14. ταῦτα ἐλάλησεν ὁ Ἰησοῦς τοῖς ἀκολουθοῦσιν αὐτῷ ἔτι περιπατῶν
    μετ' αὐτῶν ἐν τῇ χώρᾳ τῶν Ἰουδαίων.

    a. τοῖς ἀκολουθοῦσιν: the article precludes P.A.I., 3 pl.
        What is the form of this contract verb and how is it used (36
        and 235)?

  b. περιπατῶν: careful identification here. What contraction (cannot identify without this; 316.2.4)?
  c. Give the infinitival equivalent of this adverbial ptc. (305.3).

15. ἐὰν μὴ περιπατῶμεν κατὰ τὰς ἐντολὰς τοῦ Ἰησοῦ, οὐ θεωρήσομεν τὸ πρόσωπον αὐτοῦ.

  a. περιπατῶμεν: can you distinguish between indicatives and subjunctives with ε- stem contract verbs? Why (316.2.4)?
  b. Why not take this as a horatory subjunctive (288)?
  c. Could a present adverbial participle convey the thought of this condition (μὴ περιπατοῦντες. . .)? See No. 13b above.

16. μετὰ τὸ καλέσαι αὐτοὺς τὸν Ἰησοῦν οὐκέτι περιεπάτουν ἐν ταῖς ὁδοῖς τοῦ πονηροῦ οὐδὲ ἐποίουν τὰ πονηρά.

  a. μετὰ τὸ καλέσαι (293) αὐτούς: why accusative (304)? What is the equivalent adverbial ptc. expression (305.2)?
  b. οὐκέτι περιεπάτουν . . . οὐδὲ ἐποίουν: remember 148. With augmented present stems (123) and -ου- contraction on ε- stem verbs, these forms are to be identified how (316.2.4 and 139.1)?

17. ταῦτα ἐποιεῖτε ἡμῖν διὰ τὸ ἀγαπᾶν ὑμᾶς τὸν καλέσαντα ὑμᾶς εἰς τὴν βασιλείαν αὐτοῦ.

  a. διὰ τὸ ἀγαπᾶν: full identification (318).
  b. Why accusative on first ὑμᾶς (304)?

18. τῷ Ἰησοῦ λαλήσαντι ταῦτα μετὰ τὸ ἐγερθῆναι ἐκ νεκρῶν προσεκύνησαν οἱ κληθέντες ὑπ' αὐτοῦ.

  a. τῷ Ἰησοῦ λαλήσαντι: the article goes with Ἰησοῦ. Must be what use of the ptc. then?
  b. προσκυνέω takes what case for its object (313)? Where is that object here?
  c. μετὰ τὸ ἐγερθῆναι: subject understood. Gives what information (305.2)? -θῆναι must be what form (293)?

19. ἐθεώρουν τὸν Ἰησοῦν σταυρούμενον ὑπὸ τῶν στρατιωτῶν αἱ ἀκολουθήσασαι αὐτῷ ἐκ τῆς Γαλιλαίας.

20. οὐ θεωρήσομεν αὐτὸν ἐὰν μὴ ἀκολουθῶμεν αὐτῷ περιπατοῦντι ἐν τῇ Γαλιλαίᾳ.

324.II NEW TESTAMENT READING

Review the contract verb forms encountered in your NT reading so far and analyze their contractions accurately now in light of your study of chapter XXIII.

μαρτυρεῖ (Jn. 1.15), βοῶντος (1.23), περιπατοῦντα (1.36), περιπατῶμεν (I Jn. 1.6, 7), ποιοῦμεν (1.6, 10), πλανῶμεν (1.8), ὁμολογῶμεν (1.9).

Translate I Jn. 2.7-11.

2.7 (ἐντολήν). . .ἣν εἴχετε (ἔχω) "(A commandment) which you have had. . "

Relative pronoun ἣν links the adjective clause to ἐντολήν, the antecedent which is modified by this relative clause. Note 395 and 397.

ὃν ἠκούσατε "Which you have heard." ὃν links the relative clause to ὁ λόγος. How do you know (397)?

2.8 πάλιν "Again."

ὃ ἐστιν ἀληθές "A thing which is true." See 395-397 and, on the adjective ἀληθές, 360-362.

ἤδη "Already."

2.9 ὁ λέγων. . . μισῶν Note again the contradiction in the one individual (cf. 2.4). μισέω, "I hate" (μισε + ων; para. 316). The content of λέγω is here an infinitival expression. 306 and cf. 2.6 above.

ἕως ἄρτι "Until now."

2.11 ὁ μισῶν Continuing action?
How do you know (244.4; 283.2)?

οἶδεν Para. 603.

ποῦ "Where."

Lesson XXIV

326.1   What are "liquid verbs"? Give some examples.

327.1   How do future liquid verbs differ from regularly formed futures of non-liquid stems?

327.2   <u>Why</u> and <u>how</u> are the future active and middle liquid verbs to be compared to the <u>present</u> forms of the contract verbs with stem final -ε?

329.1   How can the future active forms, κρινῶ, κρινεῖς, κρινεῖ and κρινοῦσι(ν) (328) and future middle κρινῇ(330) be distinguished from the <u>present</u> active and middle forms of the same person and number?
Review para. 316.III.

329.2   How can the future active forms κρινοῦμεν and κρινεῖτε and the future middles, κρινοῦμαι, κρινεῖται, κρινοῦμεθα, κρινεῖσθε and κρινοῦνται be distinguished from present active and middle forms of the same person and number (327 and 316)?

331.1   Study the vocabulary and list the verbs whose present stems differ from their future stems. Study those differences to facilitate your identification of the principal parts of liquid verbs.

331.2   Comparing paras. 327 and 331 it should be obvious that liquid verb stems do not accept the <u>sigma</u> tense suffixes of either the future or the aorist—hence the "<u>irregularities</u>" which are really <u>alternative signals</u> of the future and aorist tenses.

333.2   In lieu of the normal <u>sigma</u> tense suffix what customarily indicates aorist tense in liquid verb stems?

333.3   What is meant by the statement. "The conjugation (of liquid verbs), in all the moods, is like the conjugation of other first aorists?" Study the examples.

334.1   What is illustrated by the verbs βάλλω – ἔβαλον?

334.2   What is illustrated by the verb λαμβάνω (verb stem λαβ-)?

335.1   The future indicative of εἰμί follows what conjugation pattern?

335.2   What is the sign of the future here (151)?

337–
338.1   The singular forms of the 1st and 2nd person reflexive pronoun are compounds formed from the respective personal pronoun (ἐμέ and σέ) and αὐτός (in G.D. and A., M. and F.).

337–
339.2   How are the reflexive pronouns, 1st and 2nd person plural and 3rd person sg. and pl., formed?

342.1   Greek parallels English in correct use of the reflexive pronoun. "My
        brother and myself serve the church" is unacceptable in both Greek and
English. Why?

344.1   Some sentences in these exercises have structures which include <u>object
        complements</u>. In such sentences (with the verb, e.g. "to preach," "to
call," "to think") the direct object (1) and the object complement (2) are both
in the accusative case, the direct object being the more definite of the two.
Jn. 15.15   οὐκέτι λέγω ὑμᾶς δούλους
        "No longer do I call you (1) servants (2)."

In translation one must sometimes introduce the object complement with the words
"as, for, to be." Some object complements include the Greek words ὡς (as), or
εἰς (for).

344.2   Adjectives may also function as object complements.
        Mt. 28.14 ἡμεῖς. . . ὑμᾶς <u>ἀμερίμνους</u> ποιήσομεν
        "We shall make you (1) <u>free from care</u> (2)"

344.3   For further information consult Goetchius, pp. 140-144, or DM, p. 94
        (there as the "double accusative").

344.I   Aids to exercise I, Lesson XXIV.

1.   οὐ γὰρ ἑαυτοὺς κηρύσομεν ἀλλὰ Χριστὸν Ἰησοῦν κύριον, ἑαυτοὺς δὲ
     δούλους ὑμῶν διὰ Ἰησοῦν.

        a.   What verb is assumed in the second (ἀλλά) and third (δέ) clauses
             of this sentence?
        b.   Why take ἑαυτούς as <u>first</u> person plural reflexive, "ourselves,"
             instead of "yourselves" or "themselves"? See 342 again.
        c.   Identify clearly the direct object and the object complement
             in clause two (ἀλλά). Review 344.1-4. Then find the parallel
             to these in clause three (δέ).

2.   ὁ ἐγείρας τὸν κύριον Ἰησοῦν ἐγερεῖ καὶ ἡμᾶς σὺν Ἰησοῦ.

        a.   ὁ ἐγείρας: parse fully. Why no <u>sigma</u> on this aorist (333)?
             What construction is this (255.1)? How used here (34)?
        b.   ἐγερεῖ: what signs of the future are here?
             1. (327) _____   2. (331) _____

3.   εἶπεν ὁ μαθητὴς ὅτι ἀποθανεῖται ὑπὲρ τοῦ Ἰησοῦ.

        a.   ὅτι clause is related to εἶπεν in what way (306)?
        b.   ἀποθανεῖται: compare the 2A stem ἀποθαν - (2A.A.I. ἀπέθανον).
             Why not identify this word as second aorist (327, with 152)?
        c.   Explain the tense and mood of ἀποθανεῖτε (306-307).

162

4. οὐκ ἐγεροῦμεν αὐτοὶ ἑαυτούς, ὁ δὲ Ἰησοῦς ἐγερεῖ ἡμᾶς ἐν τῇ ἐσχάτῃ ἡμέρᾳ.

    a. ἐγεροῦμεν
        ἐγερεῖ
        Parse both of these; note the clear signs of tense and mood (327-330).

    b. The word "ourselves" appears twice in the translation of the first clause. A completely different Greek construction stands behind each one. Explain (105.2 and 342).

5. εὐθὺς ἦρεν ὁ πονηρὸς τὸ παρὰ τὴν ὁδὸν σπαρέν.

    a. ἦρεν: movable <u>nu</u>, -ε secondary ending (173, 176 and 139.1). Expect either _____ or _____ tense (197.1). One expects an augment in ηρ-. Why (127.1: 123.3)? ηρ- (augmented) must either be ερ- or αρ-. Which is it here (325)?

    b. τὸ . . . σπαρέν: σπαρέν is not A.A.I. 3 sg. Why? See the vocabulary, 325, and the principal parts there. What form of σπείρω has tense stem σπαρ-? See again para. 206 and 259.

6. ἐὰν ἀγαπᾶτε ἀλλήλους, ἔσεσθε μαθηταὶ τοῦ ἀποθανόντος ὑπὲρ ὑμῶν.

    a. With ἐάν, ἀγαπᾶτε is most likely _____ mood (288)? Explain its contraction (316).

    b. ἔσεσθε: para. 335.

    c. (τοῦ) ἀποθανόντος: -οντος has to be what verb form (576-580)? How does the irregular accent help in parsing (250.1)?

7. ἐὰν πιστεύσητε εἰς τὸν Ἰησοῦν, μετ' αὐτοῦ μενεῖτε εἰς τὸν αἰῶνα.

    a. πιστεύσητε: why not future indicative (152 and 269)?

    b. μενεῖτε: there is obviously a contraction (μεν + ε + ετε). Is μένω a contract verb (314.2)? What kind of verb stem is it (326)? What then does the contraction signal (327)?

8. ὁ ἀγαπῶν τὸν υἱὸν ἀγαπᾷ καὶ τὸν ἀποστείλαντα αὐτόν.

    a. Parse fully and explain the contractions (316).
        ὁ ἀγαπῶν
        ἀγαπᾷ

b. ἀποστείλαντα: -αντα, with alpha connecting vowel, this should be an obvious clue to the main verb form as well as the tense (242). Parse fully.

ἀποστειλ-: why no <u>sigma</u> tense suffix (333)?

Why long stem vowel (ει not ε) (333)?

What else separates this from the present stem?

9. χαρὰ ἔσται ἐπὶ τῷ ἁμαρτωλῷ τῷ ἐπὶ τῷ ῥήματι τοῦ Ἰησοῦ μετανοήσαντι.

     a. Remember 336.
     b. Parse fully.
     ἔσται (335).
     τῷ. . .μετανοήσαντι (322 and 242).

10. οἱ ἀποκτείναντες τὸν Ἰησοῦν καὶ διώξαντες τοὺς μαθητὰς αὐτοῦ ἐκβαλοῦσι καὶ ἡμᾶς.

     a. ἀποκτείναντες: -αντες should be decisive clue. Parse fully (242). Why no σα- (333)?
     b. ἐκβαλοῦσι: parse. βάλλω is not a contract verb in the present. Why the circumflex accent (327-328)?

11. ἐπιστρέψαντες οὗτοι ἐπὶ τὸν θεὸν ἔμειναν ἐν τῇ ἐκκλησίᾳ αὐτοῦ.

     a. Parse ἐπιστρέψαντες (242).
     ἔμειναν (333).
     b. Why the change from μεν- to μειν- (333)?
     What sign of 1st aorist is missing (333)?

12. ἐγείραντος τοῦ θεοῦ τοὺς νεκροὺς ἐσόμεθα σὺν τῷ κυρίῳ εἰς τοὺς αἰῶνας τῶν αἰώνων.

     a. Parse the verb forms.
     ἐγείραντος. Can't be present; why (333)?
     ἐσόμεθα (335).
     b. Adverbial participle and its subject in the genitive case; what construction (266)? How is the construction functioning here (232.9)?
     c. Review third declension endings quickly if αἰῶνας is not easily declined for you (ch. XVII).

13. οὐκ εἰς ἐμαυτὸν ἐπίστευσα, ἀλλ' εἰς τὸν κύριον.

14. ἔξεστιν ἡμῖν λαβεῖν δῶρα ἀπ' ἀλλήλων, ἀλλ' οὐκ ἀποκτεῖναι οὐδὲ διῶξαι ἀλλήλους.

    a. ἔξεστιν is followed by the _____ and the _____ (292).
    b. Parse fully.
       λαβεῖν (296).
       ἀποκτεῖναι (333)
       διῶξαι (293)
    c. What is assumed in the second clause?

15. οὗτος μέν ἐστιν ὁ ἄρχων ὁ ἀποκτείνας τοὺς προφήτας, ἐκεῖνος δέ ἐστιν ὁ ἁμαρτωλὸς ὁ μετανοήσας ἐπὶ τῷ ῥήματι τοῦ Ἰησοῦ.

    a. Contrast and parse ἀπέκτεινας (333 and 172).
       ἀποκτείνας (333 and 242).
    b. The participle constructions have what function in this sentence (255.1)?

16. ἐὰν δὲ τοῦτο εἴπωμεν κατ' αὐτοῦ, φοβούμεθα τοὺς ὄχλους, λέγουσι γὰρ εἶναι αὐτὸν προφήτην.

    a. Parse fully.
       εἴπωμεν (278).
       φοβούμεθα (explain the ου, 316).
       εἶναι (297).
    b. Identify these constructions:
       ἐάν . . . εἴπωμεν (280).
       λέγουσι . . . εἶναι αὐτὸν προφήτην (306).

17. ἀποστελεῖ πρὸς αὐτοὺς διδασκάλους καὶ προφήτας, ἵνα μετανοήσωσιν καὶ φοβῶνται τὸν θεόν.

    a. ἀποστελεῖ: two plain signs that this is <u>not</u> P.A.I. 3 sg. What are those signs (327, 331)? Parse.
    b. φοβῶνται: with ἵνα, expect _____ mood (287). Parse and justify the identification by explaining the contraction (316).

18. μακάριοί εἰσιν οὐχ οἱ ἑαυτοὺς δοξάζοντες ἀλλ' οἱ δοξάζοντες τὸν ἀποστείλαντα τὸν υἱὸν αὐτοῦ εἰς τὸν κόσμον.

    a. μακάριοι: does this word <u>identify</u> οἱ. . . δοξάζοντες or describe (characterize) them? How can you tell (99.3; 107.I.6b)?
    b. ἀποστείλαντα: parse fully. See 17a. What is the function of this ptc.?

19. ἐρχομένου πρὸς αὐτοὺς τοῦ Ἰησοῦ περιπατοῦντος ἐπὶ τῆς θαλάσσης
    ἐφοβοῦντο οἱ ἰδόντες αὐτὸν μαθηταί.

    a. ἐρχομένου. . . τοῦ Ἰησοῦ: what construction (266)?
    b. περιπατοῦντος: parse (576); explain the contraction (316).
       Who is doing the action of this ptc. (232.3)?
       The participle tells <u>how</u> Jesus <u>came</u>. Adverbial or adjectival
       (232.7-8)? Modifies what other verbal form in the sentence?

20. ταῦτα ἐροῦμεν τοῖς ἀποσταλεῖσι πρὸς ἡμᾶς προφήταις.

    a. Parse ἐροῦμεν (327-28).
    b. ἀποσταλ- (εῖσι): what principal part of ἀποστέλλω?
       Parse (325 and 579).

344.II NEW TESTAMENT GREEK READING

Translate Jn. 1.38-42.

1.38	στραφείς	Identify fully (206 and 259). στρέφω, "I turn."
	ἀκολουθοῦντας	Why not relate to ὁ Ἰησοῦς...λέγει with the previous participles (232.3)? See
	424.1 again.	
	λέγει	See 165.II on μαρτυρεῖ.
	εἶπαν	Para. 521. So on forms in 1.39 below.
	ὃ λέγεται	"Which (395) is called," i.e., "which means" (AG, p. 471, II.3).
	μεθερμηνευόμενον	μεθερμηνεύω, "I interpret." Long, but simple. Identify fully. Adverbial
	or adjectival?	See also in 1.41.
1.39	ἔρχεσθε	Paras. 408 and 420 (420.4).
	ἔμειναν	Para. 333.
	τὴν ἡμέραν	Para. 382.
1.40	Ἦν	Remember para. 133.
	Σίμωνος	M.G. sg. Compare the accusative Σίμωνα (1.41), and nominative Σίμων (1.42), forms
		of this third declension proper name. See para. 212 and compare the forms of αἰών, - ῶνος.
	εἷς	Para. 371. Not the prep.
	τῶν ἀκουσάντων . . . καὶ ἀκολουθησάντων	Modifies _____. See 240.I.11b.

1.41 πρῶτον   N.A. sg. adjective used as adverb, "First."

      εὑρήκαμεν   From εὑρίσκω, "I find." <u>Kappa</u> tense
                                    suffix, <u>alpha</u> connecting vowel? Identfy
             (426). One would expect lengthening of the initial
             vowel.

1.42 ἔμβλεψας   See Jn. 1.36.

      κληθήσῃ   κληθη -σ -ῃ. What form of καλέω (202)?

345.1 To facilitate vocabulary mastery, several of these vocabulary words
       should be related to words you already know. To what words already
studied would you relate the following?

ἀληθής, ές   _____ (46)
ὁ ἀρχιερεύς, έως   _____ (24) and
and ὁ ἰερεύς, έως   _____ (210)
ὁ βασιλεύς, έως   _____ (46)
ὁ γραμματεύς, έως   _____ (16)
ἡ πίστις, εως   _____ (60)

345.2 Third declension masculine nouns declined like ὁ βασιλεύς, -έως, "king,"
       name persons of certain professions or offices (e.g. "scribe," ὁ γραμματεύς,
"priest," ὁ ἰερεύς). Compare the first declension masculine nouns like ὁ μαθητής
and ὁ βαπτίστης which also name persons characterized by certain activities.

347.1 How does this noun differ from the third declension nouns in para. 211
       (See 348 after your own study.)?

347.2 Is nu (-ν) a new accusative singular ending for you? Where has it
       appeared before? Review 49.2!

349.1 Again compare the endings in 49.2 with the declension of ἡ πόλις, πόλεως.

349.2 Note that the genitive has lengthened "o-vowel" (omega) in both singular
       and plural. The genitive singular -ως is simply lengthened -ος (212).

349.3 What is the sign of the dative? of the accusative?

349.4 What exception to the rules of noun accent (para 11) do you observe in
       this paradigm (see 50 for answer)?

352.1 How is this neuter paradigm like other neuter nouns you have studied (42)?

352.2 N.A.V.pl. ending -η is the familiar neuter plural ending -α contracted
       (ε + α = η). Genitive sg. -ους is also just a contracted form of the
regular third declension gen. sg. -ος (ε + ος = ους).

355.1 Accusative sg. -α should be noted (contrast -ν in the other nouns of this
       chapter). You have already seen this third declension ending in nouns
like νύξ, νυκτός, and σαρξ, σαρκός: σάρκα and νύκτα (211).

355.2 Note again 345.2

357.1 Observe that the paradigms given in this chapter present three major third
       declension noun types (all of them vowel or sigma stem nouns). Many im-
portant nouns follow each of these patterns.

357.2 Learn the gender of these several patterns. Nouns like (ἡ) πόλις, -εως
       are all feminine, like (τό) γένος, -ους all neuter, and (ὁ) βασιλεύς,
-έως all masculine.

360.1 Adjectives like ἀληθής, -ές have only two sets of endings, one for
       masculine and feminine and one for neuter. Some second declension
adjectives are also bi-form adjectives, e.g., δόκιμος, δόκιμον and σωτήριος, -ον.

363.1 Continue your independence in translation (para. 165.1 and the introduction
       to the answer sheets). If you correctly understand the sentence, and
if you have learned the grammar and syntax in the preceding lessons, you will
know several alternative translations for many parts of the text and will not
be bound by the "answers," which are merely aids to learning.

363.2 General suggestions for exercise I, Lesson XXV.
       a. Learn the new noun paradigms before doing the sentences.
       b. Fully identify every word. Write identifications for words you do
           not easily identify. This is a prerequisite to intelligent transla-
           tion.
       This suggestion is to be remembered with every lesson's sentences.

363.I Aids to exercise I, Lesson XXV.

       1. ἀληθῆ ἐστὶ τὰ λαλούμενα ὑπὸ τοῦ ἱερέως τούτου.

           a. ἀληθῆ: remember 99.3. Identity or description here?
           b. What use of the participle (235.1)?
           c. What is the subject of the sentence? the predicate?
           d. Remember the reason for the singular verb here (145)?

       2. συνελθόντων τῶν ἀρχιερέων καὶ γραμματέων ἵνα ἀποκτείνωσι τὸν ἄνδρα
           τοῦτον, προσηύξαντο οἱ μαθηταὶ ἐν τῷ ἱερῷ.

           a. Participle and subjects in genitive. Probably what construction
               (266)?
           b. Of what act does the ἵνα clause give the purpose?
           c. προσηύξαντο? What signs of first aorist (172, 175)? What is
               the eta (172)? If you haven't fully parsed this verb, do it.

       3. ἀπεκρίθη ὁ βασιλεὺς ὁ ἀγαθὸς λέγων ὅτι οὐ θέλει ἀποκτεῖναι τοῦτον.

           a. ὁ βασιλεύς: reveiw again the paradigm in 355.
           b. λέγων modifies what verb? How?
           c. ἀποκτεῖναι: fully parsed (333)?

       4. χάριτι δὲ ἐσώθησαν ἐκεῖνοι οἱ ἁμαρτωλοὶ καὶ ἠγέρθησαν ἐν δόξῃ.

           a. χάριτι: what use of the dative (115)?
           b. -θησαν: sure sign of what tense, voice, mood, person and
               number (201)?

5. τῇ γὰρ χάριτι σωζόμεθα διὰ πίστεως ἵνα δοξάζωμεν τὸν θεόν.

    a. χάριτι and πίστεως: identify carefully, reviewing the paradigms in 347 and 349.

    b. Comment on the exegetical implications of tense in this sentence (283.2).

    c. Of what does the ἵνα clause give the purpose?

6. ἰδὼν τὸν πατέρα καὶ τὴν μητέρα αὐτοῦ ἐν τῇ πόλει ἔμεινεν σὺν αὐτοῖς.

    a. If you can't figure out πατέρα and μητέρα from your knowledge of third declension endings in general, see para. 565.

    b. ἔμεινεν: why aorist and not imperfect (333)?

    c. ἰδών: parse fully (249).

7. εἰς τὰ ἔθην ἀποστελεῖς τοὺς ἀποστόλους σου, ἵνα κηρύσσωσιν αὐτοῖς τὸ εὐαγγέλλιον τῆς χάριτός σου.

    a. ἔθην: how does context clinch your parsing of this form?

    b. ἀποστελεῖς: present or future? How do you know (328-327)?

    c. Why is χάριτος articular? In what sense is "grace" specific here?

    d. κηρύσσωσιν: parse fully. What would the corresponding aorist form be?

8. ἀγαθὸς ἦν οὗτος ὁ ἀνὴρ καὶ πλήρης πνεύματος ἁγίου καὶ πίστεως.

    a. ἀγαθός . . . καὶ πλήρης together are the predicate. Both words words are identified as: _____, _____, _____. How do they differ (360)?

    b. πλήρης πνεύματος. . . καὶ πίστεως
What does the genitive convey in πνεύματος and πίστεως (obviously not possession). See DM 78, CEG 30, and Para. 45.I.17c.

9. ἰδόντες δὲ τὴν χάριν τοῦ θεοῦ παρεκάλεσαν τὰ ἔθνη μένειν ἐν τῇ χάριτι σὺν χαρᾷ καὶ ἐλπίδι.

    a. Review the types of third declension nouns used here: τὴν χάριν, τῇ χάριτι (347), τ. ἔθνη (353), ἐλπίδι (211).

    b. μένειν: parse. Implications of the tense (299.1)?

    c. ἰδόντες: what adverbial information does this participle clause give (305.2)?

10. καταβαινόντων δὲ αὐτῶν ἐκ τοῦ ὄρους ἐλάλει ταῦτα ὁ Ἰησοῦς.

a. ἐκ τοῦ ὄρους: G.sg. in -ους? The N.A. and V. sg. must be _____ (352). Learn this neuter paradigm now!

b. ἐλάλει: why not P.A.I. 3 sg. (124)? -ει cannot be a primary active ending then. Explain this personal ending (316.2.2; 591).

11. ἀγαπήσωμεν τοὺς πατέρας καὶ τὰς μητέρας ἡμῶν, ἵνα τηρήσωμεν τὴν ἐντολὴν τοῦ θεοῦ.

    a. ἀγαπήσωμεν
       τηρήσωμεν
       Parse these fully (274).

    b. How is each verb used (285 and 286)?

    c. Meaning of the tenses (283.2)?

12. τῶν ἀρχιερέων ἰδόντων τοὺς συνερχομένους εἰς τὸ ἀκούειν τοῦ ἀνδρὸς εἶπον πρὸς ἑαυτοὺς οἱ ἄρχοντες ὅτι δεῖ αὐτὸν ἀποθανεῖν.

    a. Identified each word?

    b. What other nouns decline like ἀρχιερέως (355)?

    c. Noun and adverbial participle in genitive case? probably what construction (266)?

    d. τοὺς συνερχομένους: direct object of what?

    e. εἰς with articular infinitive expresses what (305.6)? Related to what verb or participle?

    f. What is the main verb and subject?

    g. εἶπον . . . ὅτι: "Said . . . that . . ."

    h. (δεῖ) ἀποθανεῖν: why not present? Accent helps identify as _____ (296).

13. οἱ βασιλεῖς οἱ πονηροὶ ἀπέκτειναν καὶ τοὺς ἄνδρας καὶ τὰ τέκνα.

    a. ἀπέκτειναν: parse. Signs of first aorist (333, 172, 175)?

    b. τοὺς ἄνδρας: -ας in third declension indicates _____ _____ (212).

14. ὁ δὲ θεὸς ἤγειρεν αὐτούς, ἵνα δοξάζωσιν αὐτὸν εἰς τὸν αἰῶνα.

    a. ἤγειρεν: what signs of aorist are present (139.1; 172; 333)?

    b. (ἵνα) δοξάζωσιν: gives precisely what information with respect to ἤγειρεν (286)? Meaning of the tense here (283.2)?

15. Diagram sentence:
Translate:

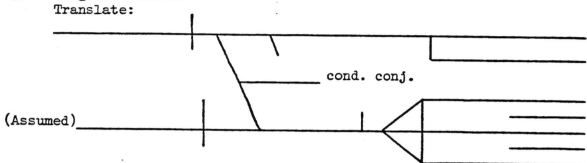

a. ἔχωμεν: why subjunctive (288.3)?
b. μετανοήσουσι: <u>sigma</u> tense suffix, primary active ending?
   Parse fully (154).

16. τοῖς ἀνδράσι τοῖς πεμφθεῖσιν ὑπὸ τοῦ βασιλέως προσηνέγκαμεν τὸν
    πατέρα καὶ τὴν μητέρα ἡμῶν.

a. The attributive participle modifies what noun? How do you know?
   -θεισιν should signal what tense, and voice (259)?
b. Study the third declension nouns used here. τοῖς ἀνδράσι,
   τὸν πατέρα and τὴν μητέρα in the course of identifying them (565).
c. προσηνέγκαμεν: ἤνεγκα is irregular enough that the student
   should commit its tense stem to memory (186).

17. ἐλθὼν πρὸς τὸν βασιλέα ταύτης τῆς χώρας παρεκάλεσας αὐτὸν μὴ
    ἀποκτεῖναι τὸν ἄνδρα τοῦτον.

a. ἐλθών (249): nominative singular. Who must be doing the
   action of this ptc.?
b. παρεκάλεσας: -σας = either A.A.I. 2 sg. or A.A. ptc. M.N. sg.
   Which here and why (172)?
c. Why no <u>sigma</u> suffix on ἀποκτεῖναι (331.2)? Parse.

18. εἰ ἀληθῆ ἐστι τὰ λεγόμενα ὑπὸ τῶν ἀκολουθησάντων τῷ ἀνδρὶ ἐν τῇ
    Γαλιλαίᾳ ἀποκτενοῦσιν αὐτὸν οἱ ἀρχιερεῖς.

a. Does the εἰ- clause have a verb? What kind of condition is
   this (288.2)?
b. (ἀκολουθη-) σαντων has to indicate what verb form (242)?
c. ἀποκτενοῦσιν: two signs of future. What are they (331.1-2)?

19. διὰ πίστεως σώσει τοὺς πιστεύοντας εἰς τὸ ὄνομα αὐτοῦ.

20.   ἐδέξαντο δὲ καὶ τὰ ἔθνη τὸ ῥῆμα τοῦ Ἰησοῦ τὸ ἀληθές.

Why relate τὸ ῥῆμα. . . τὸ ἀληθές (66)?

363.II NEW TESTAMENT GREEK READING

Translate Jn. 2.13-16.

2.13	το πάσχα	Indeclinable proper noun, "The Passover."
	ἀνέβη	2A.A.I., 3 sg., of ἀναβαίνω, "I go up."
2.14	εὗρεν	2A.A.I., 3 sg., of εὑρίσκω. Cf. the forms in 1.41.
	πωλοῦντας	πωλέω, "I sell." Para. 316. What use of this construction (235.1)?
	βοάς	βοῦς, βοός, ὁ/ἡ, "Ox, cow."
	τοὺς κερμάτιστας	Review para. 79 and 79.2.
	καθημένους	From κάθημαι, "I sit." See 424.1 again, if the use of this ptc. is not clear to you.
2.15	ποιήσας. . . ἐξέβαλεν	See 424.2 on use.
	πάντα	Para. 365-369.
	ἐξέχεεν	ἐκχέω, "I pour out."
2.16	ἄρατε	Alpha-connecting vowel without <u>sigma</u> tense suffix. What verb type (<u>325</u>, <u>333</u>)? Why not ἤρατε (420.2)?
	μὴ ποιεῖτε	Paras. 420.4 and 422. Exegetical translations (420.4)?
	ἐμπορίου	What use of the genitive (Cf. 45.I.17c)?

364.1 Note the obvious derivatives from words in this lesson's vocabulary,
as an aid to vocabulary learning. Fill in the vocabulary word from
which the terms on the right are derived.

_____ (+   ) henotheism, the worship of one god as supreme
among gods.

_____ a duo, and the "duo-" words (related through
Latin)

(+) Diatessaron, the second century "harmony"
of the gospels by Tatian.

_____ the "penta-" words

_____ (+   ) hexagram, a six pointed figure

_____ catharsis, from the related noun, ἡ κάθαρσις,
a "cleansing."

_____ (+   ) megaphone, and the other "mega-" words.

_____ (+   ) oligarchy (what would this mean?)

_____ plethora, from a related noun, ἡ πληθώρη,
"fullness"

_____ (+   ) polygraph; note the u to y (review 1.2).

365.1 πᾶς, πᾶσα, πᾶν, "every, all." The masculine and neuter follow _____
declension patterns; the feminine follows _____ declension patterns.

365.2 πᾶς, πᾶσα, πᾶν is declined just like what participle already learned (366)?

365.3 Explain the accent on the ultima in παντός, παντί (366 and 221).

367-
368.1 Machen uses "attributive position" and "predicate position" here as some
other grammarians do to refer solely to the position of the adjective
πᾶς, πᾶσα, πᾶν with respect to the article. "The attributive position" is
articular; the "predicate position" is anarthrous. None of the examples given
are predicative in the sense of the discussion in para. 71; all the examples
given in paras. 367-369 are attributive or substantive uses of the adjective,
regardless of the word order (position).

370.1 πολύς, πολλή, πολύ has the stem πολλ- and in the main follows _____
declension patterns in all genders (574).

370.2 μέγας, μεγάλη, μέγα has the stem μεγάλ- and follows with minor changes
the _____ declension patterns in all genders (575).

371.1 Translate Eph. 4:4-6, noting use of the numeral one in all three genders.
ἓν σῶμα καὶ ἓν πνεῦμα, καθὼς καὶ ἐκλήθητε ἐν μιᾷ ἐλπίδι τῆς κλήσεως ὑμῶν.
εἷς κύριος, μία πίστις, ἓν βάπτισμα· εἷς θεὸς καὶ πατὴρ πάντων, ὁ ἐπὶ πάντων
καὶ διὰ πάντων καὶ ἐν πᾶσιν.

374.1 The declension of τρεῖς, τρία and τέσσαρες, -ρα follow _____ declension plural endings (588). What nouns are similarly declined in the plural?

376.1 By the use of a preceding article nearly any word or set of words in
Greek can be made into an attributive expression to modify a noun or
into a substantive expression to stand by itself like a noun. We have already
observed this phenomenon in the use of attributive adjectives (70) and attributive participles (234) and in the substantive adjectives (75) and substantive
participles (235).

376.2 Make sure you understand first the literal translation of the attributive
and substantive uses of the prepositional phrases in Machen's examples.
Then be able to turn that literal translation into the normal translation equivalent, a relative clause. Work at it until you can go both ways (from the literal
to equivalent and back to the literal) with ease (cf. 234.3).

376.3 Rom. 8:3; ὁ θεός . . . κατέκρινεν τὴν ἁμαρτίαν ἐν τῇ σαρκί. Does
ἐν τῇ σαρκί tell where the act of condemning occurred (the phrase is
then adverbial) or does it tell the location of the sin which God condemned
(the phrase is then attributive)?

378.1 Again, first understand the literal translation of genitive expressions
used attributively or substantively. Then convert the literal translation
into the normal translation equivalent, a relative clause. You must be able to
do this. If you cannot, ask the instructor for clarification after a reexamina-
tion of para. 376-377.

380.1 How is the discussion in this paragraph related to the constructions
learned in 376?

381.1 If you have any difficulty at all with the basic concepts of the attributive, substantive and predicate use of adjectives and other constructions,
review paras. 68-75 thoroughly and ask for clarification of any remaining confusion.

382.1 The accusative used to express extent of space or time shows clearly
the accusative's basic function of setting limits. The student has already
seen this function of the accusative in its use with directional, pointing prepo-
stions like εἰς and πρός, the goal or extent of whose movement is marked by the
accusative.

382.2 The emphasis in these accusatives of extent of time and space is on the
duration or the length of the time or space. (τ. νύκτα = "through the
night"). One may contrast genitive expressions of time whose point is not the
extent but the kind of time (τῆς νυκτός = "by night, of a night"). Cf. D.M.,
pp. 77, 93.

383.I Aids to exercise I, Lesson XXVI

1. μείνας σὺν αὐτῷ ἔτη τρία ἦλθεν εἰς ἐκείνην τὴν πόλιν.

a. μείνας: parse fully (257.1; 333; 242).
Modifies what word? how (305.2)?

b. πόλιν: parse. Nominative and genitive singular forms are
_____, _____ (349).

c. ἔτη: parse. Nominative and genitive singular forms are
_____, _____ (353).
What use of the accusative (382.1-2).

2. ἰδὼν δὲ τοὺς ἐν τῇ μεγάλῃ πόλει ἔγραψε καὶ τοῖς ἐν τῇ μικρᾷ.

a. ἰδών: parse (249). Modifies what word? how (305.2)

b. τοὺς ἐν τ...πόλει and τοῖς ἐν τῇ μικρᾷ: identify these constructions (377 and 380). Make sure you can translate literally
before writing a "smooth" translation.

c. πόλει: N. and G. sg. are _____, _____ (349).

3. πορευθέντες δὲ οἱ τοῦ Ἰακώβου σταδίους ὡς πέντε εἶδον τὸν Ἰησοῦν
καὶ πάντας τοὺς μετ' αὐτοῦ μαθητάς.

a. πορευθέντες: parse (259). Modifies what word, how (305.2)?

b. οἱ τοῦ Ἰακώβου: what construction (378)? Function (34)?

c. σταδίους: use of the accusative (382)?

d. Where is the attributively used prepositional phrase here (376)?

4. ἀκούσαντες δὲ ταῦτα πάντα οἱ ἐν τῇ συναγωγῇ εἶπον ὅτι θέλουσιν
ἰδεῖν τὸν ταῦτα ποιοῦντα.

a. ἀκούσαντες: parse fully. Modifies what word? how?
τον...ποιοῦντα (591): what use of the participle (235)?

b. οἱ ἐν τῇ συναγωγῇ: identify this construction (377).
Article in nominative signals what function in the sentence?

c. What is the object of εἶπον?

d. θέλουσιν: why present tense (308)?

5. ἐθαύμασεν πᾶν τὸ πλῆθος ἐν τῷ βλέπειν αὐτοὺς τὰ ποιούμενα ὑπὸ τοῦ
Ἰησοῦ.

a. πᾶν τὸ πλῆθος: put this whole expression in the genitive
singular (365; 352).

b. ἐν τῷ βλέπειν αὐτούς: name this construction (303).
How is it used here (305.3)? Modifies what word?

6. οὐκ ἔμεινε μίαν ἡμέραν ὁ μετὰ δύο ἔτη ἰδὼν τὸν ἀπόστολον τὸν
εὐαγγελισάμενον αὐτόν.

a. ἔμεινε: _epsilon_ connecting vowel serving as secondary active ending, augment, internal lengthening in liquid stem, all point to what identification? Parse fully (333).

b. μίαν ἡμέραν: does a direct object really make sense with ἔμεινε? Why accusative here (383 and 383.1-2)? Remember para. 371?

c. ὁ . . .ἰδών : attributive (234.1), substantive (235.1), or adverbial (232.5) ptc.? Here it functions as the subject (34) of what verb?

d. τὸν ἀπόστολον τὸν εὐαγγελισάμενον Ptc. construction for what function (232)?

7. τῶν ἀρχιερέων ὄντων ἐν ἐκείνῃ τῇ μεγάλῃ πόλει ἔμεινεν ὁ Ἰησοῦς ἐν τῇ κώμῃ ἡμέρας ὡς πέντε ἢ ἕξ.

a. τῶν ἀρχιερέων ὄντων: why genitive (266.1-5 and 580)?

b. ἐν. . .πόλει modifies what verb (232)?

c. How do the main verbs of sentences 6 and 7 differ (129)?

d. ἡμέρας: G.sg. or A.pl.? The form is the same. How can you decide here (383)?

8. δεῖ τοὺς ἐν ταῖς πόλεσιν ἐξελθεῖν εἰς τὰ ὄρη.

a. After δεῖ you should expect an _____ verb (292.1) and a subject in the _____ case (304). Parse carefully ἐξελθεῖν (296). What two items distinguish it from a present active infinitive? _____ and _____ (296).

b. τοὺς ἐν ταῖς πόλεσιν: name this construction (376-377). Functions as what part of this sentence (304)?

9. θεραπευθέντος ὑπὸ τοῦ Ἰησοῦ τοῦ ὑπὸ τῶν τεσσάρων προσενεχθέντος αὐτῷ ἐδόξασαν πάντες οἱ ἐν τῇ οἰκίᾳ τὸν ποιήσαντα τὰ μεγάλα ταῦτα.

a. Set the prepositional phrases aside until you have identified the main items in the sentence core.

b. θεραπευθέντος (1) . . . τοῦ . . . προσενεχθέντος (2). The whole unit is what ptc. construction (266)? Ptc. (2) functions how in it (266.2 and 235)?

c. οἱ ἐν τῇ οἰκίᾳ: name this construction (377). What is its function in the sentence (34)?

d. πάντες: identify fully (365). Modifies what?

10. πρὸ δὲ τοῦ ἐλθεῖν τοὺς ἐκ τῶν πόλεων ἦν ὁ Ἰησοῦς μετὰ τῶν μαθητῶν αὐτοῦ ἐν τῇ ἐρήμῳ.

a. πρό: what is the object of this preposition (302; 302.1 and 305.4)?
b. τοὺς ἐκ τῶν πόλεων: name the construction (377).
   What function in this sentence (304)?
c. ἦν: remember 133?

11. ἐποιήθη μὲν δι' αὐτοῦ ὁ κόσμος καὶ πάντα τὰ ἐν αὐτῷ, αὐτὸς δὲ
    ἐγένετο δι' ἡμᾶς ὡς δοῦλος.

a. Where is the substantival prepositional phrase here (377)?
b. Functions as the subject of what verb?
c. ὡς is followed by the nominative δοῦλος, since δοῦλος would
   function as the subject in the sentence here elliptically stated,
   i.e., ὡς δοῦλος (γίνεται).
   See AG., p. 905, I.2, under ὡς, for instructive examples.
d. πάντα: identify fully (365). Modifies what here?

12. τοῦτο ἐποίησεν ἵνα σώσῃ πάντας τοὺς πιστεύοντας εἰς αὐτόν.

a. σώσῃ. Probably a form of the verb _____.
   Without augment, the -η ending could indicate either of three
   forms:
   1. (155) _____
   2. (274) _____
   3. (275) _____
   Which here and why (286)?
b. πάντας: identify fully (365). How used here?

13. πᾶς ὁ ἀγαπῶν τὸν θεὸν ἀγαπᾷ καὶ τοὺς ἀδελφούς.

a. πᾶς: full identification (365)? Modifies what?
b. ἀγαπῶν: explain the contraction (316.I.4) and identify fully (266).
c. ἀγαπᾷ: is it P.A. I., 3 sg., or P. A. S., 3 sg. (316.I.6)?
   ἀγαπα + η = _____?
   ἀγαπα + ει = _____?
   Context must distinguish here.

14. συνήχθησαν πάντες οἱ ἐν τῇ πόλει ἵνα ἀκούσωσι τὰ λεγόμενα ὑπὸ
    τῶν ἀποστόλων.

a. συνήχθησαν: -θη (σαν) should be an obvious sign of _____
   _____ by now (200).
   Before theta tense suffix, either _____ or _____ could have
   produced the -χθ- combination (204 and 204.2).

178

    b. οἱ ἐν τῇ πόλει: this is the _____ (377) use of the prepositional phrase. The construction functions as the _____ of the main verb.

    c. Of what act specifically does the _____ clause here give the purpose (286.3)?

15. ταῦτα ἔλεγον οἱ ἐν τῷ οἴκῳ πᾶσι τοῖς ἀρχιερεῦσι καὶ γραμματεῦσι διὰ τὸ γινώσκειν αὐτοὺς πάντα τὰ περὶ τοῦ Ἰησοῦ.

    a. Locate the two substantival prepositional phrases (377). How do they function here?

    b. πᾶσι and πάντα: full identification (365). How used (367)?

    c. ἀρχιερεῦσι and γραμματεῦσι: give the nominative and genitive singular forms and the gender of these nouns (355).

    d. Preposition with the articular infinitive gives what information about ἔλεγον (305.5)?
        The subject of γινώσκειν (304)? _____

16. ταῦτα ἐποίει ὁ βασιλεὺς τῶν Ἰουδαίων, ἤθελε γὰρ ἀποκτεῖναι τὰ ἐν τῇ κώμῃ παιδία.

    a. ἐποίει: -ει here cannot be the primary active ending, 3 sg., of the non-past tenses. What clue on the verb excludes primary endings (123.2-3)?
        What contraction could produce - ει (316.I.3)?
        Accent here tells you the contracting element was short. How (316.III)?

    b. βασιλεύς: the genitive sg. would be _____ (355).

    c. ἤθελε: see the note in para. 364.

    d. ἀποκτεῖναι: identify fully (333).
        τὰ (ἐν τῇ κώμῃ) παιδία: does this construction differ essentially from τὰ (ἀγαθὰ) παιδία? Name the construction (376).

17. οὐδεὶς γινώσκει πάντα τὰ ἐν τῷ κόσμῳ εἰ μὴ ὁ ποιήσας τὰ πάντα.

    a. τὰ ἐν τῷ κόσμῳ: name the construction (377).

    b. πάντα (used twice): identify fully in each case (365).
        How is each one used? attributively? substantively? See 367-369.

    c. Read the footnote!

18. σωθήσεται οὐδεὶς ἐὰν μὴ διὰ πίστεως. ἐτήρησε γὰρ οὐδεὶς πάσας τὰς ἐντολὰς τοῦ θεοῦ.

    a. ἐὰν μή = "if not," or, better, "_____" (see footnote).

    b. πάσας: identify and specify use (365-369).

c. σωθήσεται, -σεται: <u>sigma</u> tense suffix, primary middle ending, all on an aorist passive stem, have to signal what identification (200)?

19. προσευχώμεθα ὑπὲρ τῶν διωκόντων ἡμᾶς, ἵνα γενώμεθα υἱοὶ τοῦ πατρὸς ἡμῶν τοῦ ἐν οὐρανοῖς.

    a. προσευχώμεθα: long connecting vowel probably signals what mood (272.1)? 1 pl. used how in that mood (285)?
    b. γενώμεθα not hortatory after ἵνα. What instead (286)?
    c. Where is the attributive prepositional phrase (376)? What noun does it modify, and how do you know (66; 565)?

20. μακάριοι οἱ καθαροί, αὐτοὶ γὰρ τὸν θεὸν ὄψονται.

    a. οἱ καθαροί: attributive or predicative use (70-71)? How do you know (70.2)?
    b. Does anarthrous μακάριοι here specify identify or describe kind of person (99.3)? What about υἱοί in sentence 19?
    c. ὄψονται. -ονται primary (for non-past) middle ending. <u>Psi</u> carries in it what tense suffix (156)?

383.II   NEW TESTAMENT GREEK READING

Translate Jn. 2.17-21

2.17 γεγραμμένον	-μενον can only be what verb form (589)? Reduplicated stem means _____ tense.

    See paras. 430, 444, 446-47, 452. Read DM, pp. 231-233, on the periphrastic participle.

καταφάγεται	κατεσθίω: why κατα-? Cf. ἐσθίω and read CEG, p. 40. Cf. English "eat <u>up</u>/eat!"
2.18 δεικνύεις	δείκνθμι/ω, "I show." Uses both -<u>mi</u> forms and -<u>omega</u> verb forms in present.
2.19 λύσατε	-σατε without augment must be _____ _____ (411).
τρίσιν	Para. 588 (cf. 371).
ἐγερῶ	Circumflex accent on ultima (from contraction) of liquid verb is sign of _____ tense (327-328). Cf. ἐγερεῖς in 2.20.

2.20   ἔτεσιν   ἔτος, ἔτους, τό: if you don't know
                                the pattern, review para. 352.

       οἰκοδομήθη   Note carefully the aorist used to
                                summarize activity carried on over
           four decades (168.3 and DM, p. 196(1)).

2.21   τοῦ σώματος   What relationship between τ. ναοῦ and
                                σώματος is here expressed by the genitive
           case? See DM, p. 79, or CEG, p. 29.

386.1 Exactly how do the forms of the interrogative and indefinite pronouns
in 385 and 388 conform to third declension patterns you already know (212)?

387.1 The interrogative and the indefinite pronouns obviously can<u>not</u> be distinguished from one another by form. What two facts about their accent
patterns provide clues for separating them (see also para. 389)?
1.
2.

390.1 Study Machen's examples here carefully. Observe that in examples (2)
and (3) these "pronouns" modify nouns attributively and could just as
well be called adjectives.

392.1 Define "indirect question," and distinguish it from a "direct question."

392.2 In what respects are indirect questions like indirect discourse?
Review para. 308.

394.2 Do you see why a deliberative question would be expected to use the
subjunctive mood? If not, review para. 269.5.

395.1 Does the relative pronoun present you with a <u>new</u> set of endings to learn?
Why not? If it appears strange to you, don't proceed until you have
reviewed para. 96 or 102.

395.2 How can you differentiate the nominative plural forms, M. and F., from
corresponding definite articles (567)?

397.1 From whence does the relative pronoun derive its gender and number?
From whence does it derive its case?

397.2 If you do not readily see the answers to the following questions, find
the answer and write it out here.
Example (1). Why is ὅν masculine and singular?
Why is ὅν accusative?
Example (2). The antecedent of ἅ is the adjective, _____.
How do you know?

397.3 One can often understand better a relative pronoun's function in its
clause (and hence its case) by turning the relative clause around,
converting it into an independent clause. For example, when "whom you saw,"
is converted to "you saw whom," the pronoun's function as the direct object of
"saw" is clear and it's accusative case quite understandable. Practice this
conversion of relative clauses from dependent to independent statements to
increase your facility in analyzing them.

397.4 Observe that relative clauses (clauses introduced by relative pronouns)
function as <u>noun</u> clauses and adjective clauses. That is, their entire
clauses function as nouns and adjectives, e.g., as subjects, objects, objects
of prepositions, or as modifiers of nouns.

398.1 Explain the term "attraction" as it pertains to the relative pronoun. What forms are affected?

399.1 What is the point of Machen's comparison of ὅς οὐκ ἔστιν and ὁ μὴ ὤν?

400.1 What effect does the addition of the particles ἐάν or ἄν have on a relative clause? Compare the influence of ἄν on εἰ, "if" (268.1).

400.2 Why then does the subjunctive appear in such a clause (269.5)?

402.1 The exercises in this chapter contain examples of a type of adverbial participle frequently encountered in the NT, namely the "appositional participle." Such participles modify the verb by repeating its act in only slightly different terms, virtually the same, and thus in apposition with the main verb.

> (A) ἀπεκρίθη/ἐλάλησε. . . (B) λέγων

> (A) "He answered/spoke". . (B) saying. . ."

Here (B) = (A), i.e., is in apposition to (a).

See further CEG, p. 67.

402.I. Aids to Exercise I, Lesson XXVII

1. ὃς ἐὰν μὴ δέξηται ὑμᾶς τοῦτον οὐ δέξεται ὁ βασιλεύς.

   a. δέξηται: parse (275). What is the subject of this verb (397.4)? Why is the verb subjunctive (400 and 269.5)?
   b. ὅς. . .ὑμᾶς: name the construction (400).
   c. δέξεται: parse (155). Compare and contrast with δέξηται.

2. ἃ ἐὰν ποιήσωμεν ὑμῖν, ποιήσετε καὶ ὑμεῖς ἡμῖν.

   a. Is ἃ N.N. pl. or N.A. pl.? Remember 297.3 and use it!
   b. ποιήσωμεν: can this be F. A. I., 1 pl. (note the sigma)? Why not (272.1 and 269)?
   c. Compare and contrast the two verbs of this sentence (275 and 155).

3. ἐρωτήσαντός τινος αὐτοὺς τί φάγῃ ἀπεκρίθησαν αὐτῷ λέγοντες ὅτι δεῖ αὐτὸν φαγεῖν τὸν ἄρτον τὸν ἐν τῷ οἴκῳ.

   a. Opening adverbial ptc. is part of what construction (266)?
   b. τινος: must be indefinite pronoun. Why (389)?
   c. Parse carefully (384).
      φάγῃ (278)
      φαγεῖν (296)
   d. τί φάγῃ: subjunctive suggests what sort of question (394)? What was the direct question behind this reported, deliberative question (393)?

    e. λέγοντες: function of the ptc. (402.1)?
    f. Where is the attributive prepositional phrase here (376)?
       What does it modify?

4. τίνος ἔσται ταῦτα πάντα ἐν τῇ ἐσχάτῃ ἡμέρᾳ;

    a. Remember that "of whom" = "whose" in English (397.3).
    b. τίνος: interrogative or indefinite? How do you know (387.1)?
       Identify fully.
    c. ἔσται: parse (602).

5. ὅταν ἔλθῃ ὁ υἱὸς τοῦ ἀνθρώπου τίνες ἔσονται οἱ πιστεύοντες;

    a. Why subjunctive after ὅταν (384; 400.1 and 269.5)?
    b. τίνες: interrogative or indefinite (387.1)? Identify fully.
    c. ἔσονται: parse (602).

6. ὃς ἂν λύσῃ μίαν τῶν ἐντολῶν ποιεῖ ὃ οὐκ ἔξεστιν ποιεῖν.

    a. ὅς: identify (395) Why nominative (397)?
    b. What is the subject of ποιεῖ (397.4)?
    c. What is the object of ποιεῖν?
    d. Of what is the clause, ὅ . . . ποιεῖν, the object (397.3)?

7. ἃ εἶπεν ὑμῖν ὁ προφήτης ἔτι ὢν μεθ' ὑμῶν ταῦτα ἐροῦσι καὶ οἱ
   εὐαγγελισάμενοι ἡμᾶς.

    a. ἃ εἶπεν: remember 399.
       Is the relative pronoun here nominative or accusative (397)?
    b. ὢν: parse this verb form (602). What differentiates it from
       the genitive plural of the relative pronoun (395)?
       Construction modifies what verb?
    c. ἐροῦσι: parse fully. Circumflex accent indicates contraction
       which signals what (327)?
    d. ταῦτα: direct object of what verb?
       Stands in apposition to what construction?
    e. The subject of ἐροῦσι? On καί, recall para. 146.

8. ἐάν τις ἀπὸ νεκρῶν πορευθῇ πρὸς αὐτούς, μετανοήσουσιν.

    a. Why acute, not grave accent on ἐάν?
       See para. 389 and 92.I (1).
    b. ἐάν. . .πορευθῇ : name the construction (288).
    c. μετανοήσουσιν, -ουσιν: if it is a finite verb, this can only
       indicate what form (154)?

9. ὃς ἐὰν μὴ ἀκούσῃ τῶν προφητῶν οὐδὲ μετανοήσει ἐάν τινα ἴδῃ τῶν νεκρῶν.

    a. Parse all the verbs.
        (274) ἀκούσῃ
        (154) μετανοήσει
        (278) ἴδῃ
    b. Locate the subject of each of these verbs.
       The object of ἴδῃ (388)?
    c. τῶν προφητῶν: why genitive (108)?
    d. Of what is ἐάν. . . ἴδῃ the condition (288.5)?

10. οἳ ἂν εἴπωσιν ἃ οὐκ ἔστιν ἀληθῆ οὐ λήμψονται καρπόν τινα τοῦ ἔργου αὐτῶν.

    a. Parse all the verbs.
    b. Explain the cases of the relative pronouns (397).
        οἳ
        ἃ
    c. How is the relative clause, οἳ ἂν. . .ἀληθῆ, related to the main verb λήμψονται (397.4)?
    d. How is the relative clause, ἃ οὐκ. . .ἀληθῆ, related to the verb, εἴπωσιν?
    e. τοῦ ἔργου: what information is here given by the genitive case? Neither possession (35), nor description (45.I.17c), nor content (267.II, on Jn. 1:14).
       This "genitive of source," tells the <u>source from which</u> the fruit is to come. See further CEG, p. 28 and DM, p. 82.

11. ἔλεγεν ὅτι ἐάν τις ἐγερθῇ ἐκ νεκρῶν μετανοήσουσιν.

    a. τις, interrogative or indefinite? How can you tell (387.4)?
    b. ἐγερθῇ: subjunctive or indicative? How can you tell by the form (279)? Compare form in 201 and note 277. By context (400.1 and 269.5)?
    c. μετανοήσουσι: english reports a direct future statement ("will") indirectly with "would."

12. ἠρώτησαν τὸν προφήτην οἱ ἐν τῇ Γαλιλαίᾳ εἰ οἱ νεκροὶ ἀκούσουσι τῆς φωνῆς τοῦ κυρίου.

    a. οἱ ἐν τῇ Γαλιλαίᾳ: name the construction (377). Why nominative οἱ?
    b. εἰ: remember the note in 384?

13. εἶπεν οὖν αὐτοῖς ὅτι ἐν τῇ κρίσει ἀκούσουσιν πάντες τοῦ
κυρίου.

    a. πάντες: identify fully (365). Is it attributive?
       substantive? predicative?
       What function in the sentence?
    b. ὅτι ἐν. . .κυρίου: what relation does this entire ὅτι-
       clause have to the verb εἶπεν (397.4)?

14. ἐλθόντες οἱ Φαρισαῖοι εἴς τινα κώμην ἐπηρώτησαν τοὺς ἐν αὐτῇ
λέγοντες Ποῦ εἰσιν οἱ τοῦ προφήτου· ἃ γὰρ λέγουσι περὶ αὐτῶν
οἱ ἐν τῇ Γαλιλαίᾳ οὐκ ἔστιν ἀληθῆ.

    a. τινα κώμην: what use of the indefinite pronoun (390.1)?
    b. Name the constructions (377 and 378-79).
       τοὺς ἐν αὐτῇ
       οἱ τοῦ προφήτου
    c. Function of λέγοντες (402.1)?
    d. ἃ. . . λέγουσι: is ἃ accusative or nominative (397)?
       The relative clause itself has what function (397.4)?

15. ἔλεγε δὲ ὁ ἐπερωτηθεὶς Τί ἐπερωτᾷς με; οὐ γὰρ θέλω ἀποκρίνεσθαί
σοι οὐδέν.

    a. ἐπερωτηθείς: parse (259). How used here?
       ἐπερωτᾷς. Explain the contraction (316.I.6 and II.2) and
       identify fully (590).
    b. τί: remember 391.
    c. ἀποκρίνεσθαι. -σθαι has to be what verb form (293)?

16. ἔλεγεν οὖν τῶν μαθητῶν τις τῷ ἀποστόλῳ Τί ποιήσει οὗτος; ὁ δὲ
ἀπόστολος εὐθὺς ἀπεκρίθη αὐτῷ λέγων Ποιήσει ὁ θεὸς ἃ θέλει
καὶ πάντα ἃ θέλει ἐστὶν ἀγαθά.

    a. ἔλεγεν: imperfect here is perhaps "continued" action in
       the sense of "repeated" action, i.e., "He kept saying."
       (Cf. 195.I.3c and No. 11 above.) See further CEG, p. 54
       and DM, p. 188.
    b. τί: contrast with use in the last sentence.
    c. ἀπεκρίθη. . . λέγων (402.1)?
    d. ἃ (twice): account for gender, number and case in both (397).

17. ἃ ἔβλεπε τὸν κύριον ποιοῦντα ταῦτα ἤθελε καὶ αὐτὸς ποιεῖν.

a. τ. κύριον ποιοῦντα: the ptc. functions as an object complement.
   Review 344.1-2.
b. καὶ αὐτός: (146 and 105.2).
c. ἔβλεπε: comment on the possible meanings of "continued
   action" here in light of your reading for 16a above.

402.II   NEW TESTAMENT GREEK READING

Review the relative clauses encountered thus far in your NT reading:
Jn. 1.3, 9, 12 (see para. 403), 13, 15, 26, 27, 38 (Cf. 41, 42);
I Jn. 1.5; 2.5, 7(2), 8.
Identify and explain the reason for each pronoun's gender, number and case
(397.1).

Survey again also the interrogative pronouns encountered:
Jn. 1.19, 21, 22(2), 25, 38(2), 39; 2.18. Remember paras. 392-393 in this review.

Translate Jn. 2.22-25.

2.23   θεωροῦντες   What adverbial idea is here expressed
                            by the participle--time, reason, means,
            condition, attendant circumstance? Read carefully
            again paras. 237.2 and 257.I.13d and see CEG, pp. 65-67,
            on the adverbial participle.

2.24   ἐπίστευεν   Why imperfect?
                            Check a lexicon on the various meanings
            of πιστεύω (not the same here as in 2.23).

        αὐτόν   A contracted form of ἑαυτόν (339).

        διά. . . γινώσκειν Review para. 305.5.

2.25   ἵνα τις μαρτυρήσῃ   Not purpose. See para. 477, and compare
                            the use in 1.27.

        περὶ τοῦ ἀνθρώπου   CEG. p. 24(6).

        τί ἦν ἐν   See para. 393 on use of the interrogative
                            here.

403.1   Note the Greek words from which the following English words are derived.

opthalmologist _____ + _____
photo(graphy) _____ + _____
agronomy _____ + _____
hydro- _____
Why the "y" in "hydro-" words (1.2)?

403.2   With what other third declension nouns do you associate the following words:

το οὖς, ὠτός (211)
το φῶς, φωτός
το σκότος -ους (352)

405.1   <u>Tense and tense stem</u>. Does this outline present a departure from the pattern of tense indication previously learned (244.1)?

406.1   What construction would you guess serves as a first person "imperative" (285)?

407-
17.1   Be able to analyze every imperative form, seeing all its components.

Tense stem		Connecting Vowel		Personal ending	
λυ	–	ε	–	τω	λυέτω
λυσ	–	α	–	τε	λύσατε

407-
17.2   Survey the paradigms of the imperative verbs on pp. 178-179. Observe that the <u>tense suffix</u> and <u>variable vowel</u> systems learned for the aorist and present indicatives are repeated here.

Present   o/ε
Aorist   σ - α
Second aorist   o/ε
Aorist passive   θ - η (ε lengthened)

407-
17.3   <u>Imperative endings</u>. Now make your own paradigm for easy reference and memorization by writing the personal endings used for the following voices. Notice that, for the student who can spot the tense stems and variable vowels, the remaining endings form <u>two paradigms, not eight</u>!

A.   ACTIVE IMPERATIVES
        Present, Aorists,
        <u>and</u> Aorist passive

2 sg. ___#___   2 pl. _____

3 sg. _____   3 pl. _____

B.   MIDDLE-PASSIVE
        Present
     AND MIDDLE IMPERATIVES
        Aorists

2 sg. ___#___   2 pl. _____

3 pl. _____   3 pl. _____

188

What morpheme signals plural in the third person endings, both active and middle (-passive)? Recall that the same element is used for the same purpose in some secondary endings (127).

407-
17.4   The second person singular forms must be individually learned.

418-
19.1   What two features of the second aorist imperative forms allow one to differentiate them from the present imperatives which use the very same endings?

        1.
        2.

420.1   <u>Tense and time in the imperative mood</u>. By its very nature the imperative has minimal time reference in itself. There is no narrative of an act—past, present, or future—only a command whose reality hinges on the response of the hearer.

420.2   In this connection observe the <u>lack</u> of <u>augment</u> on the aorist imperatives. Why so (cf. 245.1)?

420.3   In the imperative mood, what is point of the tenses, if not time?

420.4   <u>Tense and kind of action</u>. Commands and prohibitions (negative commands, para. 422) are best considered together here. Both use the present and aorist tenses in essentially the same way.

PRESENT TENSE
    Commands: continue an act now in progress
      πιστεύετε   "Continue, keep on believing!"
    Prohibitions: cease an act now in progress
      μὴ πιστεύετε   "Stop believing!"

AORIST TENSE
    Commands: simply do (or begin) the act commanded
      πιστεύσατε   "Believe!"
    Prohibitions: simply don't do (or begin) the act pro-
      μὴ πιστεύσητε   hibited. "Don't believe!"

See further the very helpful presentations in DM., pp. 299-303, and Goetchius, pp. 261-263.

421-
22.1   <u>Mood and relation to fact</u>. As one moves from

      (1) indicative   (1) fact
to (2) subjunctive   one moves progressively   to (2) possibility
to (3) imperative   away from statement of   to (3) command
to (4) optative   fact: to (4) wish

421-
22.2   The uses of the imperatives and prohibitions outlined in 421 and 422 and further discussed in 420.4 may be graphed as follows:

REFERENCE	COMMAND FORM	PROHIBITION FORM
Continuing act	Present imperative	μή + Present Imperative
Simple reference	Aorist imperative	μή + Aorist subjunctive*

*Remember 422 and the change in pattern there.

423.1   Compare with your paradigms in 407-17.2.

424.1   <u>Anarthrous participles as object complements</u>. Review para. 344.1-3 before proceeding. Participles can function as object complements just as other adjectives and nouns can. Note the following:

εἶδον τὸν ἄνθρωπον διδάσκοντα, "I saw the man teaching."

Here the participle, διδάσκοντα, modifies ἄνθρωπον, but not as a regular attributive participle would, i.e., not "I saw the man <u>who was</u> teaching." Note the lack of an article. Instead it modifies the object by completing it, as reflected in the translation. Such participles are sometimes called secondary predicates (CEG, p. 65).

424.2   <u>The aorist participle to indicate coordinate circumstance</u>. The adverbial participle is frequently used to describe an action prior to, coordinate in thought with, and of the same mood as the leading verb of a sentence. Such a participle normally precedes the leading verb, and is normally aorist. It is best translated as a finite verb of the same mood and tense as the leading verb, connected with that verb by "and" (from CEG, p. 67).

ποιήσας φραγέλλιον . . . πάντας ἐξέβαλεν Jn. 2.15
   "He made a whip . . . and cast them all out
   (having made a whip . . . he cast them all out)"

424.3   Where possible, give "exegetical translations" which make the meaning of the tenses explicit.

424.I   Aids to exercise I, Lesson XXVIII.

   1. ἐὰν δὲ μὴ ἀκούσῃ, παράλαβε μετὰ σοῦ ἔτι ἕνα ἢ δύο.

      a. ἐὰν . . . ἀκούσῃ: what kind of condition here (288.3)? Specifically what act is dependent upon this condition? παράλαβε: why not present (405.1)? Why not 2A.A. <u>Indicative</u>, 3 sg. (420.2)? Identify fully (407-17.4).
      b. ἕνα ἢ δύο: "one" what? person or thing (371 and 373)? Is it ἤ (63), ἤ (395), or ἦ (364)?
      c. Comment on the significance of the tenses of both verbs (283.2; 420.4).

2. ὃ ἐὰν ἴδητε τὸν Χριστὸν ποιοῦντα, τοῦτο ποιήσατε καὶ ὑμεῖς.

    a. ὃ ἐὰν . . . ποιοῦντα: what kind of construction (400)?
       With ὃ ἐαν, what mood do you expect (400 and 400.1-2)?
       ἴδητε: identify fully and review ιδ- (189.2) and the signifi-
       cance of the long connecting vowel (272.1).
    b. τὸν Χριστὸν ποιοῦντα: identify the participle fully (313 and
       226; 257.1) and remember 424.1.
    c. Identify ὃ fully (395). How is it related to ποιοῦντα?
       If you don't see, read 397.3 and apply here.
    d. ποιήσατε: can't be indicative, in spite of standard sigma-
       alpha tense indicators. Why not (420.2)?
       What kind of action (420.4)?

3. κύριε, ἐλέησον ἡμᾶς, οὐ γὰρ ἐποιήσαμεν ἃ ἐκέλευσας.

    a. κύριε: Remember para. 37.
    b. ἐλέησον: if initial epsilon is an augment, then this is an
       imperfect. If not, what is it (411)?
    c. ἃ: identify fully (395). How related to ἐκέλευσας (34)?
    d. What is the direct object of ἐποιήσαμεν (397.4)?
       What is the function of the whole γάρ clause (286.3; 288.5)?

4. μὴ εἰσέλθῃ εἰς τὴν πόλιν ὁ ἐν τῷ ὄρει.

    a. μὴ εἰσέλθῃ: no augment, lengthened primary active ending
       (ει to η) (277.1; 276.2). Identify fully.
       How used here (420.4 and 421-22.2)?
    b. ὁ ἐν τῷ ὄρει (377): this substantive unit functions how in
       this sentence (34)?

5. οὕτως οὖν προσεύχεσθε ὑμεῖς Πάτερ ἡμῶν ὁ ἐν τοῖς οὐρανοῖς·
    Ἁγιασθήτω τὸ ὄνομά σου· ἐλθάτω ἡ βασιλεία σου· γενηθήτω
    τὸ θέλημά σου, ὡς ἐν οὐρανῷ καὶ ἐπὶ γῆς.

    a. προσεύχεσθε: could either be _____ or _____ mood, but
       in light of parallel verbs, is probably _____.
       Exegetical translation (420.4)?
    b. ὁ ἐν τοῖς οὐρανοῖς: how related to Πάτερ (376)?

c. Identify fully. Read the footnotes.
   ἁγιασθήτω   (204.2; 407-17.2)
   ἐλθάτω
   γενηθήτω
   What clinches tense identification of these forms (244.1)?

6. ἀπόλυσον οὖν, κύριε, τὰ πλήθη· ἤδη γὰρ ἔρχεται ἡ νύξ.

   a. ἀπόλυσον: learn -σον and remember 407-17.4 and 411.
   b. τὰ πλήθη: what other neuter nouns do you know declined like this
      (352 and 345)?

7. μηδεὶς ἐξέλθῃ εἰς τὰ ὄρη, προσευξάσθωσαν δὲ πάντες τῷ πατρὶ
   αὐτῶν τῷ ἐν τοῖς οὐρανοῖς.

   a. μηδεὶς ἐξέλθῃ: how different from μὴ εἰσελθῃ in No. 4 above?
      Check paras. 371, 372, and 422 if μηδείς is not clear to you.
   b. τὰ ὄρη: like what noun is No. 6?
   c. προσευξάσθωσαν, -σασθωσαν: tense, person, number, and mood are
      all clear from this ending (407-17.3). Identify fully.
   d. τῷ ἐν τοῖς οὐρανοῖς: how related to τῷ πατρί (376)?

8. λαβὼν αὐτὸν ἄγε πρὸς ἡμᾶς

   a. λαβών: if it isn't clear, review para. 249 before proceeding.
   b. ἄγε: identify fully (407-17.4) and translate exegetically
      (420.4). English needs a repeated object here.

9. μηδενὶ εἴπητε ὃ εἴδετε.

   a. μηδενὶ εἴπητε (421-22.2): See Nos. 4a and 7a above if unclear.
      What case and why on μηδενί (371)?
   b. What is the direct object of εἴπητε (397.4)?
   c. ὃ: why accusative (397.3)?

10. ἐγέρθητε καὶ μὴ φοβεῖσθε· ὁ γὰρ κύριος σώσει ὑμᾶς.

    a. ἐγέρθητε: what would the indicative form be (420.2)?
       See the footnote?
    b. μὴ φοβεῖσθε: why not indicative (422 and 256)?
       Exegetical translation given (420.4 and 421-22.2)?
    c. σώσει: sigma tense suffix, primary active endings; must be
       what principal part (197.1)?

11. πάντα οὖν ὅσα ἐὰν εἴπωσιν ὑμῖν ποιήσατε καὶ τηρεῖτε κατὰ δὲ
    τὰ ἔργα αὐτῶν μὴ ποιεῖτε· λέγουσιν γὰρ καὶ οὐ ποιοῦσιν.

    a. ὅσα ἐὰν (εἴπωσιν): similar to ἃ ἐάν, except for added
    meaning, "as much as (ever)" with ὅσ-α. With ἐάν you ex-
    pect what mood (400)? Identify εἴπωσιν fully (278).

    b. Identify and contrast tense meaning and constructions in
    the following (420.4 and 421-22.2).
    ποιήσατε
    τηρεῖτε   (316.2)
    μὴ ποιεῖτε (316.2)

12. ἔλεγεν αὐτῷ μαθητής τις Κύριε, κέλευσόν με ἐλθεῖν πρὸς σὲ
    ἐπὶ τὰ ὕδατα. ὁ δὲ Ἰησοῦς εἶπεν Ἐλθέ.

    a. ἔλεγεν: the imperfect is sometimes repeated action in the
    past. So here perhaps. If so, how would you translate,
    and what would be the nuance? See DM, p. 188(3) or CEG, p.
    54(2b) if you are interested.

    b. κέλευσον: compare ἐκέλευσας in No. 3 above.
    What sign of aorist here (171-80.3)?
    -σον ending on <u>unaugmented</u> form must be what verb (411 and
    407-17.4)?

    c. με ἐλθεῖν: why accusative με (304)?
    Verb fully identified (296)?

    d. ἐλθέ: compare and contrast ἦλθε (419; 405; 407-17-4 and
    193).

13. ὅσα ἐὰν ἀκούσητε τοῖς ὠσὶν ὑμῶν καὶ ἴδητε τοῖς ὀφθαλμοῖς ὑμῶν
    εἴπετε καὶ τοῖς ἔθνεσιν.

    a. ἀκούσητε: not aorist indicative; why (245)?
    Not future indicative; why (272.1)? No augment, <u>sigma</u>
    tense suffix, long connecting vowel; what must it be (274)?

    b. τοῖς ὠσίν. Note οὖς, ὠτός, τό in the vocabulary (403).
    Write it's declensional forms (cf. 222).

    c. εἴπετε: "You said" or "Say!"? How can you tell on this
    form which does not lose its augment in subordinate moods?

14. ἃ ἐὰν ἀκούσητε ἐν τῷ σκότει κηρύξατε ἐν τῷ φωτί.

    a. τῷ σκότει: declined like what other neuter nouns (352)?

    b. κηρύξατε: how distinguished from indicative (420.2)?
    Identify fully?

    c. Of what is the pronoun ἅ the object (397.3)?
        Of what is the whole relative clause the object (397.4)?

15. μακάριος ὅστις φάγεται ἄρτον ἐν τῇ βασιλείᾳ τοῦ θεοῦ.

    a. φάγεται: primary or secondary endings? active or middle
        (139.1)? 2A was ἔφαγον.
    b. ὅστις is nominative singular. How do you know (388)?
        How do you know it is masculine. (99)?
    c. μακάριος ὅστις etc. is a verbless clause, with ἔστιν
        assumed.

16. ἐν ἐκείνῃ τῇ πόλει εἰσὶν ἱερεῖς πονηροί, οἵτινες οὐ ποιοῦσι
    τὸ θέλημα τοῦ θεοῦ.

    a. If any of the noun forms in this sentence are unfamiliar
        to you, review their paradigms now.
        ἐκείνη (568)   ἱερεῖς (564)
        πονηροί (568)   θέλημα (561)
        πόλει (563)
    b. οἵτινες: why the change from ὅς on ὅστις to οἵ on οἵτινες?
        Remember the vocabulary note on this word (403).
    c. ποιοῦσι: why the apparently irregular accent, i.e., non-
        recessive on a verb (316.III)?

17. ἐξελθόντες εἴπετε πᾶσι τοῖς ἔθνεσι τοῖς ἐπὶ πάσης τῆς γῆς ἅ
    ἐποίησεν ὁ θεὸς τοῖς ἀγαπῶσιν αὐτόν.

    a. εἴπετε: recall No. 13c.
    b. ἐξελθόντες: full identification (257.1)? Review 424.2.
    c. τοῖς ἐπί . . .γῆς : how related to τοῖς ἔθνεσι (376)?
    d. What is the full indirect object of εἴπετε?
        What is its full direct object (397.4)?
    e. ἀγαπῶσιν: identify fully (226) and review the contraction
        here: _____ + _____ = ἀγαπῶσιν (316.2.4).
        The construction has what relationship to ἐποίησεν (36)?

18. ὅταν κληθῇς ὑπό τινος, πορεύθητι.

    a. ὅταν (ὅτε + ἄν): you would expect what mood (384)?
        This is a <u>conditional temporal</u> clause (cf. conditional rela-
        tive clauses in para. 400).
    b. Identify fully: κληθῇς   (279)
                      πορεύθητι (414 and 407-17.4)

19. ὅταν ἴδητε ταῦτα γινόμενα, γνώσεσθε ὅτι ἐγγύς ἐστιν ἡ κρίσις.

    a. Why not εἴδετε?

    b. γινόμενα: remember 424.1.

    c. γνώσεσθε: primary middle endings, <u>sigma</u> tense suffix; must be what form (197.1 and 150)?

20. ἴδετε πάντες ὑμεῖς τὰς χεῖράς μου· οὐ γαρ ἐποίησαν αὗται αἱ χεῖρες ὧν λέγουσιν ἐκεῖνοι οὐδέν.

424.II   NEW TESTAMENT GREEK READING

Review the imperative forms encountered in your NT reading thus far: Jn. 1.36, 39; 2.16(2), 19. See also 1.43, 46 and 2.5, 7,8. Identify them fully and give exegetical translations.

Translate Acts 4.1-2.

4.1 λαλούντων δὲ αὐτῶν	Why genitive (266)?
ἐπέστησαν	From ἐφίστημι (ἐπί + ἵστημι), "I approach." Review paras. 600 and 601 carefully and identify this form.
4.2 διαπονούμενοι	-ουμενοι must be not only a middle or middle-passive ptc., but what type of verb (321 and 316)? πονέομαι, "I am troubled." How would you expect the compound, διαπονέομαι to effect that meaning? See <u>Lexical Aids</u>, p. 79, and then p. 82 on δία (cf. CEG, p. 35).
διὰ τὸ διδάσκειν . . . καὶ καταγγέλλειν	Para. 305.5 and 304.
ἀνάστασιν	Para. 349.
τὴν ἐκ νεκρῶν	Modifies _____ (376)?

Diagram these two verses, showing the main verb, and the relationship of the subordinate clauses to it and to each other.

Lesson XXIX

425   Take this occasion to review all the principal parts of these verbs, as you learn the fourth and fifth principal parts (perfect active and perfect middle-passive).

426-
31.1   Be able to analyze every perfect active form just as you have other verb forms.

          λελυκ   -   α   -   μεν   λελύκαμεν

Pf. A. tense stem (verb root plus reduplication and tense suffix)	Connecting vowel	Personal ending

426-
31.2   Personal endings in the perfect (review 139.1).
Perfect active uses _____(!) endings (431).
Perfect middle-passive uses _____ endings (447).

426-
31.3   Illustrate standard reduplication from the vocabulary words in para. 425.

433.1   How is the M.N. sg. differentiated from the N.N. sg. active ptc.? Is this new to you? It shouldn't be (259.3; 228.2; 242.2).

433.2   How do the masculine and neuter endings of the Pf. A. ptc. differ strikingly from the present and aorist active, or even aorist passive ptc. endings (576-579)?

433.3   Connecting vowel for the Pf.A ptc., feminine gender, is the diphthong _____. Why no change from -α (nom.) to -ης, -η in the genitive and dative (55)?

435.1   "Reduplication" is sometimes equivalent to _____.

437.1   Where have you seen these two sets of consonants related before in phonetic development (156.1)?

439.1   Graph this phonetic change (as in 156.1).
_____, _____, _____, or _____ + _____ = _____

440.1   How is a "second perfect" like a "second aorist passive" (206)?

442-
47.1   In what two obvious features of form do the Pf. M-P forms differ from perfect actives?
1. _____ (430, 444)
2. _____ (447)

442-
47.2   On ─σαι recall para. 181.1.

442-
47.3   What forms of the perfect receive irregular accent?

1. (433) _____   3. (427) _____
2. (444) _____   4. (443) _____

In what way is the accent irregular (13)?

442-
47.4   Review the principal parts now in 197.1, and then fill out the chart
        below to add to that summary.

Conjugation Derived	Tense suffix	Var. vowel	Personal endings
IV. Principal part _____			
1. _____	_____	_____	_____
2. _____(450.1)	_____	_____	_____
V. Principal part _____			
1. _____			
2. _____			_____
3. _____(450.1)			_____
4. _____(450.1)			_____

450.1   The conjugations of the pluperfect tense are formed on the fourth and
        fifth principal parts, parallel to the perfect (Plpf. A. on IV, Plpf.
M-P on V). Built on the fourth and fifth principal parts, the pluperfect often
has, in addition, an augment, for the pluperfect designates a past result of a
prior action. The pluperfect uses the diphthong ____ as connecting vowel in
the active (589).

452.1   Tense and kind of action. The type of reference made by the several
        Greek tenses to an action may be graphed as follows:

Present and imperfect   continuing or repeated _____ or - - - - -

Aorist   simple or undefined

Perfect   present condition
                        resulting from a past
                        act   _____

452.2   The perfect tense focuses attention both on a past completed (perfected)
        act and on a present condition resulting from that act. In some contexts
the writer's attention is more on the former and in others more on the latter,
and sometimes on both with equal force. Cf. DM, pp. 200-206.

453.1   Do it!

454.I   Aids to exercise I, Lesson XXIX.

1. οὐδείς ἐστιν δίκαιος κατὰ τὸν νόμον εἰ μὴ ὁ ποιήσας πάντα τὰ
    γεγραμμένα ἐν τῷ βιβλίῳ τοῦ νόμου.

    a. Remember paras. 371-72 and review 99.3.
    b. γεγραμμένα: identify fully (257.1). Signs of the perfect tense?
        1. (430)
        2. (447)
        3. (444)

        How used (235)?
        What is the force of the perfect here?
    c. τοῦ νόμου: cf. the use of the genitive on τοῦ σώματος,
        Jn. 2.21 (383.II).

2. εὐηγγελίσατο πάντα τὸν λαὸν λέγων ὅτι ἤγγικεν ἡ βασιλεία τῶν
    οὐρανῶν.

    a. εὐηγγελίσατο: -sato is unmistakable sign of _____(178).
        Where is the augment (131)?
    b. λέγων: adv. ptc. used how (402.1)?
    c. ἤγγικεν (pronounced, ēng-gi-ken, 1.1). Signs of perfect?
        1. (435)
        2. (430)
        How would the aorist alter the meaning of this sentence here?

3. ὃ ἑωράκαμεν καὶ ἀκηκόαμεν λέγομεν καὶ ὑμῖν, ἵνα καὶ ὑμεῖς πιστεύσητε
    εἰς τὸν Χριστόν.

    a. ἑωράκαμεν: identification? All signs of tense spotted (435 and
        430)?
        Note the double augment: ὁρα - to ὡρα + ε.
    b. ἀκηκόαμεν: what is reduplicated here?
        Cf. 2A of ἄγω (241), as well as _____ and _____ from the
        present vocabulary (425).
    c. Can you give an exegetical translation, incorporating the
        significance of the tenses of all four verbs, along with the
        clause meanings and emphatic words?

4. καὶ ἐν τούτῳ γινώσκομεν ὅτι ἐγνώκαμεν αὐτόν, ἐὰν τὰς ἐντολὰς
    αὐτοῦ τηρῶμεν.

    a. What whole construction is the direct object of γινώσκω?

198

b. Differentiate practically the meaning of the tenses of γινώσκομεν and ἐγνώκαμεν.

c. ἐάν . . . τηρῶμεν: review 288.4-5. Comment on the significance of the tense of τηρῶμεν.
Must it be subjunctive? _____ Why (316.I.3-4)?

5. ὁ ἀγαπῶν τὸν γεννήσαντα ἀγαπᾷ τὸν γεγεννημένον ἐξ αὐτοῦ.

a. $\dfrac{\rule{2cm}{0.4pt}}{\text{How used (235)?}}$ + _____ = ἀγαπῶν (226 and 316): identify fully.

_____ + _____ = ἀγαπᾷ (18 and 316).

b. γεγεννημένον: three signs of tense (430, 444, 447)?

c. Differentiate the significance of the tenses of the three ptcs.

6. πᾶς ὁ γεγεννημένος ἐκ τοῦ θεοῦ οὐχ ἁμαρτάνει, ἀλλ' ὁ γεννηθεὶς ἐκ τοῦ θεοῦ τηρεῖ αὐτόν.

a. Identify the two participles fully (444, 259) and contrast the focus of their respective tenses.

b. _____ + _____ = τηρεῖ (316 and 324).

7. τοῦτο γέγονεν, ὅτι οὕτως γέγραπται διὰ τοῦ προφήτου.

a. γέγονεν: sign of perfect? Remember para. 440. Is γέγονεν deponent (116)?

b. γέγραπται: two signs of perfect M-P (430 and 447)?

c. ὅτι - clause is related how to γέγονεν?

8. τὸ γεγεννημένον ἐκ τῆς σαρκὸς σάρξ ἐστιν, καὶ τὸ γεγεννημένον ἐκ τοῦ πνεύματος πνεῦμά ἐστιν.

a. How would the meaning change if the ptc. were τὸ γεννηθέν (452.1-2)?

b. Use this sentence as review of important third declension noun patterns (211, 222).

9. αὕτη δέ ἐστιν ἡ κρίσις, ὅτι τὸ φῶς ἐλήλυθεν εἰς τὸν κόσμον καὶ ἠγάπησαν οἱ ἄνθρωποι τὸ σκότος.

a. αὕτη: why feminine sg.? What is in apposition to αὕτη in this sentence?

b. Identify the nouns fully and review chapter XXV if there is difficulty. On κρίσις, see again Lexical Aids, pp. 42-43 (A2).

c. ἐλήλυθεν: identify fully. How would the sentence's meaning be altered if it were ἦλθεν (454)?

10. ἔλεγον οὖν οἱ Ἰουδαῖοι τῷ τεθεραπευμένῳ Οὐκ ἔξεστιν ποιῆσαι τοῦτο.

   a. ἔλεγον: see 424.I.12a on tense meaning. Were they "grilling" the man?

   b. τεθεραπευμένῳ: identify fully? Three tense signals? What is the meaning of the perfect in this case?

   c. ποιῆσαι (293).

11. ἐγὼ ἐλήλυθα ἐν τῷ ὀνόματι τοῦ πατρός μου καὶ οὐ δέχεσθέ με.

   ἐλήλυθα: signs of the tense (3b above and 440)?
   Where is the semantic focus here?

12. ἀλλ' εἶπον ὑμῖν ὅτι καὶ ἑωράκατέ με καὶ οὐ πιστεύετε.

   Remember para. 148.

13. ἐὰν μὴ φάγητε τὴν σάρκα τοῦ υἱοῦ τοῦ ἀνθρώπου καὶ πίητε αὐτοῦ τὸ αἷμα, οὐκ ἔχετε ζωὴν ἐν ἑαυτοῖς.

   a. φάγητε, πίητε: ἐάν plus long connecting vowel clinch identification of the mood. What is it (272.1; 288.3)? Without tense suffix they are either presents or _____ (384; 186).

   b. ἐν ἑαυτοῖς: reflexive pronoun must refer to whom (342)?

14. τὰ ῥήματα ἃ ἐγὼ λελάληκα ὑμῖν πνεῦμά ἐστιν καὶ ζωή ἐστιν.

   a. λελάληκα: identify fully. All the signs of the tense of this verb should be obvious to you by now. If they are not, master para. 430 now!

   b. ἅ: identify and explain the gender, number and case (397). What is the function of this relative clause?

   c. On πνεῦμα and ζωήν, see again para. 99.3.

15. ἀπεκρίθη αὐτῷ Πέτρος Κύριε, πρὸς τίνα ἀπελευσόμεθα; ῥήματα ζωῆς ἔχεις, καὶ ἡμεῖς πεπιστεύκαμεν καὶ ἐγνώκαμεν ὅτι σὺ εἶ ὁ ἅγιος τοῦ θεοῦ.

    a. ἀπελευσόμεθα: identify fully, noting tense suffix (150; 151).
    b. Identify fully and contrast according to paras. 436 and 430.
       πεπιστεύκαμεν
       ἐγνώκαμεν
       How would the meaning be altered if these were aorists?
    c. ὁ ἅγιος: significance of the article in this predicate
       nominative (99.3)?

16. ταῦτα αὐτοῦ λαλοῦντος πολλοὶ ἐπίστευσαν εἰς αὐτόν.

    αὐτοῦ λαλοῦντος: participle and subject in genitive case?
    Review para. 266.1-4 if this construction is unclear to you.

17. γέγραπται ὅτι δύο ἀνθρώπων ἡ μαρτυρία ἀληθής ἐστιν.

    a. γέγραπται: what signs of tense (430)?
       What indicators of voice (447)?
       What is the subject of this verb?
    b. ἀληθής: M.N. sg., or F.N. sg.? Which one and why (360; 66)?
       Why acute accent (92.I.(1))?

18. ταῦτα εἶπεν πρὸς τοὺς πεπιστευκότας εἰς αὐτὸν Ἰουδαίους.

    a. πεπιστευκότας: identify fully. Remember 433.1-2 and spot
       the other two tense indicators (430). How used?
    b. What is the significance of the tense here (452 and 452.1-2)?

19. νῦν δὲ ζητεῖτέ με ἀποκτεῖναι, ἄνθρωπον ὅς τὴν ἀλήθειαν ὑμῖν λελάληκα, ἥν ἤκουσα παρὰ τοῦ θεοῦ.

    a. ἀποκτεῖναι: identify fully (333). How related to ζητεῖτε?
    b. ἄνθρωπον: why accusative sg.? How related to με?
       See the footnote.
    c. ἥν: why feminine sg. (397)? Why accusative?

20. εὐλογημένος ὁ ἐρχόμενος ἐν ὀνόματι κυρίου.

    a. εὐλογημένος: spot the two tense signals (444,447).
    b. The first participle serves as a <u>predicate</u> adjective.
       What part of the sentence is assumed?

454.II NEW TESTAMENT GREEK READING

Review the perfect verb forms you have seen thus far in the NT Greek readings: Jn 1.3: 6, 15(2), 18, 24; 2.17.

Identify them fully and give translations which reflect the perfect's meaning as fully as possible. Read DM, para. 184 on the perfect to assist you at this point.

Translate Acts 4.3-6.

4.3 τὰς χεῖρας

See CEG, p. 25(9) on the article. Also para. 566.

ἔθεντο

Study paras. 598 and 599. Note as many patterns as you can and identify this verb. English will need an object ("them") here.

τήρησιν

Compare ἀνάστασιν in 4.2. Third declension feminine nouns declined after the pattern, -σις, -σεως, -σει, -σιν, etc., name actions and processes. Here related to τηρέω. See Lexical Aids, pp. 42-43(A2) or CEG, p. 19.

4.4 ἀνδρῶν

Para. 565.

4.5 συναχθῆναι

-θῆναι can only be _____ (293). See also 204.2. Note the compound subjects in the accusative case (204).

4.5-6

For nouns, review paras. 352 and 355.

456–

57.1   Greek adjectives regularly form their comparative and superlative degrees following two main patterns, adding the following endings to the "positive" (regular) word stem.

	Comparative	Superlative
Pattern 1 adds:	-τερος, α, ον	-τατος, η, ον
Pattern 2 adds:	-(ι)ων, -(ι)ον	-ιστος, η, ον

Examples:

	Positive	Comparative	Superlative
Pattern 1:	ἰσχυρος "strong"	ἰσχυρότερος "stronger"	ἰσχυρότατος "strongest"
Pattern 2:	πόλυς "much"	πλείων "more"	πλεῖστος "most"

458.1   "Irregular" comparatives and superlatives are irregular for the same reason that second aorists are "irregular." Words from two or more roots have combined to form a single pattern for comparison of a given idea. Note in the example in NTGFB that μικρός, from one source, and ἐλάσσων and ἐλάχιστος, from a second source, combine to form a single pattern for the native speaker. In that sense "good" (from one source), "better" and "best" (from a second source) are irregular.

458.2   Watch for the endings learned in paras. 456 and 467 to appear on these so-called irregular forms as well, e.g., ἐλάσσων and ἐλάχιστος.

462.1   The idea of separation contained in the genitive case (cf. its use with ἐκ and ἀπό) leads it to be used to designate the item with which something else is being compared. In such a case the actual Greek word for "than" (ἤ) will not appear.

462.2   When comparison is stated using ἤ, what other syntactic clue must accompany it?

463.1   Compare para. 101.3 on the adverbial ending, -ως.

464.1   Fill in the comparative and superlative adverbial forms which would correspond to the following adjectives.

	Positive	Comparative	Superlative
Adjectives	δίκαιος "righteous"	δικαιότερος "more righteous"	δικαιότατος "most righteous"
Adverbs	"righteous<u>ly</u>"	"more righteous<u>ly</u>"	"most righteous<u>ly</u>"

466.1 Words like ἔξω and ἔμπροσθεν perform diverse functions, as the student
may readily see by surveying AG, pp. 278-279 on ἔξω. It is enough here
to note that
1) such words may stand alone as adverbs,
e.g. ἔξω (ἐπ᾽ ἐρήμοις τόποις) ἦν, Mk. 1.45, "He was . . . outside."
or 2) may function as a preposition, with an object in the genitive case.
(Hence the antiquated designation "improper preposition")
e.g. ἔξω τῆς παρεμβολῆς, Heb. 13.11, "outside the camp."

467.1 Three different temporal expressions with differing nuances should be
understood and related to the understanding of the cases involved.

1. The accusative of time during which (382.1-2) an act occurs.
The focus is on the extent or length of time. Cf. DM, p. 93.
Mt. 4.2. νήστευσας. . . ἡμέρας τεσσεράκοντα καὶ νύκτας
"Fasting, throughout/during 40 days and 40 nights"

2. The genitive of time within which an act occurs.
The focus is on the kind of time, the distinction of one time as
opposed to another one. Cf. DM, p. 77.
Mt. 2.14 παρέλαβεν τὸ παιδίον . . . νυκτός.
"He took the young child. .by night/of a night/at night
time."

3. The dative of time when an act occurs.
The focus is on locating in a point of time. Cf. DM, p. 87.
Lk. 12.20 ταύτῃ τῇ νυκτὶ τὴν ψυχὴν σου αἰτοῦσιν ἀπὸ σοῦ.
"In/on this night they will demand your soul from you."

The dative quite naturally occurs then with the preposition ἐν to
express temporal location (472).

468.1 Learn the "genitive of the articular infinitive to express purpose" as
a set syntactic construction. It is another instance where one must
abandon any word-for-word translation (e.g. using "of" for the genitive) and
phrase a translation equivalent, a purpose clause using the act named by the
infinitive.

468.2 What English words in the example denote purpose?

469.1 This use of the dative is sometimes called the "dative of reference."
Exegetical translations can be phrased with the words "as far as _____
is concerned," "with respect to _____," or "with reference to _____."

470.1 A very loose adverbial use of the accusative case, sometimes known as
an "adverbial accusative of reference." The uses of the dative and
accusative presented in paras. 469 and 470 are very similar, insomuch that the
exegetical phrases suggested under 469.1 apply here as well.

471.1 See 467.1 above.

472.1 See 467.1(3) above.

473.1   How are these possessive adjectives declined?

473.2   Possessive adjectives <u>emphasize possession</u>. Make sure you are able to
         give an expanded literal translation of such expressions ("the - belongs
to me - word") as well as the equivalent ("my word") so that this emphasis is
clear.

473.3   As memory aids, be sure to relate these possessive adjectives to the
         corresponding personal pronoun forms.
              e. g. ἡμέτερος, "our" to ἡμεῖς, "we"
                    ὑμέτερος, "your" to ὑμεῖς, "you"

476.1   Why μή and not οὐ after ἵνα? See para. 256.

477.1   In most of the cases here referred to, ἵνα introduces "<u>noun</u> clauses,"
         that is, clauses which function (as nouns do) as objects or subjects.
With words of exhorting, wishing, hoping, praying, the ἵνα clause often states
the content of that exhortation, wish, hope or prayer--in reality, the object
of the verbs involved. These are objects of content.
         εἰπὲ   τῷ λίθῳ τούτῳ   ἵνα γένηται ἄρτος
         verb - indirect object   - direct object or object of content

         Note that in Machen's second exmaple the ἵνα clause is in apposition to
αὕτη. Apposition is also a noun function.

477.2   ὅτι is used in the same way for noun clauses that involve indicative
         verbs, to introduce clauses that serve subjects, or objects as in other
noun functions.

479.1   Questions with μή + indicative expect a _____ answer.
         Questions with οὐ + indicative expect a _____ answer. Cf. I Cor.
12.29-30.

480.I   Aids to Exercise I, Lesson XXX

    1. παρακαλῶ δὲ ὑμᾶς ἵνα τὸ αὐτὸ λέγητε πάντες.

         a. Why the circumflex accent (316.III.1) on παρακαλῶ? Identify.
         b. What is the object of παρακαλῶ (477.1)?
         c. Why ἵνα and not ὅτι (477 and 477.2)?

    2. ὅσα ἐὰν θέλητε ἵνα ποιῶσιν ὑμῖν οἱ ἄνθρωποι, οὕτως καὶ ὑμεῖς ποιεῖτε·
        οὗτος γάρ ἐστιν ὁ νόμος καὶ οἱ προφῆται.

         a. With ὅσα ἐάν and ἵνα, what mood do you expect in the verbs (447;
             400)? Identify the verbs fully.
         b. Is ποιεῖτε indicative or imperative? Which is more decisive
             in the identification, form or context (591)?
             What significance to the tense here (420.4)?

c. What relationship does the final clause have to those preceding?

3. κέλευσον οὖν τηρηθῆναι τὸ σῶμα ὑπὸ τῶν στρατιωτῶν, μήποτε ἐλθόντες οἱ μαθηταὶ λάβωσιν αὐτὸ καὶ εἴπωσιν τῷ λαῷ ὅτι ἠγέρθη ἐκ τῶν νεκρῶν.

a. Identify fully.
   κέλευσον (411)
   τηρηθῆναι: -θῆναι should be a sure sign (293).
b. το σῶμα: why accusative (304)?
c. After μήποτε, what mood is expected (256)?
   Give the corresponding indicative forms of
   λάβωσιν: _____ (272.1)
   εἴπωσιν: _____
d. ἐλθόντες . . . λάβωσιν: how is this participle best translated (424.2)?
e. How does the ὅτι clause relate to εἴπωσιν (477.1-2)?

4. οὐκ ἔστι δοῦλος μείζων τοῦ πέμψαντος αὐτόν.

a. Why relate μείζων to δοῦλος (459; 66)?
b. τοῦ πέμψαντος : why genitive (462)?

5. μείζονα ταύτης ἀγάπην οὐδεὶς ἔχει, ἵνα τις ἀποθάνῃ ὑπὲρ τῶν ἄλλων.

a. What is the core (S-V-O) of the first clause?
   What modifies ἀγάπην (459)?
b. ταύτης: why genitive and why feminine (462)?
c. With what in the first clause do you relate the ἵνα clause?
   How (477)?

6. πάλιν ἀπέστειλεν ἄλλους δούλους πλείονας τῶν πρώτων.

a. ἀπέστειλεν: identify fully (333). Main clue of tense here?
b. πλείονας: modifies what word? How do you know (459; 66)?
   Review 456-57.1.

7. εἰ δίκαιόν ἐστιν ἐνώπιον τοῦ θεοῦ ὑμῶν ἀκούειν μᾶλλον ἢ τοῦ θεοῦ, κρίνατε.

a. Translate the condition exegetically (288.4).

206

b. ὑμῶν: why genitive (108)?
τοῦ θεοῦ: why genitive in the second occurrence (462.2)?
What is assumed?

c. κρίνατε: why aorist (333)?
What mood? Why not indicative (420.2)?

8. ἐγὼ δὲ λέγω ὑμῖν Ἀγαπᾶτε τοὺς ἐχθροὺς ὑμῶν καὶ προσεύχεσθε
ὑπὲρ τῶν διωκόντων ὑμᾶς, ὅπως γένησθε υἱοὶ τοῦ πατρὸς ὑμῶν
τοῦ ἐν οὐρανοῖς.

a. ἀγαπᾶτε and προσεύχεσθε: identify fully and comment on the
significance of the tense (420.4; 316.I.6 on the contraction).

b. ὅπως γένησθε: how related to the first clause (286.1)?

c. τοῦ ἐν οὐρανοῖς: how used (376)?

9. εἶπεν αὐτοῖς ὁ Ἰησοῦς ὅτι ἔξεστι τοῖς σάββασι καλῶς ποιεῖν.

a. ἔξεστι is normally followed by the _____ (292.1).

b. How is the ὅτι clause related to εἶπεν (477.2)?

c. τοῖς σάββασι: how different from a similar expression in
the accusative or genitive (467.1)?

10. ἔμεινεν δὲ ὁ Ἰησοῦς ἐκεῖ διὰ τὸ εἶναι τὸν τόπον ἐγγὺς τῆς πόλεως.

a. ἔμεινεν: remember para. 333. Why not imperfect of μένω (123.5)?

b. διὰ τὸ εἶναι: what construction (305.5)?
Related to what in clause one?

11. τότε συναχθήσονται ἔμπροσθεν αὐτοῦ πάντα τὰ ἔθνη.

a. συναχθήσονται: <u>theta-eta</u> plus <u>sigma</u> tense suffix.
If the tense and voice of this is not clear on sight, review 202
immediately.

b. ἔθνη: review the noun pattern in para. 352.

12. μὴ ποίει τοῦτο· οὐ γὰρ ἱκανός εἰμι ἵνα εἰς τὴν οἰκίαν μου εἰσέλθῃς.

a. μὴ ποίει: is it ποιε + ε (407) or ποιε + ει (591)?
How can you tell (316.III.1)? Meaning of construction (420.4)?

b. The ἵνα clause defines or qualifies a previous word. Which
one (CEG, p. 74)?

13. ἐλθόντες οἱ στρατιῶται νυκτὸς ἔλαβον τὸν ἄνδρα καὶ ἀγαγόντες
    αὐτὸν ἔξω ἀπέκτειναν.

    a. ἐλθόντες and ἀγαγόντες: what two signs of the tense (249.1)?
    b. How are these participles used (424.2)?
    c. ἀπέκτειναν: remember para. 333 and identify fully along with
    ἔλαβον.
    d. ἔξω: review 466.1, both examples. Which pattern here?
    e. νυκτός: how would the meaning be changed by either νύκτα or
    νυκτί (467.1)?

14. τῇ μὲν σαρκὶ οὐκ ἐστε μεθ᾽ ἡμῶν, τῇ δὲ καρδίᾳ ἐστὲ ἐγγύς.

    a. τῇ σαρκί and τῇ καρδίᾳ: translate exegetically (469.1).
    b. What other constructions in the sentence are modified by each of
    these dative phrases?

15. μὴ περιπατοῦμεν κατὰ σάρκα; οὐκ ἔχομεν τὸ πνεῦμα τοῦ θεοῦ;

    a. The first question demands what answer? How do you know (479)?
    b. The second question demands what answer?
    What element must be included in the English translation of the
    question, in order to elicit this answer to the translated question?
    c. Review the contraction in περιπατοῦμεν (316).

16. εἰσῆλθεν εἰς τὴν οἰκίαν τοῦ ἀρχιερέως τοῦ εἶναι ἐγγὺς τοῦ τόπου
    ὅπου ἦν ὁ Ἰησοῦς.

    a. How is τοῦ εἶναι related to εἰσῆλθεν (468 and 468.1)?
    b. τοῦ τόπου: why genitive (466)?
    c. What is the nominative singular of ἀρχιερέως?
    Review its paradigm (355).
    d. The ὅπου clause modifies what word?

17. εἰς τὰ ἴδια ἦλθεν καὶ οἱ ἴδιοι αὐτὸν οὐ παρέλαβον.

How are the adjectives used here (473; 75): See 107.II again on
Jn. 1.11.

18. ἐγὼ ἐλήλυθα ἐν τῷ ὀνόματι τοῦ πατρός μου, καὶ οὐ λαμβάνετέ με·
    ἐὰν ἄλλος ἔλθῃ ἐν τῷ ὀνόματι τῷ ἰδίῳ, ἐκεῖνον λήμψεσθε.

a. ἐλήλυθα: identify fully (425). How would the meaning be altered if this were ἦλθον (452.1-2)?
b. Study the uses of the personal pronouns carefully.
c. λήμψεσθε: identify (155). If the tense signals are not immediately clear to you, review 197.1 and learn them.
d. ἔλθῃ: name two obvious signs of subjunctive (272.1; 276.2; 277.1). To what verb is this ἐάν clause related (288.5)? How?

19. μὴ ἐποίησα τὸ ἴδιον θέλημα; οὐ μᾶλλον ἐποίησα τὸ σόν;

a. Do these questions demand any certain answer? How do you know (478)?
b. To what person does τὸ ἴδιον relate? Compare its use in 17 above. Note that the person whose "own" is meant varies from context to context.
c. τὸ σόν: substantive expression assumes what specific noun?

20. εἰ ἐμὲ ἐδίωξαν, καὶ ὑμᾶς διώξουσιν· εἰ τὸν λόγον μου ἐτήρησαν, καὶ τὸν ὑμέτερον τηρήσουσιν.

a. ἐδίωξαν/διώξουσιν and ἐτήρησαν/τηρήσουσιν
Compare and contrast their forms, noting augments, endings
Identify fully (197.1).
b. To which elements do you relate each of the εἰ clauses? How? Translate exegetically (288.4).

480.II NEW TESTAMENT GREEK READING

Translate Acts 4.7-10

4.7 στήσαντες   See ἵστημι in para. 538 and 544.
Is this transitive or intransitive?
Contrast the forms in 600 and 601. Identify fully (242). How used?

ἐπυνθάνοντο   Imperfect or second aorist? How do you know (123.5)? What might indicate a real cross-examination? Cf. CEG, p. 54(2b).

δυνάμει and   Review para. 349 and 222 if unclear.
ὀνόματι   What was pressing in the interrogators' minds, judging by word order?

4.8 πλησθείς   -θείς, -θέντος: identify fully this form of πίμπλημι (259). How used (254.3? 424.2?)?

4.9 ἀνακρινόμεθα   Do you see how the compounding with ἀνα- intensifies or alters the meaning of κρίνω (DM, p. 99, on ἀνά)?

εὐεργεσίᾳ   Note the compound with ευ- (Lexical Aids, p. 47(1b).

ἀνθρώπου   Use of the genitive?

ἀσθενοῦς   Para. 360.

σέσωσται   Reduplication with <u>epsilon</u>, primary
                                            middle ending without connecting vowel?
            Must be what form (442)? The tense focuses attention
        on what fact (452) here?

4.10 ἔστω   -τω should be obvious sign of _____
                                            mood (407-17.3 and 423). Identify fully.

      γνωστόν   Read <u>Lexical Aids</u>, p. 44, (B5) carefully.

      παρέστηκεν   See παρίστημι in AG, p. 633. Significance
                                            of the tense?

      τούτῳ and οὗτος   They have different antecedants?
                                            Trace them back accurately.

      ἐνώπιον   Para. 466.

Lay these sentences out in a diagram, locating the independent clause
and arranging the subordinate items in order under the items they modify.

481.1 Which vocabulary words in this lesson do you relate to the following English words?

antidote   _____ + _____
    Contrast "anti-" words and "ante-" words. What is the
    difference in meaning and derivation?
monologue   _____ + _____
aeon/eon   _____
gynecology   _____ + _____

Why are English "gynecology" and "mystery" spelled with "y" (1.2)?

481.2 On πειράζω, check Richard C. Trench, SYNONYMS OF THE NEW TESTAMENT
(Grand Rapids: Eerdmans, 1953; reprint of 1880 edition), pp. 278-281,
before you complete the study of this lesson. Look over Trench's work for your
own information.

482.1 Where does the μι conjugation get its name?

484.1 Study these six principal parts and make all the observations you can
about tense stem formation, use of tense suffixes, connecting vowels,
means of reduplication, and anything else that seems important.

487.1 Where else have you seen <u>kappa</u> used as an aorist tense suffix (186)?

483-
90.1 Summarize the irregular and regular features of the forms of the <u>mi</u>-
verbs presented in paragraphs 483 to 490.
    Irregular features:

    Regular features:

491.1 How is the reduplication used to form the present stem of the <u>mi</u>-verbs
different from that used to form the perfects (430; 484)?

493.1 Do you see the lengthening of the present stem vowel to which Machen
is referring? Look at paras. 598 and 600 and observe the same lengthening in the stem vowels of τίθημι and ἵστημι. Do it!

495.1 Learn these personal endings now! And remember what happens to the
vowel preceding them in the singular forms.

496.1 <u>Mi verbs</u> use the <u>same endings</u> to form the <u>subjunctives</u> that you learned
for the subjunctives in the <u>omega conjugations</u> (269).

Explain the contractions to which Machen refers (316.I).

_____ + _____	= διδῶ	_____ + _____	= διδῶμεν
_____ + _____	= διδῷς	_____ + _____	= διδῶτε
_____ + _____	= διδῷ	_____ + _____	= διδῶσι

498.1 How do these present active imperative forms compare with those of
the <u>omega</u> verbs (407)?

499.1 Compare the forms of the present subjunctives (496), the present
imperatives (498), the present infinitive (499) and the present
participles (500) with the aorist subjunctives (509), the aorist imperatives
(511), the aorist infinitive (513), and the aorist participles (514). What
is the main difference between these two sets of forms (510)?

This underscores the importance of something you have already learned about
the basis of tense identification. What is that (20.1)?

503.1 Study these imperfect active forms. What personal endings are used
(504; 127.1)? Where have you seen -σαν used before as a third person
plural, secondary active ending (199 and 133)?

504.1 In what linguistic change does the imperfect active parallel the present
active?

505.1 Study carefully the middle-passive forms of the present and imperfect
of δίδωμι in para. 596. Do it! What endings are used on the presents
and the imperfects respectively (139.1)?

506.1 Your study of δίδωμι outside of the first principal part, and especially
of the non-indicative forms here in the aorists, should show you the
great importance of learning the <u>verb</u> root of each of the most frequent <u>mi</u> verbs
in the New Testament (you'll encounter them all in Machen).

506.2 The <u>verb</u> roots to be learned are: δο for δίδωμι, θε for τίθημι, στα for
ἵστημι.

Review the principal parts in para. 484 as well as the various verb forms
here in paras. 507-514 and observe the consistent appearance of this
unit δο-.

516.1 Considering the materials in paras. 506.1-2 and studying para. 601, do
you see why Machen refers to the second aorist of γινώσκω as a <u>mi</u> form?

518.1 Used as introduced in para. 518, the article usually refers to some
person(s) or thing(s) in the immediate context. Study the examples
here on this point. Compare Eph. 4.11 for a related use of the article.

518.2 This is why Machen says (519) that the article used with μέν and δέ is
functioning as a _____.

520.1 Review your previous study of the aorist participle for co-ordinate
action (424.1). The use is virtually the same as that presented here in
paragraph 520, differing only in the semantics of the verbs involved, referring
to acts on the one hand which are co-ordinate, and on the other hand which are
synonymous.

521.1 Review John 1.38-39 again (344.II) on this point.

522.I Aids to exercise I, Lesson XXXI.

1. παρέδωκα γὰρ ὑμῖν ἐν πρώτοις ὅ καὶ παρέλαβον, ὅτι Χριστὸς ἀπέθανεν
   ὑπὲρ τῶν ἁμαρτιῶν ἡμῶν κατὰ τὰς γραφάς.

   a. Identify all the verbs fully.
      (507) παρέδωκα   ἀπέθανεν
            παρέλαβον
   b. ὅ καὶ παρέλαβον: identify ὅ and explain its case (397.3).
      This whole clause functions as the object of what verb (397.4)?
   c. How does the ὅτι clause relate to the relative clause,
      ὅ καὶ παρέλαβον (477.1-2)?

2. μὴ ἔχοντος δὲ αὐτοῦ ἀποδοῦναι ἀπέλυσεν αὐτὸν ὁ κύριος αὐτοῦ.

   a. ἔχοντος δὲ αὐτοῦ: trouble fitting the genitive into the
      context? Remember para. 266.
   b. ἀποδοῦναι: identify fully (513). Why not present (499.1)?
   c. How does the adverbial participle modify ἀπέλυσεν? By giving
      its time, or means, or circumstance, or cause, or result, or
      condition of action (See 257.I.13d)?

3. καὶ ἀποκριθεὶς πᾶς ὁ λαὸς εἶπεν Τὸ αἷμα αὐτοῦ ἐφ' ἡμᾶς καὶ ἐπὶ
   τὰ τέκνα ἡμῶν.

   a. ἀποκριθείς: identify fully (259). How used (520)?
   b. πᾶς: identify fully and review its paradigm in para. 365.
   c. What is understood in the quote as given? What is subject and
      what is predicate in the statement?

4. θέλω δὲ τούτῳ τῷ ἐσχάτῳ δοῦναι ὡς καὶ σοί.

   a. τῷ ἐσχάτῳ: how used (75)?
   b. δοῦναι: identify fully (513). Why not present (499.1)?
      What would the corresponding middle form and passive form be
      (596-97)?
   c. ὡς καὶ σοί: modifies what other unit in the sentence?

5. ἐσθιόντων δὲ αὐτῶν λαβὼν ὁ Ἰησοῦς ἄρτον καὶ εὐλογήσας ἔκλασεν καὶ
   δοὺς τοῖς μαθηταῖς εἶπεν Λάβετε φάγετε, τοῦτό ἐστιν τὸ σῶμά μου.
   καὶ λαβὼν ποτήριον καὶ εὐχαριστήσας ἔδωκεν αὐτοῖς λέγων Πίετε
   ἐξ αὐτοῦ πάντες.

a. Identify all the verb forms fully.

ἐσθιόντων	(226)	φάγετε	(416)
λαβών	(249)	ἐστίν	(98)
εὐλογήσας	(242)	εὐχαριστήσας	(242)
ἔκλασεν	(ft. nt. 1?)	ἔδωκεν	(507)
δούς	(514)	λέγων	(226)
λάβετε	(416)	πίετε	(384)

b. ἐσθιόντων...αὐτῶν: why genitive (266)? Modifies what? how?

c. On the aorist participles, remember para. 424.2! What two words are coordinated by the first καί? by the fourth καί?

d. πάντες: all of what, the people or the cup? How do you know (66)?

6. καὶ εἶπαν λέγοντες πρὸς αὐτόν Εἰπὸν ἡμῖν ἐν ποίᾳ ἐξουσίᾳ ταῦτα ποιεῖς, ἢ τίς ἐστιν ὁ δούς σοι τὴν ἐξουσίαν ταύτην. ἀποκριθεὶς δὲ εἶπεν πρὸς αὐτούς Ἐρωτήσω κἀγὼ λόγον, καὶ εἴπατέ μοι.

a. λέγοντες: how used (402.1)?

b. εἰπόν: identify fully. By form, what two identifications are possible?
   1. (193) _____
   2. (521; 419) _____
   Context and accent indicate which here?

c. ὁ δούς: full identification and use (514; 265)?

d. ἀποκριθείς: identification and use (259; 520)?

e. εἴπατε: indicative or imperative? Remember that εἶπον, appears not to lose its augment in subordinate verb forms (cf. 251).

7. ὁ γὰρ ἄρτος τοῦ θεοῦ ἐστιν ὁ καταβαίνων ἐκ τοῦ οὐρανοῦ καὶ ζωὴν διδοὺς τῷ κόσμῳ.

a. Do you see the compound predicate in this sentence? Do καταβαίνων and διδούς modify the same person? Why or why not (240.I.11b)? Identifications?

b. Is the point of the predicate identity or characterization (99.3)?

8. λέγει αὐτοῖς Ὑμεῖς δὲ τίνα με λέγετε εἶναι; ἀποκριθεὶς δὲ Σίμων Πέτρος εἶπεν Σὺ εἶ ὁ Χριστὸς ὁ υἱὸς τοῦ θεοῦ τοῦ ζῶντος.

a. Ὑμεῖς . . .εἶναι: what two indications of interrogative (7; 386/89)?
b. με: why accusative (304; 306)?
c. What aspects of the question would you say are to be emphasized and why?
d. ζῶντος: explain the contraction and identify fully.
_____ + _____ = ζῶντος (316.I; 590)

9. λέγει αὐτῷ ὁ Ἰησοῦς Πορεύου· ὁ υἱός σου ζῇ. ἐπίστευσεν ὁ ἄνθρωπος τῷ λόγῳ ὃν εἶπεν αὐτῷ ὁ Ἰησοῦς καὶ ἐπορεύετο.

a. Identify fully:
πορεύου (why not Impf. M-P. I, 2 sg? 123.3; 408)
ζῇ (481)
b. ἐπίστευσεν and ἐπορεύετο: identify and contrast the tense meanings. Why do you think the imperfect is used on the second form? Read CEG, p. 54(d) or DM, p. 190(3).
c. ὅν. . . αὐτῷ: why is the relative pronoun accusative (397.3)? Why masculine singular (397)?

10. ὁρᾶτε μή τις κακὸν ἀντὶ κακοῦ τινὶ ἀποδῷ.

a. ὁρᾶτε: identify: what is the force of the tense (420.4)?
b. μή . . . ἀποδῷ: identify the verb fully (509).
On μή, see paras. 475-476.

11. ἦλθεν ἡ ὥρα, ἰδοὺ παραδίδοται ὁ υἱὸς τοῦ ἀνθρώπου εἰς τὰς χεῖρας τῶν ἁμαρτωλῶν. ἐγείρεσθε, ἄγωμεν. ἰδοὺ ὁ παραδιδούς με ἤγγικεν.

a. παραδίδοται and παραδιδούς: identify fully (505).
Why not perfect (491.1)? Is the personal ending suitable for perfect?
b. ἐγείρεσθε: imperative or indicative? Context will have to show.
c. ἤγγικεν: augment and kappa tense suffix? Identify fully and reflect on tense implication (430; 435).

12. καὶ ἰδοὺ εἷς προσελθὼν αὐτῷ εἶπεν Διδάσκαλε, τί ἀγαθὸν ποιήσω ἵνα σχῶ ζωὴν αἰώνιον; ὁ δὲ εἶπεν αὐτῷ Τί με ἐρωτᾷς περὶ τοῦ ἀγαθοῦ; εἷς ἐστιν ὁ ἀγαθός· εἰ δὲ θέλεις εἰς τὴν ζωὴν εἰσελθεῖν τήρει τὰς ἐντολάς.

a. Watch these: εἷς not εἰς (371); τί not τι (385 and see 391 too). διδάσκαλε (remember para. 37).

b. προσελθών . . . εἶπεν: is the participle best understood as modifying the main verb temporally (254.3) or as giving an act logically co-ordinate with the verb, with temporal significance minimized (424.2)?

c. σχῶ: after ἵνα you expect what mood (286)?

d. ὁ δὲ εἶπεν: how can it be translated, "And he said" (518.1)?

e. τήρει: if not 3 sg., what can -ει be?
_____ + _____ = τήρει (316.I).
How is this verb modified (288.2)?

13. καὶ προσελθὼν ὁ πειράζων εἶπεν αὐτῷ Εἰ υἱὸς εἶ τοῦ θεοῦ, εἰπὲ ἵνα οἱ λίθοι οὗτοι ἄρτοι γένωνται. ὁ δὲ ἀποκριθεὶς εἶπεν Γέγραπται Οὐκ ἐπ' ἄρτῳ μόνῳ ζήσεται ὁ ἄνθρωπος.

a. προσελθών: identify and use (424.2)?

b. ὁ πειράζων: the substantive participle is often used to name a member of a class. Cf. ὁ σπείρων, "The sower."

c. εἰπὲ ἵνα: verb identification (416)?
ἵνα after verbs of saying often does not state purpose. Rather, how is it used here (477 and 477.1)?

d. γένωνται: primary middle ending, long connecting vowel, γεν – tense stem? Full identification (278)?

14. καὶ προσελθόντες οἱ μαθηταὶ εἶπαν αὐτῷ Διὰ τί ἐν παραβολαῖς λαλεῖς αὐτοῖς; ὁ δὲ ἀποκριθεὶς εἶπεν ὅτι ῾Υμῖν δέδοται γνῶναι τὰ μυστήρια τῆς βασιλείας τῶν οὐρανῶν, ἐκείνοις δὲ οὐ δέδοται.

a. προσελθόντες . . . εἶπαν and ὁ δε ἀποκριθεὶς εἶπεν: participle use (424.2; 520)?

b. δέδοται: primary middle ending, reduplication with epsilon? Identification should be obvious (484 and 442).

c. γνῶναι: para. 601 and 516.

15. ἔλεγον αὐτῷ οἱ μαθηταὶ ᾿Απόλυσον αὐτούς. ὁ δὲ ἀποκριθεὶς εἶπεν αὐτοῖς Δότε αὐτοῖς ὑμεῖς φαγεῖν.

a. ἔλεγον: was there repeated urging from the disciples? Review 424.I.12a and 452.1.

b. ἀπόλυσον: if the sigma is a tense suffix, the -σον ending can only indicate _____ (411).

c. δότε: verb root δο-, no augment, no reduplication, with 2 pl. active ending, must be _____ (597).

522.II NEW TESTAMENT GREEK READING

Translate Acts 4.11-14.

4.11   The words may be unfamiliar, but they are all quite regular.

      ὑφ᾽   Why the phonetic change in the preposition (NTGFB, p. 51, n. 1-2)?

4.12 ἄλλῳ οὐδενί   Literally, "Not one other." Did you identify οὐδενί fully (371-372)? Double negative simply strengthens the negative, contrary to English idiom.

      ἄλλῳ/ἕτερον   How do these synonyms differ? See Trench, NEW TESTAMENT SYNONYMS, para. 95.

      δεδομένον   Verb root δο-, reduplication with _epsilon_? Must be what form (444; 484)? Modifies what word here?

      δεῖ σωθῆναι   Para. 292.1. -θῆναι can only be _____ (293).

4.13 θεωροῦντες . . .
      καὶ καταλαβόμενοι   Modify what verbs?

      τήν. . .παροησίαν   Don't let the word order bother you.

      τε   Postpositive conjunction, so that what two words are actually joined here?

      ἐπεγίνωσκον   How different from γινώσκω, without ἐπί? Dee DM, p. 106, on the preposition in compound.

4.15 ἑστῶτα   ἑστά + οτα = ἑστῶτα: participle ending without _nu_ indicates what tense (433.2)? See AG on ἴστημι. Modifies τον ἄνθρωπον. How (424.1)? What other construction must go with τὸν ἄνθρωπον?

      τὸν τεθεραπευμένον   What signs of perfect (430; 444; 447)? What is the significance of that tense here?

523.1 Note the two verbs given with the commonly associated syntactic patterns, ἀφίημι and ἐπιτίθημι. Standard lexicons indicate such patterns using the appropriate forms of the indefinite pronoun, τις, τι, as follows:

ἀφίημι τί τινι, "I forgive something (N.A.sg.) to/for someone (M.D.sg.)," indicates that "ἀφίημι takes the accusative of the thing forgiven and the dative of the person to whom it is forgiven."

ἐπιτίθημι τί τινι, "I lay something (N.A.sg.) upon someone (M.D.sg.)," would indicate that ἐπιτίθημι takes the "accusative of the thing laid and the dative of person or thing upon which it is laid." Compare AG, pp. 302-303, on ἐπιτίθημι.

523.2 The adverb, μόνον, "only," is actually the neuter accusative singular of the adjective, μόνος, -α, -ον, "alone." Several N.A. sg. adjective forms function in the same way, as adverbs. Compare πρῶτον, "first of all," N.A. sg. of the adjective, πρῶτος, -η, -ον, "first."

524.1 Study these principal parts and make all the observations you can about their tense suffixes, methods of reduplication, personal endings, points of apparent regularity or irregularity.

525.1 Compare each of these points carefully with the patterns, of δίδωμι, in paras. 596-597. Where are they alike? Where different in essential pattern?

525.2 Remember to analyze the forms of τίθημι in terms of the stem θε- (as in para. 506.2), additions to it, alterations in it. Carefully study the forms in paras. 598-599 from this perspective. Do it! It will pay!

527.1 Note that the second aorist participle (para. 599) is identical to the endings of the regular aorist passive participle of the omega verbs (259), as is the present participle of τίθημι, with the addition of the τι- reduplication (598).

529.1 What does Machen mean by the statement that τίθημι has a first aorist active in the indicative mood, but a second aorist active in the other moods and subordinate forms? Compare the forms of δίδωμι at this point, para. 597.

532.1 How can the present and second aorist forms of ἀφίημι be distinguished?

534.1 Again one must abandon a word-for-word translation in this construction. Knowing that "ὥστε with the infinitive expresses result," translate with an English equivalent that clearly expresses result. Clauses introduced by "so that . . ." or even "with the result that . . ." are good. As with other subordinate clauses, make sure you see specifically of which other verb the result is here being given in the ὥστε clause (286.3; 288.5).

535.1 How do ὥστε and ὥσπερ and οὔτε appear to violate the general rules of accent (11.2)?

536.1 Do you understand why ἕως (ἄν) would take the subjunctive when it referred to an act yet to be accomplished, "Until I come?" If not, review 269.5.

537.I Aids to exercise I, Lesson XXXII

1. διὰ τοῦτό με ὁ πατὴρ ἀγαπᾷ ὅτι ἐγὼ τίθημι τὴν ψυχήν μου, ἵνα πάλιν λάβω αὐτήν. οὐδεὶς ἦρεν αὐτὴν ἀπ' ἐμοῦ, ἀλλ' ἐγὼ τίθημι αὐτὴν ἀπ' ἐμαυτοῦ. ἐξουσίαν ἔχω θεῖναι αὐτήν, καὶ ἐξουσίαν ἔχω πάλιν λαβεῖν αὐτήν.

    a. λάβω: primary ending, second aorist verb stem; must be what mood (269.3)?
    b. ἀγαπᾷ = _____ + _____ (316.I). Full identification (590)?
    c. ἦρεν: rho plus secondary ending should give clue to identity (333).
    d. What clause is in apposition to, is roughly equal to, the pronoun, τοῦτο (477.1-2)?
    e. θεῖναι: full identification (599). Why not present (530)?

2. αὕτη ἐστὶν ἡ ἐντολὴ ἡ ἐμή, ἵνα ἀγαπᾶτε ἀλλήλους καθὼς ἠγάπησα ὑμᾶς. μείζονα ταύτης ἀγάπην οὐδεὶς ἔχει, ἵνα τις τὴν ψυχὴν αὐτοῦ θῇ ὑπὲρ τῶν φίλων αὐτοῦ.

    a. ἀγαπᾶτε: which is it? ἀγαπα + ετε or + ητε (316.I; 286)? The implication of the tense here (283.1-2)?
    b. καθὼς clause modifies what verb? καθὼς introduces statements of comparison (as do ὡς, ὥσπερ). In such cases be sure you see what is being modified by the comparison, and how that comparison illuminates the word modified.
    c. μείζονα: why this gender, number and case (459)? Why genitive in ταύτης (462)?
    d. θῇ: identification (599)? θε + _____ = θῇ (316.I; 269)?
    e. Note the two ἵνα clauses, used as described in para. 477.1. Each of them stands in apposition to a different, single word, giving its content. Which word does each thus modify?

3. ἀλλὰ ἐλθὼν ἐπίθες τὴν χεῖρά σου ἐπ' αὐτὴν καὶ ζήσεται.

    a. ἐλθὼν ἐπίθες: remember 424.2. On ἐπίθες: no augment, but also no reduplication with iota; para. 599.
    b. αὐτήν presupposes the gospel context where a little girl is involved.

4. ὁ δὲ Ἰησοῦς εἶπεν Ἄφετε τὰ παιδία καὶ μὴ κωλύετε αὐτὰ ἐλθεῖν
πρός με· τῶν γὰρ τοιούτων ἐστὶν ἡ βασιλεία τῶν οὐρανῶν. καὶ
ἐπιθεὶς τὰς χεῖρας αὐτοῖς ἐπορεύθη ἐκεῖθεν.

   a. Don't miss the footnotes on these sentences.
   b. ἄφετε: why not present (531) Why not indicative (532) or
      subjunctive (599)?
   c. μὴ κωλύετε: give an exegetical translation (420.4).
   d. ἐπιθείς: -θείς should give clue to identify (527.1).
      Why not present (530)?
   e. τὰς χεῖρας: such expressions, where possession is obvious, often
      omit the possessive pronoun (αὐτοῦ, here), with the article alone
      giving sufficient specification, (Cf. CEG, p. 23(9)).

5. καὶ προσευξάμενοι ἐπέθηκαν αὐτοῖς τὰς χεῖρας.

   a. ἐπέθηκαν: what element points to τίθημι form (525.2)?
      Why not present (530)? Tense suffix = _____ (525)?
   b. -ξάμενοι: review paras. 183 and 156.1 on form if necessary;
      Para. 232.7 and 257.I.13d on syntax.

6. τότε ἐπετίθεσαν τὰς χεῖρας ἐπ᾽ αὐτούς, καὶ ἐλάμβανον πνεῦμα ἅγιον.

   a. ἐπετίθεσαν: sign of tense (525)?
      -σαν ending appears where on the mi verbs (598)?
   b. ἐλάμβανον: what implication from the tense here? Does it
      catch the "one by one," or "one after another" sense of the
      event in "repeated" action?

7. ἀκούσαντες δὲ ἐβαπτίσθησαν εἰς τὸ ὄνομα τοῦ κυρίου Ἰησοῦ· καὶ
ἐπιθέντος αὐτοῖς τοῦ Παύλου χεῖρας ἦλθε τὸ πνεῦμα τὸ ἅγιον ἐπ᾽
αὐτούς.

   a. ἐπιθέντος . . . τοῦ Παύλου: why genitive (266)?
      Why not present (530)? -θέντος by itself should clinch the
      identification (529.1).

8. ζωοποιεῖ ὁ υἱὸς τοῦ θεοῦ ὃν θέλει.

   a. Footnote? Explain the contraction on ζωοποιεῖ (316.I).
   b. ὃν θέλει: relative clauses functions as what part of the
      sentence (397.4)? Why is the relative pronoun accusative (397.3)?

9. ὑμεῖς ὃ ἠκούσατε ἀπ' ἀρχῆς, ἐν ὑμῖν μενέτω. ἐὰν ἐν ὑμῖν μείνῃ ὃ
ἀπ' ἀρχῆς ἠκούσατε, καὶ ὑμεῖς ἐν τῷ υἱῷ καὶ ἐν τῷ πατρὶ μενεῖτε.

    a. Full identification of these verbs?
        μενέτω (407-17.3) Remember 420.4!
        μείνῃ (333; 288)
        μενεῖτε (328)
    b. What <u>clause</u> is the subject of μενέτω (397.4)? Of μείνῃ?

10. καὶ ἐγένετο ὡσεὶ νεκρός, ὥστε τοὺς πολλοὺς λέγειν ὅτι ἀπέθανεν.

    a. ὥστε plus the infinitive expresses what (534)? Give an
        exegetical translation. Was the report repeated or continuing
        (299)?
    b. τοὺς πολλούς: why accusative (304)?

11. ἴσθι ἐκεῖ ἕως ἂν εἴπω σοι· μέλλει γὰρ Ἡρῴδης ζητεῖν τὸ παιδίον
τοῦ ἀπολέσαι αὐτό.

    a. ἴσθι: para. 602.
    b. εἴπω: why this mood (536; 278)?
    c. τοῦ ἀπολέσαι: genitive with the _____ _____ expresses
        _____ (468). -σαι had to be what form here (293)?
    d. αὐτό: why neuter?

12. Κύριε, σῶσον, ἀπολλύμεθα.

    a. σῶσον: full identification (401)?
    b. ἀπολλύμεθα: review 533 and relate to ἀπολέσαι of last sentence.
        The present tense is sometimes used for events which are about
        to happen (CEG, p. 53f). Would that work here? How translated
        then?

13. καὶ ἀνοίξας τὸ βιβλίον εὗρεν τὸν τόπον.

    ἀνοίξας: which is best, temporal or co-ordinate circumstance
    (254.3 or 434.2)?

14. τὰ δὲ ἐκπορευόμενα ἐκ τοῦ στόματος ἐκ τῆς καρδίας ἐξέρχεται.

15. οὐ περὶ τούτων δὲ ἐρωτῶ μόνον, ἀλλὰ καὶ περὶ τῶν πιστευόντων διὰ τοῦ λόγου αὐτῶν εἰς ἐμέ, ἵνα πάντες ἓν ὦσιν, καθὼς σύ, πατήρ, ἐν ἐμοὶ κἀγὼ ἐν σοί, ἵνα καὶ αὐτοὶ ἐν ἡμῖν ὦσιν, ἵνα ὁ κόσμος πιστεύῃ ὅτι σύ με ἀπέστειλας.

    a. ἐρωτῶ: full identification? Circumflex indicates what (316.III.1)?
          _____ + _____ = ἐρωτῶ (316.I)?
    b. τῶν πιστευόντων: use of the participle (235.1)? Implication of the tense (233.5)?
    c. ἓν ὦσιν: not ἐν (371)! Verb form which is comprised only of the lengthened primary ending? What is it (282.1 and 602)?
    d. ἀπέστειλας: full identification (333)?
    e. Review the emphatic use of pronouns here.
    f. Diagram the sentence's main clause structure here.

16. εἶπεν οὖν ὁ Ἰησοῦς Ἔτι χρόνον μικρὸν μεθ᾽ ἡμῶν εἰμι καὶ ὑπάγω πρὸς τὸν πέμψαντά με.

17. ὅτι δὲ ἤγγισεν ὁ καιρὸς τῶν καρπῶν, ἀπέστειλεν τοὺς δούλους αὐτοῦ.

    a. Review simple third principal part formation if the main verbs give you trouble (171-177; 333).
    b. How does the ὅτε clause modify the main verb?

18. αὐτὸς δὲ σωθήσεται, οὕτως δὲ ὡς διὰ πυρός.

537.II NEW TESTAMENT GREEK READING

Translate Acts 4.15-18

4.15 κελεύσαντες . . . αὐτούς . . . ἀπελθεῖν	How is the content of the command given here (306)? Why accusative αὐτούς (304)?
συνέβαλλον	Why the imperfect? Consult DM, pp. 188-189. The lively inter-change of one member participating after another comes through.
4.16 λέγοντες	Para. 402.1
τί ποιήσωμεν	Para. 394

(1) ὅτι (2) μὲν   "For (3) the fact that (1) indeed
(3) γὰρ   (2) . . ."

ὅτι . . . αὐτῶν   This whole ὅτι clause is the subject of
a verbless clause (477.2). Such a
clause is grammatically neuter when modified. What
is the predicate adjective then?

κατοικοῦσιν   Paras. 226 and 591

ἀρνεῖσθαι   -σθαι can only be what (293)?
Review that paragraph for several forms
coming up here.

4.17 ἐπὶ πλεῖον   "Any further (of place)"

ἀπειλησώμεθα   New but regular. Look it up. Use (285)?

λαλεῖν   "To go on speaking." Why so (299)?

4.18 παρήγγειλαν   Remember para. 333?

Lesson XXXIII

538.1 Continue the habit of relating new words encountered in Greek to known English derivatives or near derivatives.
   Docetic/Docetism   _____
   dynamo (note the "y")   _____
   "hetero" words (Cf. Gal. 1.6-7) _____
   Homoiousian (Cf. Homoousian)   _____

539.1 Study the principal parts of this <u>mi</u> verb as you did those in the preceding two lessons, making all the deductions of your own which you can before proceeding in Machen's explanation.

540.1 Notice the normal lengthening of the stem vowel (alpha) before the tense suffixes. Compare para. 321 and the patterns observed for δίδωμι (484) and τίθημι (524).

542.1 Exactly <u>how</u> is the present conjugation of ἵστημι like that of δίδωμι and τίθημι (600; 596; 598)? Spell it out!

544.1 How do the first aorist and second aorist forms differ in meaning for ἵστημι?

548.1 It is understandable that the perfect of ἵστημι would come to have a meaning roughly equivalent to the present, since the perfect states a present condition, "I have come to stand," or "I stand (having taken my stand)." How is the regular present used?

548.2 How do the second perfect forms differ from the regular perfects in the participle forms (Cf. the second aorist passive, 206)?

550.1 For a more extensive introduction to the optative mood, consult DM, pp. 53, 172-174, and the pull-out table of conjugations for the full conjugational patterns.

551.1 How can you identify a condition contrary to fact? Note the implied reversal of the statement: "If you had been (but you were not). . ."

551.2 Summarize your knowledge of Greek conditional statements here.
   <u>Condition of fact</u> is expressed by (288.2):
   <u>Condition of contingency</u> is expressed by (288.3):
   <u>Condition contrary to fact</u> is expressed by (551):

552.1 What may be a clue that γίνομαι means something other than "become?" Cf. Jn. 1.3,6.

554.1 Aids to exercise I, Lesson XXXIII.

   1. διὰ τοῦτο ὁ κόσμος οὐ γινώσκει ἡμᾶς ὅτι οὐκ ἔγνω αὐτόν. Ἀγαπητοί, νῦν τέκνα θεοῦ ἐσμεν, καὶ οὔπω ἐφανερώθη τί ἐσόμεθα. οἴδαμεν ὅτι ἐὰν φανερωθῇ ὅμοιοι αὐτῷ ἐσόμεθα, ὅτι ὀψόμεθα αὐτὸν καθώς ἐστιν.

a. ἔγνω: augment, lengthened verb root γνο- (150.2), without personal ending (i.e., zero morpheme)? Identify fully (601).

b. ἀγαπητοί: see Lexical Aids, p. 44 (B.5), on such adjectives.

c. τέκνα θεοῦ: what significance to lack of articles (99.3)?

d. How is each ὅτι clause used here (477.2)?

e. Identify the being verbs here correctly, along with the others (602).

2. ἔλεγον οὖν αὐτῷ Ποῦ ἐστιν ὁ πατήρ σου ἀπεκρίθη Ἰησοῦς Οὔτε ἐμὲ οἴδατε οὔτε τὸν πατέρα μου· εἰ ἐμὲ ᾔδειτε, καὶ τὸν πατέρα μου ἂν ᾔδειτε.

a. ἔλεγον: why imperfect? Compare Acts. 4.7, ἐπυνθάνοντο, and your observations in 480.II on that verb.

b. οὔτε . . . οὔτε: don't miss the compound, just because of the emphatic placement of the first element.

c. Contrast the forms of οἶδα and ᾔδειν here (603; and 450.1).

d. What kind of a condition is the last line? How are you sure (551)? Implications?

3. ζητήσετέ με καὶ οὐχ εὑρήσετε, καὶ ὅπου εἰμὶ ἐγὼ ὑμεῖς οὐ δύνασθε ἐλθεῖν.

δύνασθε: like δεῖ and ἔξεστιν and μέλλει, usually takes the infinitive to complete it (538; 600).

4. καὶ συνέρχεται πάλιν ὁ ὄχλος, ὥστε μὴ δύνασθαι αὐτοὺς μηδὲ ἄρτον φαγεῖν.

a. συνέρχεται: what use of the present (165.II, on Jn. 1.15)?

b. ὥστε clause modifies what word and how (534 and 534.1)?

c. μηδέ: para. 147.

5. ἠκούσατε ὅτι ἐγὼ εἶπον ὑμῖν Ὑπάγω καὶ ἔρχομαι πρὸς ὑμᾶς. εἰ ἠγαπᾶτέ με, ἐχάρητε ἂν ὅτι πορεύομαι πρὸς τὸν πατέρα, ὅτι ὁ πατὴρ μείζων μού ἐστιν.

a. ὑπάγω and ἔρχομαι: on the tense see again CEG, p. 53(f).

b. εἰ . . . ἄν, with secondary tenses in indicative mood. What construction (551)?

c. ἠγαπᾶτε: explain the contraction: _____ + _____ = ἠγαπᾶτε (316.I).

d. μου: why genitive (462)?

6. εὗρεν ἄλλους ἑστῶτας καὶ λέγει αὐτοῖς Τί ὧδε ἑστήκατε ὅλην τὴν
ἡμέραν;

    a. εὗρεν . . . λέγει: how can these tenses be paralleled
       (4.a above)?

    b. ἑστῶτας: why not present (548; 533.2)?

7. προφήτην ἡμῖν ἀναστήσει κύριος ὁ θεὸς ἐκ τῶν ἀδελφῶν ὑμῶν ὡς
ἐμέ· αὐτοῦ ἀκούσεσθε κατὰ πάντα ὅσα ἂν λαλήσῃ ὑμῖν.

    a. Identify the verbs fully; see the footnote.
       Relate ἀναστήσει to the verb root, στα- (540).

    b. ὡς is followed by a noun/pronoun in the same case as the
       word with which the comparison is being made. What two
       words are involved here?

    c. αὐτοῦ: why genitive (119)?

8. καὶ ἀναστὰς ὁ ἀρχιερεὺς εἶπεν αὐτῷ Οὐδὲν ἀποκρίνῃ;

    a. ἀναστάς: transitive or intransitive (538 and 601)? What is
       the difference in meaning?

    b. ἀποκρίνῃ: indicative or subjunctive (139.1)?

9. τότε οὖν εἰσῆλθεν καὶ ὁ ἄλλος μαθητὴς ὁ ἐλθὼν πρῶτος εἰς τὸ
μνημεῖον, καὶ εἶδεν καὶ ἐπίστευσεν· οὐδέπω γὰρ ᾔδεισαν τὴν
γραφήν, ὅτι δεῖ αὐτὸν ἐκ νεκρῶν ἀναστῆναι.

    a. εἶδεν/ᾔδεισαν: identify fully (186; 450.1 and 603).
       How do they differ in form? Signs of tense in each?

    b. ἀναστῆναι: -ναι indicates what in the mi verbs (596-603)?
       Did you see all nine forms involved in those paragraphs?
       Why not present (540)?

10. εἰ ἐν Σοδόμοις ἐγενήθησαν αἱ δυνάμεις αἱ γενόμεναι ἐν σοί,
ἔμεινεν ἂν μέχρι τῆς σήμερον.

    a. What kind of condition here? How do you know (551)? What
       are the main words involved?

    b. ἐγενήθησαν: meaning here (552)?

    c. Don't miss the footnotes here.

11. Ἔδωκεν αὐτοῖς δύναμιν καὶ ἐξουσίαν ἐπὶ πάντα τὰ δαιμόνια.

Review the forms of δύναμις encountered so far and compare the declension of πόλις, para. 349.

12. ἐγένετο δὲ ἐν τῷ βαπτισθῆναι ἅπαντα τὸν λαὸν καὶ Ἰησοῦ βαπτισθέντος καὶ προσευχομένου ἀνεῳχθῆναι τὸν οὐρανόν, καὶ καταβῆναι τὸ πνεῦμα τὸ ἅγιον.

   a. Footnote on ἅπαντα? What accusative (304)? Review para. 305.3 right now if this opening prepositional construction is not plain to you.

   b. Ἰησοῦ βαπτισθέντος καὶ προσευχομένου: why genitive (266)? If parallel to ἐν τῷ βαπτισθῆναι, what sort of adverbial clause is this (305.3)?

   c. ἀνεῳχθῆναι and καταβῆναι: -θῆναι and -ναι should be clear indicators (293; and sentence 9b above). The verb root of βαίνω is βα- (cf. 506.2 and 150.2).
Luke often uses infinitives + accusative nouns for main statements (e.g., Lk. 3.21).

13. ἐγένετο δὲ ἐν ταῖς ἡμέραις ἐκείναις ἐξελθεῖν αὐτὸν εἰς τὰ ὄρη προσεύξασθαι.

   a. ἐγένετο: see para. 552 again.

   b. τὰ ὄρη: if not clear, review para. 352.

14. ἐξῆλθον δὲ ἰδεῖν τὸ γεγονός, καὶ ἦλθον πρὸς τὸν Ἰησοῦν, καὶ εὗρον καθήμενον τὸν ἄνθρωπον ἀφ' οὗ τὰ δαιμόνια ἐξῆλθον.

   a. ἰδεῖν: para. 296.

   b. τὸ γεγονός: full identification and use (433 and 433.1)?

   c. καθήμενον: full identification (538) and use (424.1)? Modifies what word?

15. καὶ ἐγένετο ἐν τῷ εἶναι αὐτὸν ἐν τόπῳ τινὶ προσευχόμενον, ὡς ἐπαύσατο, εἶπέν τις τῶν μαθητῶν αὐτοῦ πρὸς αὐτὸν Κύριε δίδαξον ἡμᾶς προσεύχεσθαι, καθὼς καὶ Ἰωάνης ἐδίδαξεν τοὺς μαθητὰς αὐτοῦ.

   a. ἐν τῷ εἶναι αὐτόν: review 305.3 again if necessary.

   b. προσευχόμενον: used as subject complement. Relates to the subject as the participles noted in para. 424.1 relate to the object. Compare καθήμενον in 14 above.

   c. δίδαξον. -σον, if sigma is a tense suffix, must indicate _____ (411).

d. ἐπαύσατο: footnote? Is there anything puzzling about this form? Shouldn't be.

16. ὁ δὲ ἔφη αὐτῷ Ἀγαπήσεις κύριον τὸν θεόν σου ἐν ὅλῃ τῇ καρδίᾳ σου.

ἔφη: para. 538. Compare the lengthening of γνο- to γνω in the second aorist (601).

17. δοκεῖτε ὅτι εἰρήνην παρεγενόμην δοῦναι ἐν τῇ γῇ;

18. περὶ τίνος ὁ προφήτης λέγει τοῦτο; περὶ ἑαυτοῦ ἢ περὶ ἑτέρου τινός;

19. αὐτὸς ἡμᾶς βαπτίσει ἐν πνεύματι ἁγίῳ καὶ πυρί.

554.II NEW TESTAMENT GREEK READING

Translate Acts 4.19-22

4.19	See notes on 480.I.7 if you have trouble.
4.20 μὴ λαλεῖν	What is the object of this infinitive (397.4)?
4.21 προσαπειλησάμενοι DM, p. 110)?	Cf. ἀπειλέομαι in 4.17 above. What does the πρός- add here (CEG, p. 44, or
μηδέν	Para. 371, 372.
εὑρίσκοντες manner? Which	How does it modify the leading verb adverbially? Gives time, or cause, or one? See CEG, pp. 65-67.
τῷ γεγονότι	Para. 433 and 433.1.
4.22 ἐτῶν	ἔτος, ἔτους: para. 352.
τὸ σημεῖον . . . τῆς ἰάσεως	How is the genitive used here? See DM, p. 79(6), if you don't see.

STUDY GUIDE TO MACHEN'S NEW TESTAMENT GREEK FOR BEGINNERS

APPENDIX: EXERCISES TRANSLATED

David L. Thompson
Asbury Theological Seminary
Wilmore, Kentucky

Lesson II
15.I

15.I   1. ἐλύομεν, ἐλυόμην, ἐλύσω. 2. ἐλύου, ἔλυε, ἐλυσάμην. 3. δίδασκε, διδάσκονται, διδασκόμεθα. 4. λῦε, λύου, λύουσι. 5. λῦσαι, λύσω, λύετε.

15.II   1. ἀποστόλοις, ἀποστόλους, ἀποστόλου, ἀπόστολοι, ἀποστόλῳ.
    2. κώμαις, κῶμαι, κώμας, κώμῃ. 3. πλοῖα, πλοίων, πλοίοις, πλοίου, πλοίῳ, πλοῖον.

Lesson III

23.I.   1. You see, are seeing. You know, are knowing. You take, are taking.
    2. He (she, it) writes, is writing. He (she, it) is having. He (she, it) says, is saying. 3. He (she, it) looses, is loosing. He (she, it) teaches, is teaching. He (she, it) sees, is seeing. 4. We take, are taking. We have, are having. We know, are knowing. 5. You (pl.) see, are seeing. You (pl.) say, are saying. You (pl.) write, are writing. 6. They teach, are teaching. They take, are taking. They loose, are loosing. 7. You (pl.) know, are knowing. You know, are knowing. We know, are knowing. 8. We see, are seeing. They teach, are teaching. He (she, it) says, is saying. 9. You have, are having. They see, are seeing. We take, are taking.

23.II.   1. γινώσκομεν, βλέπομεν, βλέπομεν. 2. λύουσι(ν), λύουσι(ν), λύει.
    3. λύει, ἔχετε, γινώσκεις. 4. λαμβάνω, γινώσκομεν, γέγουσι.
5. ἔχει, γράφομεν, βλέπουσι(ν).

Lesson IV

45.I.   1. A brother sees (is seeing) a man.[1] 2. A servant writes (is writing) words. 3. Apostles are teaching a man. 4. Apostles are loosing servants. 5. A servant takes (or receives) gifts. 6. Sons take houses. 7. Brothers are taking servants and houses. 8. We see temples and apostles. 9. You see servants and brothers. 10. You are writing a word to an apostle. 11. He teaches a man. 12. A brother says a word to an apostle. 13. A brother of apostles knows a law. 14. Servants know a law and (they) receive gifts. 15. Men know death. 16. We take gifts and have brothers. 17. We say words of death (i.e., about death) to apostles and servants; or, To apostles and servants we say words of death. 18. Brothers and servants know and see temples and gifts. 19. An apostle is writing a law and saying words to a servant's sons (to sons of a servant.) 20. Sons of apostles (apostles' sons) say words and loose servants.

45.II.   1. δοῦλος γράφει νόμον.[2] 2. υἱὸς βλέπει λόγους. 3. ἀδελφοὶ λύουσι δούλους. 4. υἱοὶ λαμβάνουσι δῶρα. 5. δοῦλον καὶ δῶρον βλέπει ἀπόστολος. 6. δοῦλοι καὶ υἱοὶ λέγουσι λόγον ἀδελφῷ. 7. βλέπομεν

---

[1]The alternate verb translation is possible though unnecessary throughout.
[2]Remember that the Greek word order may vary slightly depending upon emphasis.

δῶρα καὶ δούλους.   8. ἄνθρωποι βλέπουσι λόγους καὶ δῶρα ἀδελφοῦ καὶ οἴκους ἀποστόλων καὶ υἱῶν.   9. λόγους καὶ νόμους γράφομεν ἀδελφοῖς· λόγον θανάτου λέγομεν δούλῳ.   10. υἱὸς βλέπει ἱερὰ καὶ οἴκους.   11. γινώσκετε θάνατον.
12. λαμβάνεις δῶρον ἀποστόλου.   13. γράφεις λόγον ἀδελφοῦ δούλῳ.   14. λύω δούλους καὶ λέγω λόγους υἱοῖς καὶ ἀδελφοῖς.   15. υἱὸς βλέπει θάνατον.
16. νόμους γινώσκουσι καὶ διδάσκουσι δούλους ἀποστόλου.

Lesson V

59.I.   1. A soul sees life. (Without a context the translation choice between the single present, "sees," and the present for continuing action, "is seeing," is purely arbitrary.)   2. A kingdom knows truth.   3. A man writes commandments and laws.   4. Apostles receive servants and gifts and churches.   5. Apostles and churches see life and death.   6. A servant's son says a parable to a church.   7. We are saying a parable and a command and a law; or, A parable we are saying, and a command and a law.   8. You know kingdoms and churches.   9. An apostle teaches a church and a servant a kingdom (i.e., a servant [teaches] a kingdom).   10. A man writes a law and a parable to a church.   11. Hearts of men have life and peace.   12. A voice of apostles teaches souls of servants.   13. An hour has glory.   14. Churches' voices teach kingdoms and men.   15. You see gifts and glory.   16. He writes a church (i.e., to a church) a word of life.   17. He is saying a parable and a law to hearts of men (men's hearts).   18. An apostle's son is writing to a church.

59.II.   1. βασιλεία λαμβάνει δόξαν.   2. ἐκκλησίαι λέγουσι παραβολὰς καρδίαις ἀνθρώπων.   3. καρδία ἀνθρώπου διδάσκει ἀπόστολον, καὶ φωνὴ ἀποστόλου (διδάσκει) δοῦλον.   4. γραφὰς ἀποστόλων ἔχομεν.   5. ἐκκλησίαι ἔχουσιν εἰρήνην καὶ δόξαν.   6. ἡμέρα βλέπει ζωήν καὶ θάνατον.   7. λαμβάνουσιν ἀπόστολοι ἱερὰ καὶ βασιλείας.   8. οἴκους βλέπομεν καὶ ἱερὰ καὶ ἐκκλησίας.   9. δοῦλος λέγει παραβολὴν καρδίαις ἀνθρώπων.   10. φωνὰς ἐκκλησιῶν γινώσκομεν καὶ λόγους ἀληθείας.   11. φωνὴ ἀποστόλου λέγει παραβολὴν ψυχαῖς ἀνθρώπων.

Lesson VI

76.I.   1. Good is the church, and the kingdom is bad; or, The church is good, and the kingdom is bad.   2. The evil heart of the men knows death.
3. The apostles see the small houses and the bad (evil) ways (roads).   4. The evil servants (i.e., the servants, the bad ones) destroy the house of the apostle (or, the apostle's house.)   5. The wicked (ones, men, persons, people) are destroying the temple.   6. The Lord of life raises the dead (ones, men, persons, people). 7. The words of truth[3] teach the other apostles.   8. The righteous (ones, men, persons, people) are receiving the good gifts of the Lord (the Lord's good gifts.)   9. The wicked man (one, person) sees the desert and the last houses.   10. First are the servants,[4] last (are) the lords.   11. The Lord is writing a good word to the small church.   12. The faithful one (man, person) sees

---

[3]"Life" and "truth" are specified in some sense in the Greek text by the article, but the English cannot easily translate that specification in this case.
[4]Greek may use semi-colon where English style demands comma.

the faithful men (ones, persons, people.)   13. The wicked servants are last; the good sons are first.   14. The son of the last brother sees the Lord's good churches (the good churches of the Lord).   15. We (are) say(ing) another parable to the evil kingdom.   16. First is the church; last is the other king-dom. (Order can be reversed of course.)   17. The Lord is saying a good (i.e., suitable) parable to the faithful women and the faithful men.   18. The good man (one, person) writes good things,[5] the bad person, bad things.   19. The servant is good and says good things.   20. The truth is faithful, and the hour is evil (bad).

76.II.   1. τῇ πρώτῃ ἐκκλησίᾳ ὁ κύριος γράφει τὴν παραβολὴν τὴν πρώτην (τὴν πρώτην παραβολήν).   2. ἡ ἀγαθὴ βλέπει τὰς ὁδοὺς τῆς ἐρήμου.
3. πρῶτα τὰ ἀγαθὰ καὶ τὰ κακὰ ἔσχατα.   4. ὁ θάνατος κακὸς καὶ ἡ ζωὴ καλή.
5. ὁ κύριος τῆς βασιλείας ἐγείρει τοὺς πιστοὺς καὶ τὰς πιστάς.   6. οἱ ἀγαθοὶ γινώσκουσι τοὺς κακοὺς καὶ οἱ κακοὶ τοὺς ἀγαθούς.   7. τοὺς ἀγαθοὺς λόγους λέγομεν τῇ ἐκκλησίᾳ καὶ τοὺς λόγους τοὺς κακοὺς γράφομεν τοῖς ἀδελφοῖς.
8. βλέπεις τὰς καλὰς ἡμέρας τοῦ κυρίου τῆς ζωῆς.   9. καλαὶ αἱ ὁδοὶ καὶ κακοὶ οἱ ἄνθρωποι.   10. τὸ πρῶτον δῶρον ἔσχατον καὶ τὸ ἔσχατον πρῶτον.
11. οἱ ἀγαθοὶ δοῦλοι γινώσκουσι τὴν ἀλήθειαν καὶ τὴν δόξαν τοῦ κυρίου.
12. ἡ ἡμέρα ἡ ἐσχάτη λαμβάνει τοὺς κακοὺς δούλους.   13. οἱ ἄνθρωποι λύουσι τὰ ἱερὰ τὰ καλὰ καὶ τοὺς μικροὺς οἴκους.   14. οἱ δίκαιοι ἔχουσιν ἄλλον οἶκον.   15. ἡ ἐκκλησία λαμβάνει τὸν ἄλλον οἶκον.   16. γινώσκω τὰς ἄλλας ὁδούς.   17. ὁ κύριος λέγει τὴν παραβολὴν τὴν ἄλλην τῇ πρώτῃ ἐκκλησίᾳ.

Lesson VII

89.I.   1. The disciples of the prophets remain (are remaining) in the world.
2. The wicked (men, ones, people) are throwing stones into the disciples' house (the house of the disciples).   3. God sends (is sending) the angels into the world.   4. The prophet is sending the Lord's disciples out of the houses into the church.   5. God raises the dead (ones, men, people) out of death. (Remember the note on 76.I.6, 7.)   6. You are receiving (taking) the good gifts from the children.   7. We are leading the children out of the houses.   8. After the angels God sends (is sending) the Son.
9. With the angels the Lord is leading the righteous into heaven.   10. Through the ways of the desert the servants are bringing the gifts into another place.
11. Through the writings of the prophets we know the Lord.   12. On account of (because of) the glory of God the Lord raises the dead.   13. They are carrying the dead into the desert.   14. The disciples are teaching (teach) the good children in the church.   15. The Lord is saying (says) a parable to the disciples in the temple.   16. On account of the truth the prophets see death (in some specific sense.)   17. The disciples are leading the good servants and the sons of the prophets from (i.e., away from) the desert to the small houses of the disciples (the disciples' small houses.)   18. On account of (because of) the kingdom of God we bear the evil (things.)   19. On account of the souls of the brethren he sees evil (things).   20. Heaven is good (beautiful); the world is evil (or with the adjectives first).

---

[5]Greek may use semi-colon where English style demands comma.

Lesson VII
89.II.1

89.II. 1. ἐν τῷ κόσμῳ ἔχομεν θάνατον καὶ ἐν τῇ ἐκκλησίᾳ ζωήν. 2. οἱ προφῆται ἄγουσι τοὺς δικαίους μαθητὰς τοῦ κυρίου εἰς τὴν ὁδὸν τῆς ἐρήμου. 3. τὸ τέκνον βάλλει λίθον εἰς τὸν μικρὸν οἶκον (τὸν οἶκον τὸν μικρόν). 4. ὁ ἄνθρωπος λέγει ἀγαθὸν λόγον (λόγον ἀγαθὸν) τοῖς μαθηταῖς καὶ ἄγει τοὺς μαθητὰς πρὸς τὸν κύριον. 5. οἱ μαθηταὶ μένουσιν ἐν τῇ ἐκκλησίᾳ καὶ λέγουσι παραβολὴν τοῖς ἄλλοις προφήταις. 6. διὰ τῆς φωνῆς τοῦ προφήτου διδάσκει ὁ κύριος τοὺς μαθητάς. 7. διὰ τὴν ἐκκλησίαν οἱ μαθηταὶ καὶ οἱ ἀπόστολοι γράφουσιν ἀγαθοὺς λόγους (λόγους ἀγαθοὺς) τοῖς ἀδελφοῖς. 8. διὰ τὰ τέκνα πέμπει ὁ προφήτης τοὺς κακοὺς εἰς τὴν ἔρημον. 9. μετὰ τὸν κύριον τὸν μαθητὴν βλέπει ὁ ἀπόστολος. 10. διδάσκουσιν οἱ προφῆται τοὺς μαθητὰς μετὰ τῶν τέκνων. 11. φέρουσι τοὺς μαθητὰς πρὸς τὸν κύριον. 12. μένει ὁ κύριος μετὰ τοῦ προφήτου ἐν ἄλλῳ τόπῳ. 13. ἄγουσιν οἱ δίκαιοι τοὺς μαθητὰς διὰ τῆς ἐρήμου πρὸς τὸν κύριον. 14. βλέπομεν τὰς ἡμέρας τοῦ υἱοῦ τοῦ θεοῦ ἐν τῷ κόσμῳ τῷ κακῷ. 15. κακαὶ αἱ ἡμέραι· ἀγαθαὶ αἱ ἐκκλησίαι. 16. διὰ τοῦ λόγου τοῦ κυρίου ἐγείρει ὁ θεὸς τοὺς νεκρούς.

Lesson VIII

100.I. 1. Your disciples know the kingdom and are leading their brothers into it. 2. I am teaching my brothers and saying a parable to them. 3. The Lord is leading me to His disciples. 4. On account of me you see death, but I say evil words to you. 5. Through you God leads the faithful into His kingdom, and through them the others. 6. On account of us the Lord remains in the world. 7. I am a servant, but you (are) an apostle. 8. The Lord is good, and you are good. 9. You are the Lord's disciples and brothers of His apostles. 10. The apostle is faithful, but his servants are evil. 11. The church is faithful, and we see her/it. 12. We see you, and we are saying a parable to you. 13. We are servants, but (and) we teach servants. 14. Our servants see us, and we teach them. 15. From you my brother receives good gifts and sends them to me through his servants. 16. We know the way, and through it we are leading you into our house. 17. With our brothers we see our Lord's disciples (the disciples of our Lord). 18. After the evil days we see the kingdom of our Lord. 19. With us you see him. 20. We are in your houses with you.

100.II. 1. οἱ δοῦλοί σου εἰσιν ἐν τῷ οἴκῳ τοῦ κυρίου. 2. ὁ οἶκός μου ἐστιν ἐν τῇ ἐρήμῳ. 3. ὁ προφήτης γινώσκει τοὺς μαθητὰς αὐτοῦ καὶ φέρει αὐτοὺς εἰς τοὺς οἴκους αὐτοῦ. 4. διὰ τοῦ λόγου μου ἔχετε δόξαν. 5. διὰ τὰ τέκνα ἡμῶν βλέπετε κακὰς ἡμέρας. 6. ἐν ταῖς ἡμέραις ἡμῶν κακὸς ὁ κόσμος (κακός ἐστιν ὁ κόσμος). 7. γινώσκει ὁ θεὸς τὰς ψυχὰς ἡμῶν καὶ φέρει/ἄγει αὐτὰς ἐκ θανάτου. 8. οἱ υἱοὶ ἡμῶν ἐστὲ ὑμεῖς καὶ οἱ μαθηταὶ ὑμῶν ἐσμεν ἡμεῖς. 9. ἐν τῇ βασιλείᾳ τοῦ θεοῦ ἐσμεν (ἡμεῖς) μετὰ τῶν μαθητῶν σου τῶν πιστῶν. 10. ἡμεῖς λέγομεν παραβολήν σοι, σὺ δὲ λέγεις ἄλλον λόγον ἡμῖν. 11. κακή ἐστιν ἡ ὁδός, ἡμεῖς δὲ ἄγομεν τὰ τέκνα ἐν αὐτῇ. 12. λαμβάνει ὁ ἀδελφός μου δῶρα ἀφ' ὑμῶν, γράφετε δὲ ὑμεῖς κακὸν λόγον αὐτῷ. 13. ὁ οἶκός μου (ἐστιν) κακός, οἱ δὲ μαθηταί σου φέρουσι (ἄγουσι) τὰ τέκνα ἐξ αὐτοῦ. 14. ἄγουσιν οἱ μαθηταί μου τοὺς ἀδελφοὺς αὐτῶν πρός με. 15. (ἐγὼ) βλέπω καὶ γινώσκω τοὺς υἱούς μου καὶ ἄγω αὐτοὺς πρὸς τὸν κύριόν μου. 16. γινώσκει ὁ θεὸς τὴν ἐκκλησίαν αὐτοῦ καὶ ἄγει αὐτὴν ἐκ (τοῦ) θανάτου εἰς τὴν βασιλείαν αὐτοῦ. 17. καλαὶ καὶ δίκαιαι (ἐισιν) αἱ ἐντολαί σου, καὶ ἄγουσιν ἡμᾶς εἰς τὴν ζωήν. 18. ὁ κύριος ἡμῶν πέμπει τοὺς ἀποστόλους αὐτοῦ πρός με. 19. ἡμεῖς πέμπομεν τοὺς δούλους ἡμῶν εἰς τὸν ὑμῶν οἶκον, ὑμεῖς δὲ λαμβάνετε τὰ δῶρα ἡμῶν ἀφ' ἡμῶν. 20. ἀγαθοί ἐστε ὑμεῖς, κακοὶ δὲ (εἰσιν) οἱ μαθηταὶ ὑμῶν.

Lesson IX

107.I. 1. These teachers are judging the apostle himself. 2. And the same teacher has the same joy in his heart. 3. Now I myself am receiving the same gospel from my Lord. 4. This man (one, person) sees that one and judges him. 5. After these things you yourselves have the love of the Lord in your hearts. 6. These men have joy, and/but those men have sin. 7. And/but this is the voice of his Lord/or the Lord himself. 8. Thus we know this man, and we see his face. 9. We receive these gifts from the same man, and we see him. 10. You (sg.) yourself are baptizing that man, and you are his brother. 11. We are leading these our good teachers (these good teachers of us) into the same church. 12. I myself have this promise of my Lord. 13. This woman sees the face of her Lord. 14. She herself knows the truth itself. 15. Your promise is good, and you (sg.) yourself are good. 16. Those men are disciples of the same teacher. 17. This man is that man's teacher, and that man (is) this man's (teacher). 18. This man teaches the good men (ones, people), and he himself is good. 19. After those days we are teachers of these servants. 20. With the faithful we have good promises, but the evil see bad days.

107.II. 1. αὗται αἱ ἐκκλησίαι γινώσκουσι τὸν κύριον αὐτόν. 2. οἱ αὐτοὶ μαθηταὶ γινώσκουσιν αὐτὸν καὶ βλέπουσιν τὸ πρόσωπον αὐτοῦ. 3. ἐκεῖνοι οἱ διδάσκαλοι κρίνουσι τὰς αὐτὰς ἐκκλησίας καὶ ἄγουσιν αὐτὰς εἰς τὴν αὐτὴν χαράν. 4. αὐτοὶ ἔχομεν ταύτην τὴν ἁμαρτίαν ἐν ταῖς καρδίαις ἡμῶν. 5. αὕτη ἐστιν ἡ ἀγάπη τοῦ θεοῦ ἡμῶν. 6. αὗταί εἰσιν αἱ πισταὶ ἐκκλησίαι τοῦ κυρίου ἡμῶν. 7. ὁ ἀπόστολος αὐτὸς βαπτίζει τοὺς ἀδελφοὺς αὐτοῦ καὶ ἄγει αὐτοὺς πρὸς σέ. 8. διὰ τούτου τοῦ εὐαγγελίου ἔχομεν (τὴν) ζωήν. 9. διὰ τούτους τοὺς διδασκάλους βλέπομεν (τὸν) θάνατον. 10. αὐτὸς γινώσκει ἡμᾶς καὶ ἀπ' αὐτοῦ λαμβάνομεν ταύτην τὴν ἐπαγγελίαν. 11. διὰ τὸ αὐτὸ εὐαγγέλιον πέμπομεν αὐτοὶ τούτους τοὺς ἀποστόλους πρὸς ὑμᾶς. 12. εἰς τοῦτον τὸν κόσμον πέμπει τὸν κύριον αὐτόν. 13. ἐγὼ βλέπω τοῦτον (τὸν ἄνθρωπον) καὶ οἱ ἀδελφοὶ βλέπουσιν αὐτόν. 14. νῦν βαπτίζομεν ἐκείνους τοὺς μαθητὰς τοῦ κυρίου ἡμῶν καὶ πέμπομεν τοὺς αὐτοὺς μαθητὰς εἰς τὴν ἔρημον. 15. οἱ μαθηταί μου γινώσκουσι τὴν φωνήν μου καὶ φέρουσι ταῦτα πρός με. 16. διὰ τούτων φέρομεν τὸ αὐτὸ εὐαγγέλιον εἰς τὸν αὐτὸν κόσμον. 17. ἡμεῖς ἐσμὲν μαθηταὶ τοῦ κυρίου, ὑμεῖς δὲ ἐστε μαθηταὶ τοῦ πονηροῦ. 18. ἄγει αὕτη ἡ ἁμαρτία τὰ τέκνα ἡμῶν εἰς (τὸν) θάνατον. 19. αἱ ἁμαρτίαι τούτων τῶν ἐκκλησιῶν ἄγουσι ἄλλους (ἀνθρώπους) εἰς τὰς αὐτὰς ἁμαρτίας. 20. οἱ μαθηταὶ αὐτοῦ ἔχουσι ταύτην τὴν ἁμαρτίαν ἐν ταῖς καρδίαις αὐτῶν καὶ διδάσκουσι ἀνθρώπους οὕτως. 21. γινώσκω τὰς ἁμαρτίας τῶν μαθητῶν καὶ τοὺς μαθητὰς αὐτούς.

120.I. 1. These servants are being released by the Lord.   2. By (means
of) the word of the Lord we are being led into the Church of God.
3. You are not hearing the voice of the prophet, but you are going out of
his house.   4. By (means of) the word of the Lord Himself you are becoming His
disciples.   5. Those good teachers are not entering (do not enter) into the
houses of the sinners.   6. The sinners are not being baptized by the apostles,
but (in strong contrast) are going out of these houses to other teachers.
7. You say to those sinners that you are being saved by God from your sins.
8. God Himself rules His kingdom.   9. The Church has peace, because she/it
is being saved by her/its Lord.   10. We are not answering the apostle, because
we do not know him.   11. Not by the disciples are you being saved from your
sins, but by God Himself。   12. You are not going in the evil way, but you are
being saved from your sins, and your brothers are hearing the voice of the Lord.
13. With his brothers he is being led into the kingdom of God by (means of) the
voice of the apostles.   14。 You are not becoming a disciple of the Lord, because
you do not enter (are not entering) His Church.

120.II. 1. σῴζονται αὗται αἱ ἐκκλησίαι ὑπὸ τοῦ θεοῦ ἀπὸ (τοῦ) θανάτου.
2. σῴζομαι ὑπ' αὐτοῦ καὶ διδάσκομαι τῷ λόγῳ αὐτοῦ.   3. μαθηταὶ τοῦ
ἀποστόλου τοῦ ἀγαθοῦ γινόμεθα ἡμεῖς, ὑμεῖς δὲ οὐκ ἀκούετε τῆς φωνῆς αὐτοῦ.
4. ἁμαρτωλὸς εἰμί, διδάσκομαι δὲ ὑπὸ τῶν ἀποστόλων τοῦ κυρίου.   5. ἐγώ εἰμι
δοῦλος πονηρός, σὺ δὲ γίνῃ διδάσκαλος ταύτης τῆς ἐκκλησίας.   6. λέγουσιν οἱ
κακοὶ ἐκείναις ταῖς ἐκκλησίαις ὅτι οἱ ἀδελφοὶ ἡμῶν οὐ βλέπουσι τὸ πρόσωπον
τοῦ κυρίου.   7. λύεται ὁ κόσμος τῷ λόγῳ τοῦ θεοῦ ἡμῶν.   8. γινώσκομεν τὸν
κύριον ὅτι δῶρα καλὰ λαμβάνομεν παρ' αὐτοῦ καὶ διδασκόμεθα ὑπ' αὐτοῦ ἐν
παραβολαῖς.   9. γράφεις ταῦτα τοῖς ἀδελφοῖς σου καὶ σῴζῃ ἀπὸ τῆς ἁμαρτίας σου.
10. διδάσκει ἄλλους καὶ αὐτὸς διδάσκεται ὑπὸ τούτου τοῦ ἀποστόλου.   11. ἐκεῖνος
ὁ μαθητὴς οὐκ ἀποκρίνεται τούτῳ τῷ προφήτῃ ὅτι οὐ γινώσκει τοὺς λόγους αὐτοῦ.
12. λέγεις ταύτῃ τῇ ἐκκλησίᾳ ὅτι δοῦλος κακὸς εἶ.   13. ἐν ἐκείνῳ τῷ ἱερῷ
μένετε, ὅτι οὐκ ἐστὲ δοῦλοι τοῦ κυρίου.   14. οὐ βλέπομεν τὰ πρόσωπα τῶν
μαθητῶν τοῦ κυρίου ἡμῶν, ὅτι οὐκ ἐσμὲν ἐν τοῖς οἴκοις αὐτῶν.   15。 ἐν τῷ οἴκῳ
τοῦ κυρίου ἡμῶν χαρὰ καὶ εἰρήνη εἰσίν.   16. τῷ λόγῳ αὐτοῦ ἄρχει ὁ θεὸς τούτου
τοῦ κόσμου.   17. οὐκ εἰσέρχονται οὗτοι οἱ ἁμαρτωλοὶ εἰς τὸν οἶκον τοῦ κυρίου,
ἐξέρχονται δὲ εἰς τὴν ἔρημον.   18. οὗτοι οἱ λόγοι γράφονται ὑπὸ τοῦ θεοῦ ταῖς
ἐκκλησίαις αὐτοῦ ταῖς πισταῖς.

Lesson XI

135.I. 1. We were hearing (not we heard) his voice in those days, but now
we no longer hear it.   2. But (and) the Lord's disciple was saying
a parable to his brothers.   3. The servants were killing the children (along)
with the disciples。   4. Then on the one hand I was going down into the house,
(but) now on the other hand I no longer am going down; or, I used to do down ....
5. You were receiving the bread from the servants and (you) were eating it.
6. On account of the truth the disciples were dying in those days.   7. This
apostle was gathering together our Lord's disciples into the church.   8. Now
on the one hand we are being taught by the apostles, but then on the other hand
we were teaching the church.   9. Our Lord was taking away our sins.   10. Then

on the one hand they were going up into the temple, but now on the other hand they no longer are going up; or, ... They used to go up ... . 11. You were evil, but you <u>are</u> good. 12. You on the one hand are good, but we on the other are evil. 13. Then I was in the temple, and the Lord was teaching me. 14. We say to you that we were in your house. 15. You (sg.) were throwing them out of the temple. 16. The men were sending their servants to me. 17. The Lord was sending angels (messengers) to us. 18. He was in the world and the world was not seeing him. 19. You were a servant of the evil one, but now no longer are you a servant. 20. This is the man's gift, but it is not good.

135.II. 1. ὁ δοῦλος ἔλεγε τούτους τοὺς λόγους κατ' αὐτῶν. 2. κατὰ τὸν λόγον τοῦ ἀποστόλου ἀνέβαινον εἰς τὸ ἱερόν. 3. ἦν ὁ κύριος ἐν τῷ ἱερῷ αὐτοῦ. 4. ἀπέκτεινον τὰ τέκνα ἡμῶν. 5. ἀπεθνήσκετε ἐν ἐκείναις ταῖς ἡμέραις διὰ τὴν βασιλείαν τοῦ θεοῦ. 6. ἦρες τὰς ἁμαρτίας τῶν μαθητῶν σου. 7. ὁ προφήτης ἔπεμπε τοὺς αὐτοὺς δούλους εἰς τὸν μικρὸν οἶκον. 8. οὐκέτι ἐσμέν ἁμαρτωλοί, σῳζόμεθα γὰρ ὑπὸ τοῦ κυρίου ἀπὸ τῆς ἁμαρτιῶν τῶν καρδιῶν. 9. τοῦτο τὸν ἄρτον παρελάμβανον παρὰ τῶν δούλων τοῦ ἀποστόλου. 10. τότε ἔγραφε ταῦτα τοῖς ἀδελφοῖς αὐτοῦ. 11. ἐν ἐκείνῃ τῇ ὥρᾳ ἦμεν ἐν τῇ ἐρήμῳ μετὰ τοῦ κυρίου (σὺν τῷ κ.). 12. ἀγαθοί εἰσιν, ἀλλ' ἦσαν πονηροί. 13. ἀγαθὸς ἦς σύ, ἡμεῖς δὲ ἦμεν ἁμαρτωλοί. 14. τότε δοῦλος ἤμην, νῦν δὲ υἱός εἰμι. 15. οἱ υἱοὶ τῶν προφητῶν συνῆγον ταῦτα εἰς τὸ ἱερόν. 16. νῦν πέμπομαι ὑπὸ τοῦ κυρίου πρὸς τὰ τέκνα τῶν μαθητῶν, τότε δὲ ἔπεμπον τοὺς δικαίους εἰς τὴν ἔρημον.

Lesson XII

149.I. 1. These words were being written in a book. 2. I was being taught by him out of the books of the prophets. 3. In those days we were both being taught by him and were teaching the others, but now we neither are being taught nor are we teaching. 4. The sinners were going away to to sea. 5. The church was going out to him, but now it no longer is going out. 6. We do not yet see the Lord in His glory, but we were being taught by Him even in the evil days. 7. A good word was being said in the temple concerning this apostle. 8. His glory was being seen around Him. 9. The gifts were being brought to the wicked (people, ones, men) also. 10. You were receiving the books from the prophets. 11. The disciples were coming together to this man. 12. The works of the evil one are evil. 13. Neither is <u>he</u> (himself) evil, nor are his works evil. 14. The Lord was dying on behalf of His church. 15. A disciple is not above his teacher, nor (is) a servant above his lord. 16. You were being led to the Lord in the boat through the sea. 17. You were going out of your houses. 18. These demons were coming out through his word. 19. They were being heard and were hearing; they are being heard and are hearing. 20. I was coming to the Lord, and/but I was leading the others also.

149.II. 1. ἠκούοντο ἐκεῖνοι οἱ λόγοι ὑπὸ τοῦ αὐτοῦ ἀποστόλου, νῦν δὲ οὐκέτι ἀκούονται. 2. ταῦτα τὰ βιβλία ἐγράφοντο ὑπ' αὐτοῦ ὑπὲρ τῶν δούλων αὐτοῦ. 3. οὔπω ἐδιδασκόμην ὑπὸ τούτου, ἀλλ' ἦγον τοὺς ἄλλους πρὸς αὐτόν. 4. ὑμεῖς οὐκ ἐστὲ ὑπὲρ ἐμέ, οὐδὲ ἐγὼ (εἰμι) ὑπὲρ ὑμᾶς. 5. ἀπέστελλες ἄλλους

πρὸς αὐτὸν καὶ ἀπεστέλλου ὑπ' αὐτοῦ πρὸς ἄλλους.   6. τὰ δαιμόνια ἐξήρχοντο/
-ετο ἐκ τῶν τέκνων.   7. εἰσήρχεσθε καὶ ἐξήρχεσθε ἐν τῇ ἐκκλησίᾳ.   8. οὔπω
ἀπηρχόμεθα πρὸς τοὺς ἁμαρτωλούς, ἔτι δὲ ἠκούομεν τὴν φωνὴν τοῦ ἀποστόλου καὶ
ἐδιδασκόμεθα περὶ τοῦ κυρίου ἐκ τῶν βιβλίων τῶν προφητῶν.   9. κατέβαινον πρὸς
τὴν θάλασσαν καὶ διήρχοντο δι' αὐτῆς ἐν πλοίοις.   10. οὐδὲ οἱ πονηροὶ οὐδὲ οἱ
ἀγαθοὶ ἀπεκρίνοντο τῷ κυρίῳ.   11. καὶ ἐβλέπομεν καὶ ἠκούομεν τούτους τοὺς
μαθητάς.   12. ἐσῴζου τῷ λόγῳ τοῦ κυρίου.   13. οὐ τοῖς ἔργοις ὑμῶν ἐσῴζεσθε
ἀπὸ τῶν ἁμαρτιῶν ὑμῶν ἀλλ' ὑπὸ τοῦ κυρίου.   14. οὐδὲ οἱ ἀγαθοὶ σῴζονται ἔργοις.
15. διὰ τοῦ λόγου τοῦ κυρίου ἐγινόμεθα μαθηταὶ ἀγαθοί.   16. οὐκ ἀπέθνησκες
σὺ ὑπὲρ αὐτοῦ, ἀλλ' αὐτὸς ἀπέθνησκεν ὑπὲρ σοῦ.

Lesson XIII

165.I. 1. The Lord will lead His disciples into the kingdom.   2. We shall
know both the good and the evil (men, ones, people).   3. You will take
the boats from the sea (lake).   4. You will release (i.e., loose) the slaves.
5. The wicked will have neither joy nor peace.   6. In that hour the Son of
Man will come with His angels.   7. You (pl.) are sinners, but you will become disciples of the Lord.   8. The wicked persecute the prophets, but in the
days of the Son of Man they will no longer persecute them.   9. You (sg.) will
pray to your God and you will glorify Him.   10. Then you will know that He is
the Lord.   11. Not even I shall know these things.   12. The servant will
teach others, but the faithful teacher will teach me.   13. The apostles will
receive those things, but/and these (things) even the brothers (the brothers also)
(will receive).   14. Through the word of the Lord these blind men will see
again (receive their sight).   15. The prophet himself will write these things
in the Scriptures (the writings).   16. Evil days will come.   17. Even you
will go away into the ways of the wicked, and thus (you) will teach the men.
Or, you also....   18. Even they themselves will preach the gospel in this
evil world; or, They also....   19. Even this woman will come to him, and he
will teach her; or, This woman also....   20. The gospel was being proclaimed
in the evil days, and even now (it) is being preached, but in that day the Lord
Himself will come.

165.II. 1. ἡ ἐκκλησία πέμψει δούλους πρός με.   2. αὗται γενήσονται ἀγαθαί.
3. τούτους τοὺς λόγους γράφω ἐν βιβλίῳ.   4. ταῦτα εἰσελεύσονται εἰς
τον κόσμον ἐν ἐκείναις ταῖς ἡμέραις.   5. νῦν οὔπω διδάσκει με, ἐν δὲ ἐκείνῃ
τῇ ὥρᾳ καὶ διδάξει (με) καὶ γνώσεται (με).   6. ταύτας ἐδίωκον ἐν ταῖς ἡμέραις
ταῖς κακαῖς καὶ διώξουσιν αὐτὰς καὶ εἰς τοὺς ἄλλους τόπους.   7. τότε
προσεύξονται τυφλοὶ τῷ κυρίῳ, πονηροὶ δὲ οὐ προσεύξονται.   8. ἐλαμβανοντο τὰ
δῶρα ὑφ' ἡμῶν ἀπὸ τῶν τέκνων, οὐκέτι δὲ λημψόμεθα αὐτά.   9. προσευξόμεθα ὑπὲρ
τῶν αὐτῶν τέκνων ἐν τῇ ἐκκλησίᾳ.   10. ἐν μὲν τούτῳ τῷ κόσμῳ ἔχομεν θάνατον,
ἐν δὲ τῇ βασιλείᾳ τοῦ θεοῦ ἕξομεν καὶ ἀγάπην καὶ δόξαν.   11. τότε ἐδιδασκόμεθα
ὑπὸ τῶν ἀποστόλων, ἐν δὲ ἐκείνῃ τῇ ἡμέρᾳ διδάξομεν καὶ ἡμεῖς.   12. ἐδίωκον
ἐγὼ ὑμᾶς ἐν ἐκείναις ταῖς ἡμέραις, νῦν δὲ ὑμεῖς διώξετέ με.   13. οὐ καταβήσῃ
πρὸς τὴν θάλασσαν, ἀλλὰ διώξεις ταύτας μετὰ τῶν τέκνων αὐτῶν εἰς τὴν ἔρημον.
14. ἐκήρυσσον τοῦτο τὸ εὐαγγέλιον, νῦν δὲ οὐκέτι κηρύξουσιν αὐτό.   15. κακά
εἰσιν ταῦτα, ὑμεῖς δὲ ἕξετε καλὰ ἐν ἐκείνῃ τῇ ἡμέρᾳ.   16. ἐλεύσεται ὁ κύριος
πρὸς τὴν ἐκκλησίαν αὐτοῦ ἐν δόξῃ.

185.I. 1. The Lord released his servant, but the servant did not release
the other man.   2. Already these men have turned to the Lord, and/
but those men will turn in the evil days.   3. We believed on the Lord, and
He will save us.   4. You both did believe on Him, and you will believe.
5. You returned to the Lord, and He received you into His church.   6. In
those days you were going in the evil ways.   7. You (pl.) turned to the Lord,
and He healed you.   8. Those men were evil, but we persuaded them.   9. I
have prepared a place in heaven for you.   10. I received you into my house,
but these wicked men did not receive (you).   11. The blind men received their
sight (not "were receiving").   12. I saved you, but you did not receive me
into your houses.   13. They themselves were evil, and they sent evil men
into the church.   14. You taught me in the temple.   15. Then we heard these
commandments, but we shall hear others (other commands) in the church.   16. In
that hour they will go out of the world, but then they received us.   17. They
heard him and marveled.   18. You received the gospel, but these men will not
receive it.   19. We neither heard the Lord, nor did we believe on Him.

185.II. 1. οὐκ ἐδεξάμεθα τὸ εὐαγγέλιου ὅτι οὐκ ἠκούσαμεν τῆς φωνῆς τοῦ ἀποστόλου.
        2. ἐν ἐκείναις ταῖς ἡμέραις οὐκ ἐπιστεύομεν εἰς τὸν κύριον, οὗτος δὲ
ὁ μαθητὴς ἔπεισεν ἡμᾶς.   3. ὁ ἁμαρτωλὸς ἐπέστρεφεν πρὸς τὸν κύριον, καὶ ἤδη
διδάσκεται ὑπ' αὐτοῦ.   4. οἱ δοῦλοι ἡτοίμασαν οἴκους ὑμῖν (σοι).   5. ἐπίστευσεν
οὗτος ὁ τυφλὸς εἰς τὸν κύριον.   6. τὰ τέκνα ἐθαύμασαν, καὶ οἱ μαθηταὶ ἐπίστευσαν.
7. οὐκ προσηύξω τῷ κυρίῳ καὶ διὰ τοῦτο οὐκ ἐθεράπευσέν σε.   8. ἐκεῖνοι οἱ
πονηροὶ ἐδίωξαν ταύτας εἰς τὴν ἔρημον.   9. ἐκήρυξα τὸ εὐαγγέλιον αὐτοῖς.
10. ὑμεῖς ἐδιώξατέ με, ἀλλ' οὐκ ἐγὼ ἐδίωξα ὑμᾶς.   11. οὗτοι οἱ τυφλοὶ ἐδόξασαν
τὸν κύριον, ὅτι ἐθεράπευσεν αὐτούς.   12. διὰ τῶν μαθητῶν αὐτοῦ ἐκήρυξε τὸ
εὐαγγέλιον αὐτοῦ τῷ κόσμῳ.   13. αἱ ἐπαγγελίαι (εἰσίν) ἀγαθαί, καὶ ἐδεξάμεθα
αὐτάς.   14. ἐδέξασθε τὰς αὐτὰς ἐπαγγελίας καὶ ἐπιστεύσατε εἰς τὸν αὐτὸν
κύριον.   15. οὐκ ἐκήρυξε τὸ εὐαγγέλιον, οὐδὲ νῦν κηρύσσει αὐτό.   16. ἐκείνη
οὐδὲ ἐδόξασε τὸν κύριον, οὐδὲ ἐδέξατο τὰ τέκνα.

Lesson XV

195.I. 1. We both saw the Lord and heard His words.   2. For you (sg.)
     neither entered their houses nor said a parable to them.   3. In that
hour they became disciples of the Lord.   4. (On the one hand) these men
became good disciples, but (on the other hand) those men were still evil.
5. They were bringing the blind men to Him.   6. The evil angels fell from/out
of heaven.   7. You cast out the demons, but (in contrast) you healed the
children.   8. You gathered together the wicked into your house, but we
(gathered together) the good. (Reverse order would allow English ellipsis as
well: The evil you gathered together, but we, the good.)   9. You did not
preach the gospel in the church, for you did not even become a disciple.
10. Now on the one hand you are saying good words but these men, on the other
hand, said the same words even in those days.   11. We believed on the Lord,
for the disciples led us to Him.   12. These things (on the one hand) I said
to you in the temple, but those things (on the other hand) I am not yet saying.
13. Then you (pl.) entered into the church, but in that day you will enter
(into) heaven.   14. Then we shall see the Lord in His glory; for we believed
on Him.   15. The Lord went out then from the world, but His disciples are
still remaining in it.   16. These commandments I received from the Lord, for

Lesson XV
195.I.17

I was His disciple.   17. Then on the one hand you received the promise from the Lord, but now you are also proclaiming it in the world.   18. You (pl.) came to the Lord, and received these things from Him.   19. He Himself gathered us together into His church.   20. The men saw the Son of God, for He Himself became a man and was abiding in this world.

195.II.   1. οὐκ εἴδομεν αὐτόν, οὔπω γὰρ ἤμεν μαθηταὶ αὐτοῦ.   2. ὁ ἀπόστολὸς προσήνεγκε τοὺς ἁμαρτωλοὺς αὐτῷ.   3. οὐκ ἠκούσατέ μου ἀλλὰ ἤλθετε πρὸς τοὺς μαθητάς μου.   4. εἰσήλθετε εἰς τοῦτον τὸν οἶκον, οἱ δὲ ἄλλοι ἐξῆλθον ἐξ αὐτοῦ.   5. εἰσήρχοντο οἱ ἁμαρτωλοὶ εἰς τοὺς οἴκους αὐτῶν, οἱ δὲ ἀπόστολοι εἶδον τὸν κύριον.   6. ἐν ἐκείναις ταῖς ἡμέραις ὀψόμεθα τὸν κύριον, ἐν δὲ ταῖς κακαῖς ἡμέραις οὐκ εἴδομεν αὐτόν.   7. ἐλάμβανον οἱ ἀδελφοί σου δῶρα ἀπὸ τῶν τέκνων οἱ δὲ ἀπόστολοι ἔλαβον τὰ τέκνα ἀπ' αὐτῶν.   8. δοῦλος ἐγένου τοῦ ἀποστόλου, ἀλλ' ὁ ἀπόστολος ἐγένετό σοι καὶ ἀδελφός.   9. ἐγένεσθε ἐκκλησία τοῦ θεοῦ, ἐπιστεύσατε γὰρ εἰς τὸν υἱὸν αὐτοῦ.   10. συνήγαγε τοὺς μαθητὰς αὐτοῦ εἰς τὴν βασιλείαν αὐτοῦ.   11. εἶπον ὁ πιστὸς διδάσκαλος ὅτι ἀγαθὸς (ἐστιν) ὁ κύριος.   12. ἐπίστευσαν εἰς τὸν κύριον καὶ προσήνεγκαν καὶ ἄλλους αὐτῷ.   13. ἤκουσαν τῶν τέκνων καὶ ἦλθον πρὸς αὐτά.   14. ἐδεξάμεθα χαρὰν καὶ εἰρήνην ἀπὸ τοῦ θεοῦ, ὅτι ἤδη εἰσηρχόμεθα εἰς τὴν βασιλείαν αὐτοῦ.   15. λέγουσιν οἱ μαθηταὶ ὅτι εἶδον οἱ ἀπόστολοι τὸν κύριον καὶ ἐδέξαντο τοῦτο ἀπ' αὐτοῦ.   16. ἐξῆλθες εἰς τὴν ἔρημον, ὁ δὲ ἀπόστολος εἶπεν ταῦτα τοῖς ἀδελφοῖς αὐτοῦ.

Lesson XVI

209.I.   1. We believed on the Lord and were known by Him.   2. These things were written in the books.   3. You taught the children, but you yourselves also were taught by the Lord.   4. The faithful were received into heaven, but the evil angels were cast out of it.   5. The dead will be raised by the word of the Lord.   6. These blind men were gathered together into the church.   7. The demons were cast out, for the Lord cast them out. 8. Even now the disciples on the one hand are being sent, but then, on the other hand, the apostles were sent, and in that day even the angels will be sent; or, ... the angels also will be sent.   9. You entered (into) the church and were baptized.   10. He was believed in the world, received up in glory.   11. The sinners were saved in that hour and became disciples of the Lord.   11. We went into another place, for these men will not receive us. 13. God was glorified by the Son, and He glorified Him.   14. The gospel was proclaimed in those days, and even now (or now also) it will be proclaimed. 15. A place will be prepared for us in heaven according to the promise of the Lord.   16. The children were brought to the Lord.   17. These men saw the face of the Lord and heard His voice.   18. In the small house the voice of the apostle will be heard.   19. I am first of (the) sinners, but even I was saved; or, ... but I also ... .   20. We will see the angels and (we) will be seen even by them; or, ... by them also.

209.II.   1. αὕτη (εστιν) ἡ ἐκκλησία τοῦ θεοῦ, οἱ δὲ ἁμαρτωλοὶ ἐφέροντο εἰς αὐτήν.   2. οὗτος ἐξεβλήθη διὰ τὸ εὐαγγέλιον.   3. ἐγὼ πρὸς τοὺς ἁμαρτωλοὺς ἐπέμφθην, ὑμεῖς δὲ πρὸς τοῦ ἀδελφοὺς ὑμῶν ἐπέμπεσθε.   (σὺ δὲ...σου

ἐπέμπου).   4. οὐκ ἐδέξω σὺ τὸ εὐαγγέλιον, οἱ δὲ ἄλλοι ἐδέξαντο αὐτὸ καὶ
ἐσώθησαν.   5. οὗτοι οἱ λόγοι ἐγράφησαν ὑπὸ τῶν ἀποστόλων.   6. οἱ δοῦλοι
εἰσελεύσονται εἰς τὸν οἶκον, οἱ δὲ υἱοὶ ἐβαπτίσθησαν ἐν ἐκείνῃ τῇ ὥρᾳ.
7. ὄψεσθε τὸν κύριον ἐν οὐρανοῖς, οἱ δὲ ἀπόστολοι ἐδιδάχθησαν ὑπ' αὐτοῦ.
8. προσήνεγκαν οἱ μαθηταὶ τοὺς τυφλοὺς τῷ κυρίῳ, τὰ δὲ τέκνα ἤχθησαν ὑπ'
ἄλλων.   9. παρελαμβάνοντο τὰ δῶρα παρὰ τῶν δούλων, ὁ δὲ νόμος ἐκηρύχθη
τῷ κόσμῳ.   10. ἡτοιμάσθη τόπος τοῖς ἀδελφοῖς.   11. ἤλθομεν πρὸς τὴν θάλασσαν
οἱ δὲ υἱοὶ ἡμῶν εἰσελεύσονται εἰς τὸ ἱερόν.   12. μετὰ ταῦτα ἀνελήμφθησαν εἰς
τὴν δόξαν.   13. ἠγέρθη ὁ υἱὸς τοῦ ἀνθρώπου ἐκ νεκρῶν καὶ ἐδοξάσθη.
14. ἠκούσθησαν αἱ ἐπαγγελίαι τοῦ θεοῦ ἐν τῷ κόσμῳ.

Lesson XVII

224.I.   1. They do not have hope, nor/neither do they have the Holy Spirit.
2. On account of the good hope the disciples of the Lord brought/bore
these things.   3. These are the words of the Holy Spirit.   4. Your names
have been written (were written) by God in the Book of Life.   5. God saved
us by (means of) the word of the Lord.   6. The evil rulers did not believe
on the name of the Lord.   7. Those men said these things to the rulers of
this age.   8. You will see the face of the Lord forever, but the wicked
will not see it, because they have not believed (did not believe) on His name.
9. No longer according to (the) flesh do we know the Lord.   10. In your
flesh you saw death, but through the Holy Spirit you have (a) good hope.
11. The letter (on the one hand) kills, but in the Spirit (on the other hand)
you have life.   12. We see the face of the Lord both at night and by day.
13. The disciples taught both the rulers and the servants.   14. In that
night you saw the evil ruler.   15. I was with the rulers in that house.
16. After that night this man went (came) in the Spirit into the desert.
17. These are words of hope and life.   18. The Holy Spirit led him into the
temple.   19. These words were preached in that night to the ruler's servants.
20. The bodies of the saints (holy ones) were raised up.

224.II.   1. τῷ θελήματι τοῦ θεοῦ ἐπιστεύσαμεν εἰς τὸ ὄνομα τοῦ κυρίου.
2. οἱ ἄρχοντες οὐκ ἐδέξαντο ταύτην τὴν ἐλπίδα ἀπὸ τοῦ ἀποστόλου,
ὅτι οὐκ ἐπίστευσαν εἰς τὸν κύριον.   3. γνωσόμεθα τὸ θέλημα τοῦ θεοῦ εἰς τὸν
αἰῶνα.   4. ἐν τούτῳ τῷ αἰῶνι ἔχομεν (τὸν) θάνατον, ἐν δὲ ἐκείνῳ τῷ αἰῶνι
(τὴν) ἐλπίδα καὶ (τὴν) ζωήν.   5. ἐν τῇ σαρκὶ ἡμῶν μένομεν ἐν τούτῳ τῷ αἰῶνι,
διὰ δὲ τοῦ πνεύματος τοῦ θεοῦ ἔχομεν ἐλπίδα καλήν.   6. τῷ θελήματι τοῦ θεοῦ
ἐσώθημεν ἀπὸ τῶν ἁμαρτιῶν ἡμῶν διὰ τοῦ αἵματος τοῦ κυρίου.   7. ἐν ἐκείναις
ταῖς ἡμέραις εἴδετε τοὺς ἄρχοντας.   8. οὗτος ὁ αἰὼν (ἐστιν) κακός, ἐν δὲ
αὐτῷ ἔχομεν ἐλπίδα.   9. ταῦτα τὰ ῥήματα ἐγράψαμεν τοῖς ἄρχουσιν.   10. ἤλθομεν
πρὸς τὸν ἀγαθὸν ἄρχοντα, καὶ πρὸς τὸν ἀπόστολον τοῦ κυρίου.   11. ἐν τοῖς ὑμῶν
σώμασιν ὀψόμεθα (τὸν) θάνατον, ἐγερθησόμεθα δὲ κατὰ τὸ ῥῆμα τοῦ θεοῦ.
12. ἐδιώχθητε ὑπὸ τοῦ ἄρχοντος, τὸ δὲ αἷμα τοῦ κυρίου σώζει ὑμᾶς ἀπὸ (τῆς)
ἁμαρτίας.   13. ἐγράψαμεν ἐκεῖνα τὰ ῥήματα τὰ καλὰ τῷ πονηρῷ ἄρχοντι.
14. αὕτη ἡ νὺξ ἐγένετο αὐτοῖς ὥρα θανάτου, ἐπίστευσαν δὲ εἰς τὸ ὄνομα τοῦ
κυρίου.   15. τὰ πνεύμα τὰ πονηρὰ ἐξεβλήθησαν τῷ ῥήματι τοῦ κυρίου.

240.I.   1. Being persecuted by the ruler, we pray to God. While being per-
         secuted/while we are being persecuted by the ruler, we pray to God.
2. The one who receives you receives the Lord also.   3. These things we
are saying to those who (the men who, the ones who) are going into the house
concerning the one who (the man who) raises the dead.   4. While we are coming
out of the church he says these things to us.   5. The churches which are
being persecuted by the rulers believe on the Lord.   6. Those who (the men
who, the ones who) believe (are believing) on the Lord are being saved.
7. God knows the things which are being written in the book of life.
8. While we were leading the children, we went out to them.   9. We saw those
who (the men who, the ones who) were receiving the gifts from the children.
10. This is the ruler who receives (is receiving) me into his house.
11. Those who believe on the Lord and are being saved by Him are holy.
12. This is the Spirit that saves (is saving) us.   13. They were in the
house which was being destroyed by the ruler.   14. They were in the house
while it was being destroyed by the ruler.   15. This is the church which
believes (is believing) on the Lord.   16. Being taught by the Lord you were
going in the way which goes up (was going up) into the desert.   While you
were being taught by the Lord, you were going... .   17. The gospel that was
saving (that saves) the sinners was preached by them.   18. This is the good
news which is being preached in the world and which saves (the) men.
19. I/they came to him while he was baptizing the disciples.   20. While he
was in the temple, we saw him.

240.II.   1. ἔτι ὢν ἐν σαρκὶ ὁ κύριος ἔσωζε τοὺς πιστεύοντας εἰς αὐτόν.
         2. διδασκόμενοι ἐν τῷ ἱερῷ ἐδιωκόμεθα ὑπὸ τοῦ ἄρχοντος.   3. οἱ
σωζόμενοι ὑπὸ τοῦ κυρίου γινώσκουσιν τὸν σώζοντα αὐτούς.   4. οἱ κηρύσσοντες
ταῦτα ἐδέξαντο καὶ αὐτοὶ τὰ κηρυσσόμενα ὑπ' αὐτῶν.   5. ἡ δεχομένη λαμβάνουσα
τὸν κύριον εἰς τὸν οἶκον αὐτῆς βλέπει τὸ πρόσωπον τοῦ σώζοντος αὐτήν.   6. ἔτι
διδάσκοντα ἐν τῷ ἱερῷ εἴδομεν αὐτόν.   7. διδάσκοντες ἐν τῷ ἱερῷ εἴδομεν τὸν
σώζοντα ἡμᾶς.   8. ἡ ἐλπὶς ἡ βλεπομένη οὐκ ἔστιν ἐλπίς.   9. ὁ κύριος εἶπεν
τοῖς πιστεύουσιν εἰς αὐτὸν ὅτι ὁ θεὸς σώζει (τοὺς) ἁμαρτωλούς.   10. οἱ ἀδελφοὶ
τῶν διωκόντων τοὺς μαθητὰς οὐκ ἔχουσιν ἐλπίδα.   11. οἱ λέγοντες ταῦτα οὐ
γινώσκουσι τὸν σώζοντα τὴν ἐκκλησίαν.   12. ἐξεβλήθημεν ὑπὸ τοῦ ἄρχοντος τοῦ
διώκοντος τὴν ἐκκλησίαν.   13. αὕτη ἐστὶν ἡ φωνὴ ἡ ἀκουομένη ὑπὸ τῶν πιστευόντων
εἰς τὸν κύριον.   14. μένων ἐν τῷ οἴκῳ εἶδον τὰς λαμβάνοντας δῶρα ἀπὸ τῶν
μαθητῶν.   15. κηρυσσόμενον ὑπὸ τῶν πιστευόντων εἰς τὸν κύριον τὸ εὐαγγέλιον
ἄξει ἀνθρώπους εἰς τὴν ἐκκλησίαν.   16. οἱ πιστοὶ ὄψονται τὸν κύριον ἀναβαίνοντα
εἰς τὸν οὐρανόν.

Lesson XIX

257.I.   1. When we had received (or, having received) these things from those
         who believed (were believing) on the Lord, we went out into the desert.
2. The women who received (have received) those being persecuted by the ruler
are faithful.   3. We saw them both while they were remaining in the house and
when (after) they had gone out of it.   4. Those who had seen the Lord came to
the ones who had led the disciple out of the temple.   5. We said these things
concerning the one who (had) saved us. 6. These are the men who preached the

Gospel, but those are the ones who persecuted the believers (the ones who were believing). 7. When you (pl.) had brought (or, Having brought) to the Lord the one who was being persecuted by the evil ruler, you went out into another place. 8. They/I came to the Lord when He had gone into the temple. 9. You (sg.) believed on him after (when) he (had) said these things. 10. These things I said when (after) I came (had come) out of the church. 11. The man who had not seen the Lord did not believe on Him. 12. While he was yet in the way, the Lord said these things to those who had gone out of the house and were going with Him; or, the Lord said these things, still being in the way, to those who... . 13. When they (had) heard the things which were being said by the Lord, they believed on Him. 14. We saw those who had become disciples of the Lord, even while they were still abiding in their first hope. 15. The children who had taken these things from those who had heard the Lord saw Him while He was yet in the house. 16. These women, having seen the one who had preached that Gospel, came to him while he was entering the house. 17. The angels who fell out of heaven were evil. 18. When they saw those who were still in the temple, they preached to them the Kingdom of God. 19. He answered these things to those who (had) brought the children to Him. 20. We went away not having seen (or, When we had not seen...) the one who (had) taught us.

257.II. 1. οἱ μὴ ἰδόντες τὸν ἀπόστολον οὐ γινώσκουσιν αὐτόν. 2. οὐκ εἶδον τὸν πιστεύσαντα εἰς τὸν κύριον. 3. (ἐγὼ) εἶδον αὐτὸν πιστεύσαντα εἰς τὸν κύριον, ὑμεῖς δὲ εἴδετε αὐτὸν ἔτι ὄντα ἐν τῇ βασιλείᾳ τοῦ πονηροῦ. 4. ἀκούσαντες ταῦτα ἐπιστεύσαμεν εἰς τὸν ἀποθανόντα ὑπὲρ ἡμῶν. 5. ἤλθομεν πρὸς τοὺς πορευομένους ἐν τῇ ὁδῷ. 6. ὀψόμεθα τὸν ἀπόστολον εἰσελθόντες εἰς τὸν οἶκον τοῦτον. 7. ἐκεῖνοι εἶπον τοῖς εἰσελθοῦσι εἰς τὸν οἶκον ὅτι ἀγαθὸς (ἐστιν) ὁ κύριος. 8. λέγοντες ταῦτα εἰσηρχόμεθα εἰς τὸν οἶκον ἡμῶν. 9. λαβόντες ταῦτα τὰ δῶρα παρὰ τῶν ἐνεγκόντων αὐτὰ συνῆλθον εἰς τὴν ἐκκλησίαν. 10. αὗταί εἰσιν αἱ λαβοῦσαι τὸν διδάξαντα αὐτάς. 11. οὗτοι ἰδόντες τὸν κύριον ἠνέχθησαν πρὸς τοὺς ἄρχοντας. 12. οἱ μαθηταὶ οἱ εἰσελθόντες εἰς τὴν ἐκκλησίαν ἐβαπτίσθησαν ὑπὸ τῶν ἀποστόλων τῶν ἰδόντων τὸν κύριον. 13. ὁ τυφλὸς ὁ δεξάμενος τοῦτον ἦν μετὰ τῶν διωκόντων αὐτόν. 14. τὰ δαιμόνια τὰ ἐκβαλλόμενα εἶπον τοῦτο τῷ ἐκβάλλοντι αὐτά. 15. διερχόμενοι διὰ τῆς ἐρήμου ἐδιδάξαμεν τοὺς ὄντας μεθ' ἡμῶν. 16. εἴδομεν τὸν δοῦλον πιστεύσαντα εἰς τὸν κύριον καὶ ἔτι ὄντα ἐν τῷ οἴκῳ.

Lesson XX

267.I. 1. When the ruler had gone to the Lord, the servants said these things to the disciples. (The ruler having gone..., the servants said....
2. When he (the ruler) had gone to them, the ruler (he) believed on the Lord.
3. After you believed on the Lord, immediately the ruler also believed.
4. When the one who had been raised by the Lord had entered (into) the house, the disciples marveled. 5. When he had been cast out of the synagogue the rulers were gathered together. 6. After he (the man) had been cast out of the synagogue the Lord taught him. 7. After the Holy Spirit had said these things the disciples proclaimed the Word of God. 8. To those who had been healed by Him you spake words of hope and life. 9. When this man had gone

into his house, immediately we said to the others the words which had been received from the Lord.   10.   Having been cast into prison on account of the Gospel which was preached to them by the apostle, they glorified there the one who had saved them.   11.   When He had been taken up into heaven the disciples went into their house.   12.   You (pl.) received those who had been cast out of the synagogue and the women who had received them into their houses.   13.   These are the women who have been persecuted and are still being persecuted by the rulers.   14.   This is the hope which has been preached in the world by those who have seen the Lord.   15.   When the soldiers had pursued us into the house, the ones who were there received (us).   16.   Those who were in the house received us after we had been persecuted by the soldiers.   17.   While you were entering (into) the house, the rulers came to you, and/but when you had entered, they threw (you) out.   18.   These things (on the one hand) I/they said to them while they were bringing the little children to the Lord, but (on the other hand) those things (I said to them) (after) they had brought them (the children to the Lord).   19.   While the Lord was going with His disciples, the apostles were saying these things, but when he had gone into the house (they were saying) those things.   20.   These things I said to you (pl.) while you were still with me.

267.II. 1. λαβόντων τῶν στρατιωτῶν τὰ ἱμάτια ἀπὸ τῶν τέκνων, οἱ μαθηταὶ ἐξεβλήθησαν ἐκ τῆς οἰκίας.   2. ἐβληθέντες ἐκ τῆς συναγωγῆς οἱ μαθηταὶ προσῆλθον ἡμῖν.   3. εἰσερχομένων ἡμῶν εἰς τὴν οἰκίαν ἡμῶν, ὁ κύριος εἶπεν ταῦτα τοῖς ἄρχουσιν.   4. ὁ κύριος εἶπεν ἐκεῖνα ὑμῖν καὶ οὖσι μετ' αὐτοῦ ἐν τῇ ὁδῷ καὶ ἐλθοῦσι πρὸς τὸν ἄρχοντα.   5. οἱ ἀκούσαντες τὸν ἀπόστολον λέγοντα ταῦτα εἶδον τὸν οἶκον τὸν λυθέντα ὑπὸ τῶν στρατιωτῶν.   6. ἀκούσαντες τὰ λεγόμενα ὑπὸ τοῦ κυρίου ἐδίωξαν οἱ ἄρχοντες τοὺς μαθητάς.   7. διωκομένων τῶν μαθητῶν ὑπὸ τῶν ἀρχόντων, οἱ ἀπόστολοι εἰσήρχοντο εἰς ἄλλην οἰκίαν.   8. οἱ ἐλθόντες εἰς τὸν οἶκον τοῦ ἄρχοντος ἦσαν οἱ ἀδελφοί μου.   9. τῶν ὀνομάτων ἡμῶν γραφέντων εἰς τὸ βιβλίον τῆς ζωῆς, ὀψόμεθα τὸν κύριον.   10. προσενεχθέντες πρὸς τὸν κύριον ὑπὸ τῶν μαθητῶν τούτων βλέπομεν αὐτὸν εἰς τὸν αἰῶνα.   11. οὗτοί εἰσιν οἱ ἄρχοντες οἱ γενόμενοι/γενηθέντες μαθηταί σου.   12. βληθέντος τοῦ ἀποστόλου εἰς φυλακήν, οἱ μαθηταὶ οἱ ἀκούσαντες ταῦτα ἀπῆλθον εἰς τόπον ἄλλον.   13. βληθεισῶν ἐκείνων εἰς φυλακήν, ἀπήλθομεν εἰς τὴν ἔρημον.   14. ἰδόντες τὸν ἐγερθέντα οἱ βληθέντες εἰς φυλακὴν ἐθαύμασαν καὶ ἐπίστευσαν εἰς τὸν κύριον.   15. τῶν μαθητῶν ἀγαγόντων πρὸς τὸν κύριον τοὺς διωχθέντας δι' αὐτόν, ἐκεῖνοι οἱ δοῦλοι ἦλθον πρὸς ἡμᾶς φέροντες δῶρα καλά· or, ...προσῆλθον ἡμῖν... .   16. οἱ μὴ λαβόντες ταύτην τὴν ἐλπίδα ἀπὸ (τοῦ) θεοῦ οὐκ εἰσελεύσονται εἰς τὴν βασιλείαν τῶν οὐρανῶν.

Lesson XXI

291.I. 1. If we evangelize you, you will receive salvation and hope.   2. If you do not receive our witness, you will not be saved.   3. If this man does not see the Lord, he will not believe on Him.   4. If (as a matter of fact) it is (being) declared to us that the Lord is good, let us also be good, in order that we may teach the rest (the remaining ones).   5. I told them the good news (proclaimed the Gospel to them), in order that they might be saved and might (continually) have life.   6. Let us no longer sin (as a practice), in

order that we may become faithful disciples.   7. Happy are the crowds, if
they hear my words.   8. If those who believe on the Lord enter into that
house, we will preach the good news to them here.   9. We proclaimed to this
people the words of life, in order that they might receive the truth and be
saved.   10. Let us go to the one who saw the Lord, in order that he may teach
us concerning Him.   11. When they had said these things in the temple, those
who heard received the things being said, in order that they might proclaim
them to the rest also.   12. Let us believe on the one who died for us, in
order that he may write our names in the book of life.   13. I will go to the
one who saved me, in order that I may neither break His commandments nor go
in the ways of death.   14. These things I/they said in the temple, in order
that those who heard might be saved from their sins and might have the
righteousness of God.   15. If (as a matter of fact) you saw these things in
the evil days, you will see the same things both now and forever.   16. If
you be not taught by the Lord, you will not know Him forever.   17. The one
who breaks the commandments of God does not have hope, if he does not return
to the Lord.   18. These things he received from the One who had died for him,
in order that, when they had received them, the rest themselves also might be
saved.   19. When we have come together into the house, let us receive the
witness of the one who told us the good news.   20. When the soldiers had
persecuted the saints in order that they might not believe on the one who saved
them, these men came together in(to) the synagogue.

291.II. 1. δεξώμεθα (παραλάβωμεν) την μαρτυρίαν τούτων ἵνα σωθῶμεν.   2. ἐὰν
μη ἐπιστρέψωμεν προς τον κύριον, οὐ γνωσόμεθα αὐτόν.   ·3. ἐὰν ἑτοιμάσῃ
ὁ κύριος τόπον ἡμῖν, εἰσελευσόμεθα εἰς (τους) οὐρανούς/(τον) οὐρανόν.   4. εἰ
ἐδεξάμεθα (παρελάβομεν) ταύτην την ἐντολὴν ἀπο τοῦ κυρίου, εὐαγγελισώμεθα
τοῖς ὄχλοις/τους ὄχλους.   5. εἰ οὗτοί εἰσιν μαθηταὶ τοῦ κυρίου, οὐ διώξουσι
τους ἁγίους.   6. ἐὰν οὗτοι οἱ ἄρχοντες διώξωσιν τους πιστεύσαντας εἰς τον
κύριον, οὐκ ἐλεύσονται προς τον κύριον ἵνα σωθῶσιν.   7. ἐὰν την δεξαμένην
τους ἁγίους ἴδῃ, λήμψεται τα τέκνα ἀπ' αὐτῆς.   8. εἰπόντες ταῦτα τοῖς ἁγίοις
οἱ μαθηταὶ ἐδιδάχθησαν ὑπο τοῦ κυρίου ἵνα μηκέτι ἁμαρτάνωσιν.   9. εἰ ὁ υἱος
τοῦ ἀνθρώπου ἦλθε(ν) ἵνα σώσῃ ἁμαρτωλους δεξώμεθα την μαρτυρίαν αὐτοῦ.   10. εἰ
γινώσκομεν τον κύριον, μηδε διώξωμεν τους ἁγίους αὐτοῦ μηδε ἐκβάλωμεν ἐκ τῆς
συναγωγῆς.   11. ἐὰν οἱ ὄχλοι οἱ ἀκούσαντες τον κύριον ἴδωσιν αὐτον ἐν ἐκείνῃ
τῇ συναγωγῇ, ἐλεύσονται προς αὐτον ἵνα εἴπῃ αὐτοῖς λόγους ἐλπίδος.   12. ἐὰν
μη εἴπῃ ταῦτα τοῖς ὄχλοις, οὐ σωθήσονται.   13. ἐὰν ἴδῃς ἐν ἐκείνῃ τῇ νυκτι
τον σώσαντά σε, ὁ ἄρχων διώξει σε ἵνα μη εὐαγγελίσῃ (εὐαγγελίζῃ κηρύξῃ το
εὐαγγέλιον) τοῖς ἄλλοις.   14. ἦλθεν ὁ κύριος προς ἡμᾶς (προσῆλθεν ἡμῖν) ἵνα
εὐαγγελισώμεθα (κηρύξωμεν το εὐαγγέλιον) ὑμῖν/σοί.   15. ἦλθον οἱ πιστοι δοῦλοι
ἵνα προσενέγκωσι ἡμῖν ἐκεῖνα τα ἱμάτια.

Lesson XXII

312.I. 1. It is not lawful for you to have her.   2. And/but having commanded
the crowds to be dismissed, He went out into the desert; or, When he had
commanded....   3. It is not good to take the children's bread and to throw it
out.   4. And/But Jesus began to say to the Jews that it was necessary for

Him to go away.   5.   For the Son of man is about to/is going to come in glory with His angels.   6.   If (as a matter of fact) he wishes to go with me, it is necessary for him to die.   7.   It is good for you to enter into life.   8.   While I was saying this (lit., in the circumstance of my saying this), the Holy Spirit fell upon them.   9.   And/but after the Lord was raised, the Jews persecuted His disciples.   10.   And/but before the prophet was cast into prison, Jesus' disciples were baptizing those who were coming to them.   11.   And/but because he was there (on account of the fact he was there) the Jews came together.   12.   For I want to see you, in order that you may receive a good gift, in order that you may become faithful disciples.   13.   Jesus died for them in order that they might be saved.   14.   God sent Jesus in order that He might die for us, in order that we might glorify (continually) the one who saved us.   15.   The blind man said that he saw the men.   16.   Jesus said that he was still in the flesh, in order that those who heard might believe on Jesus.   18.   When Jesus had commanded us to go into the village, immediately He dismissed the crowd.   19.   Having been saved (when or since we have been saved) by Jesus, we ought to suffer also on account of His name.   20.   While we are suffering these things, the brethren were saying that they saw Jesus.

312.II.   1.   ἐν τῷ εὐαγγελίζεσθαι τὸν Ἰησοῦν τῷ λαῷ, οἱ φαρισαῖοι ἐκέλευον τοὺς στρατιώτας ἐνεγκεῖν αὐτόν.   (εὐαγγελιζομένου τοῦ Ἰησοῦ)   In this exercise, the infinitive expression will be used as the preferred answer.   Other equivalent translations so far presented by Machen will follow the sentence in parenthesis.   2.   μετὰ τὸ κελεῦσαι τὸν Ἰησοῦν τοὺς ὄχλους ἀπελθεῖν, οἱ μαθηταὶ αὐτοῦ προσῆλθον αὐτῷ (πρὸς αὐτόν).   (κελεύσαντος τοῦ Ἰησοῦ)   3.   εἰ θέλομεν ἰδεῖν τὸν Ἰησοῦν, εἰσέλθωμεν εἰς τὴν κωμὴν ταύτην.   4.   εἶπον ὅτι ἔξεστιν αὐτοῖς λαβεῖν ταῦτα τὰ ἱμάτια.   5.   εἶδον ὅτι δεῖ τὸν υἱὸν τοῦ ἀνθρώπου πάσχειν ταῦτα.   6.   μετὰ τὸ τὸν Ἰησοῦν εἰπεῖν ταῦτα τοῖς φαρισαίοις, οἱ ὄχλοι ἀπῆλθον.   (εἰπόντος τοῦ Ἰησοῦ ταῦτα).   7.   διὰ τὸ ἡμᾶς μὴ εἶναι μαθητὰς τοῦ Ἰησου, ὁ ἄρχων κελεύσει ἡμᾶς ἀπελθεῖν.   8.   μετὰ τὸ τὴν σωτηρίαν κηρυχθῆναι τῷ λαῷ ὁ Ἰησοῦς ἐδίδαξε τοὺς μαθητὰς αὐτοῦ.   (κηρυχθείσης τῆς σωτηρίας)   9.   ὀφείλομεν προσεύχεσθαι τῷ σώσαντι ἡμᾶς ἐν τῷ ἡμᾶς πάσχειν ταῦτα.   (πάσχοντες ταῦτα)   10.   σωθησόμεθα ἐν ἐκείνῃ τῇ ὥρᾳ διὰ τὸ πιστεῦσαι ἡμᾶς εἰς τὸ ὄνομα τοῦ Ἰησοῦ.   11.   οἱ εἰσελθόντες εἰς ἐκείνην τὴν κωμὴν εἶδον τὸν Ἰησοῦν εἶναι ἐν τῷ οἴκῳ.   (ὅτι ὁ Ἰησοῦς ἐστίν)   12.   μὴ ἁμαρτάνωμεν, διὰ τὸ τὸν θεὸν μὴ δέξασθαι εἰς τὴν βασιλείαν αὐτοῦ τοὺς ἁμαρτάνοντας καὶ μὴ ἐπιστρεφοντας αὐτῷ.   (ὁ γὰρ θεὸς οὐ δέξεται)   13.   ἐν τῷ προσεύχεσθαι τούτους τῷ θεῷ, αἱ στρατιῶται ἐδίωκον τὴν ἐκκλησίαν.   (τούτων προσευχομένων)   14.   καὶ μετὰ τὸ αὐτοὺς εἰσελθεῖν εἰς ταύτην τὴν κωμὴν εἶπον ὅτι θέλουσι ἰδεῖν τὸν Ἰησοῦν.   (μετὰ δὲ τὸ εἰσελθεῖν αὐτούς· or, εἰσελθόντες)   15.   αὕτη ἦλθεν ἰδεῖν τὰ ἔργα τοῦ χριστοῦ.   (ἵνα ἴδη or, εἰς τὸ ἰδεῖν)   16.   οἱ ἄνθρωποι ἠνέχθησαν πρὸς τὸν Ἰησοῦν Χριστὸν εἰς τὸ αὐτὸ θεραπεῦσαι αὐτούς.   (ἵνα θεραπεύσῃ)

Lesson XXIII

324.I.   1.   God will not bless the one who does not walk (is not walking) according to the commandments of Jesus.   2.   Those who are loved by Jesus love the one who loves them.   3.   While Jesus was speaking to those who were following, the ruler began to exhort him to go away.   4.   When we have followed the one who spoke these things, let us seek his house.   5.   If (as a matter of fact) we love God, let us keep (continually) his commands and do (continually) the things spoken to us by Jesus.   6.   When Jesus had done this thing, the one who had been healed was speaking about him to the following crowd (the crowd which was following).   7.   The apostles were seeing the works which were being done by Jesus while they were walking with Him.   8.   After the prophet was cast into prison, Jesus was no longer walking in that country.   9.   Those who love God do His commands.   10.   Even those who had been healed by Him were doing these things to Jesus.   11.   The crowds were seeking Him, in order that they might see the things (which were) being done by Him.   12.   Those who do not do His commandments do not love (have friendly regard for) Jesus. (See the bibliography on φιλέω/ἀγαπάω in AG, pp. 866-867.)   13.   Let us love (in continuing sense) God with/in our hearts, while loving (while we love) the brethren also.   14.   These things Jesus spoke to those who were following him, while He was still walking with them in the country of the Jews.   15.   If we do not (continually) walk according to the commands of Jesus, we will not see His face.   16.   After Jesus called them, they were no longer walking in the ways of the evil one nor were they doing (the) evil things.   17.   You were doing these things to us because (of the fact that) you love (continuing) the one who called you into His kingdom.   18.   Those who had been called by Him worshipped (gave worship to) Jesus when He had spoken these things after being raised (after He was raised) from the dead.   19.   The women who had followed Him from Galilee were watching Jesus while He was being crucified by the soldiers.   20.   We will not see Him, if we do not (continually) follow Him (while He is) walking in Galilee.

324.II. 1. ἐκεῖνα ἐλάλησεν ὁ Ἰησοῦς τοῖς ἀκολουθοῦσιν αὐτῷ ἀπὸ Γαλιλαίας.
        2. ἐθεώρουν τὸν ἀγαπήσαντά με καὶ ἀποθανόντα ὑπὲρ ἐμοῦ.   3. προσκυνήσωμεν τὸν ποιοῦντα ταῦτα καὶ εὐλογήσωμεν τὸ ὄνομα τὸ ἅγιον αὐτοῦ.   4. οἱ θεωροῦντες αὐτὸν περιπατοῦντα ἐν τῇ Γαλιλαίᾳ ἔλεγον ὅτι οὐ θέλουσι ἀκολουθεῖν αὐτόν.
5. ἀκολουθήσαντες τὸν Ἰησοῦν ἐν τῷ περιπατεῖν αὐτὸν ἐν τῇ Γαλιλαίᾳ ἐθεώρησαν καὶ μετὰ τὸ ἐγερθῆναι αὐτὸν ἐκ νεκρῶν.   6. ζητῶμεν τὸν λαλήσαντα ἡμῖν λόγους ἐλπίδος.   7. εὐλογῶμεν τὸ ὄνομα τοῦ περιπατήσαντος σὺν ἡμῖν ἐν τῷ κόσμῳ καὶ σταυρωθέντος ὑπὲρ ἡμῶν.   8. ἐὰν ἀκολουθῇς τὸν ποιοῦντα ταῦτα, θεωρήσεις αὐτὸν ἐν τῇ δόξῃ αὐτοῦ. 9. εἰ οὐκ ἀγαπῶμεν τοὺς εὐλογοῦντας ἡμᾶς, οὐκ ἀγαπήσομεν τοὺς ποιοῦντας πονηρά· or, ἐὰν μὴ ἀγαπῶμεν... .   10. ἀγαπᾷ ἡμᾶς καὶ δηλοῖ ἡμῖν τὴν δόξαν αὐτοῦ, ἵνα εὐλογῶμεν τὸν θεὸν εἰς τὸν αἰῶνα.   11. ἐν τῷ ἀκολουθεῖν τοὺς ὄχλους τὸν Ἰησοῦν καὶ ἀκούειν τὰ λαλούμενα ὑπ' αὐτοῦ, οἱ ἄρχοντες ἔλεγον ὅτι οὐκ ἀγαπῶσι αὐτόν. (ἀκολουθούντων τῶν ὄχλων...καὶ ἀκουόντων)   12. δηλώσω τοῖς ἀκολουθοῦσί με τὰ δηλωθέντα μοί ὑπὸ τοῦ Ἰησοῦ.   13. οὗτοί εἰσιν οἱ ἀγαπῶντες τὸν Ἰησοῦν καὶ θεωρήσαντες τὰ ἔργα αὐτοῦ καὶ κληθέντες εἰς τὴν βασιλείαν αὐτοῦ.   14. παρεκάλεσεν ὁ ἀδελφὸς αὐτοῦ αὐτὸν ἀκολουθεῖν τὸν Ἰησοῦν ἵνα ᾖ σὺν αὐτῷ εἰς τὸν αἰῶνα.   15. ταύτην τὴν παραβολὴν λαλοῦμεν τοῖς ἀγαπῶσι τὸν θεὸν καὶ τηροῦσι τὰς ἐντολὰς αὐτοῦ.   16. τοῦτό ἐστιν τὸ τέκνον τὸ εὐλογοῦν τὸν θεὸν καὶ ἀγάπων αὐτόν.

Lesson XXIV

344.I.   1.   For we do not preach ourselves but (we preach) Christ Jesus as Lord, and (in contrast) ourselves (as) your servants on account of Jesus.
2.   The one who raised the Lord Jesus will raise even us (us also) with Jesus.
3.   The disciple said that he would die for Jesus.   4.   We ourselves will not

raise ourselves, but Jesus will raise us in the last day. 5. Immediately the evil one carried away the thing sown beside the way. 6. If you love (continually) one another, you will be disciples of the One who died for you. 7. If you believe on Jesus, you will remain with Him forever. 8. The one who loves the Son loves the One who sent Him, (also). 9. There shall be joy over the sinner who has repented on the basis of the word of Jesus. 10. Those who killed Jesus and persecuted His disciples will cast us out also. 11. When these men had (re)turned to God they remained in His Church. 12. When God has raised the dead, we shall be with the Lord forever and ever. 13. I did not believe in/on myself, but in/on the Lord. 14. It is right for us to receive gifts from one another, but not to kill nor to persecute each other. 15. This (on the one hand) is the ruler who slew the prophets, but that (on the other hand) is the sinner who repented at the word of Jesus. 16. (And) If we should say this against him, we fear the crowds, for they say Him to be a prophet (that He is a prophet). 17. He will send to them teachers and prophets, in order that they may repent and fear (continuing) God. 18. Not those who glorify themselves are blessed, but those who glorify the one who sent His Son into the world. 19. While Jesus was coming to them walking upon the sea, the disciples who saw Him were afraid (fearing). 20. These things we will say to those prophets who have/had <u>been</u> sent to us.

344.II. 1. ἄραντος τοῦ Ἰησοῦ τὰς ἁμαρτίας ἡμῶν, ἐσόμεθα ἅγιοι εἰς τὸν αἰῶνα.
2. μὴ ἀρξώμεθα λέγειν ἐν ἑαυτοῖς ὅτι οὐ γινώσκομεν αὐτόν. 3. οὐ φοβηθησόμεθα τὸν ἄρχοντα τὸν ἀποκτείναντα τοὺς προφήτας, ὁ γὰρ θεὸς ἀποστελεῖ τοὺς ἀγγέλους αὐτοῦ πρὸς ἡμᾶς. 4. τῶν στρατιωτῶν ἀποκτεινάντων τὸν Ἰησοῦν τὸν κύριον ἡμῶν, ἐφοβούμεθα καὶ ἀπήλθομεν ἀπ' αὐτοῦ. 5. εἶπεν ὅτι οὐ δεῖ ἡμᾶς ἰδεῖν ἀλλήλους. 6. ἐὰν διώξητε καὶ ἀποκτείνητε τοὺς πεμπομένους πρὸς ὑμᾶς, οὐκέτι ἔσεσθε οἱ λαοὶ τοῦ θεοῦ. 7. οἱ ὄχλοι ἀπῆλθον, οἱ δὲ μένοντες εἶπον αὐτὸν ἔχειν τὰ ῥήματα τῆς ζωῆς. 8. τοῦ Ἰησοῦ λαλήσαντος ταῦτα καὶ ἀποστείλαντος τοὺς μαθητὰς αὐτοῦ εἰς τὰς κώμας τῆς Γαλιλαίας, οἱ φαρισαῖοι ἐφοβοῦντο τὸν λαόν. 9. ἀποκτείναντες τὸν Ἰησοῦν ἐκβαλοῦσι ἐκ τῶν συναγωγῶν αὐτῶν τοὺς πιστεύσαντας εἰς αὐτόν. 10. ὁ ἀπόστολος αὐτὸς οὐκ ἔσωσεν ἑαυτόν, ὁ δὲ θεὸς ἦν ὁ σώσας αὐτόν. 11. μετὰ τὸ λαλῆσαι τὸν κύριον τὴν παραβολὴν ταύτην, οἱ ἄρχοντες ἐκεῖνοι εἶπον ὅτι ἀποκτενοῦσι τοὺς πεμφθέντας ὑπ' αὐτοῦ. 12. ἐὰν μὴ ὁ Ἰησοῦς αὐτὸς πέμπῃ ἡμᾶς, οὐκ ἐσόμεθα μαθηταὶ αὐτοῦ. 13. ἐὰν μὴ μετανοήσητε, μενεῖτε ἐν ἁμαρτίᾳ εἰς τὸν αἰῶνα. 14. ὁ εἰπὼν τὸν λόγον τοῦτον τῷ πέμψαντι τοὺς ἀποστόλους ἐρεῖ καὶ τὸν αὐτὸν λόγον τοῖς πεμφθεῖσι ὑπ' αὐτοῦ. 15. ἐκεῖνοι οἱ μαθηταὶ οἱ ἀγαθοὶ ἀγαπήσαντες τοὺς ἀκολουθοῦντας τῷ Ἰησοῦ ἀγαπήσουσι καὶ τοὺς ἀκολουθοῦντας τοῖς ἀποστόλοις αὐτοῦ. 16. οἱ ἰδόντες αὐτὸν ἐν τῷ αὐτὸν περιπατεῖν ἐν τῇ Γαλιλαίᾳ, θεωρήσουσι αὐτὸν ἐν τοῖς οὐρανοῖς εἰς τὸν αἰῶνα.

Lesson XXV

363.I. 1. The things (which are being) spoken by this priest are true.
2. When the chief priests and scribes had gathered together in order that they might kill this man, the disciples prayed in the temple. 3. The good king answered saying that he did not want to kill this man. 4. Those sinners have been saved by (means of) grace, and (they) have been raised up

in glory.   5.   For by grace we are being saved through faith, in order that
we (may) (continually) glorify God.   6.   When he had seen his father and mother
in the city, he remained with them.   7.   You will send your apostles into the
nations, in order that they may (continually) proclaim to them the good news
of your grace.   8.   This man was good and full of the Holy Spirit and of
faith.   9.   Having seen the grace of God, they encouraged the Gentiles to
remain in the grace (of God) with joy and hope.   10.   As they were coming down
from the mountain, Jesus was speaking these things.   11.   Let us love our
fathers and mothers in order that we may keep the command of God.   12.   When
the chief priests had seen those who were gathering together in order to hear
the man, the rulers said to themselves that he had to die (i.e., it was
necessary for him to die).   13.   The evil kings slew both the men and the
children.   14.   And God raised them up, in order that they might (in a continuing sense) glorify Him forever.   15.   If we have not grace and faith and
hope, the Gentiles will not repent at our word.   16.   We brought our father
and mother to the men who were sent by the king.   17.   Having come to the
king of this country, you besought him not to kill this man.   18.   If the
things being said by those who have followed the man in Galilee are true, the
chief priests will kill him.   19.   Through faith he will save those who believe on his name.   20.   But even the Gentiles (the Gentiles also) received
the true word (message) of Jesus; or, But the Gentiles also... .

363.II. 1. τοῦτό ἐστιν τὸ ἔθνος τὸ ἀποκτεῖναν τοὺς πιστεύοντας εἰς (τὸν)
Ἰησοῦν.   2. εἰσελθόντων τῶν γραμματέων εἰς ἐκείνην τὴν πόλιν, οἱ
μαθηταὶ ἀπῆλθον πρὸς τὰ ὄρη.   3. εἴδομεν ὅτι ἀληθὴς (ἐστιν) ὁ λόγος ὁ
λαλούμενος ὑπὸ τοῦ ἀνθρώπου.   4. τοῦ κυρίου εἰπόντος τοῦτο τοῖς ἀρχιερεῦσι,
ὁ ἄρχων ἐθαύμασεν.   5. ὁ πατὴρ τοῦ ἀποκτείναντος τοὺς ἀνθρώπους ἀποκτενεῖ
καὶ τὰ τέκνα.   6. ἐγερεῖ ὁ θεὸς ἐκ νεκρῶν τοὺς σωθέντας τῇ χάριτι αὐτοῦ.
7. σωθήσεσθε ὑπὸ τοῦ θεοῦ διὰ (τῆς) πίστεως.   8. διὰ τὴν πίστιν τῶν πατέρων
καὶ τῶν μητέρων τὰ τέκνα ἀποθανοῦνται ἐν τῇ πόλει τῇ πονηρᾷ.   9. οὖσα αὐτὴ
πλήρης (τῆς) ἁμαρτίας, ἡ πόλις ἔχει καὶ βασιλέα κακόν.   10. ἐὰν εἰσέλθωμεν
εἰς ἐκείνας τὰς πόλεις ἔχοντες τὰς καρδίας (ἡμῶν) πλήρεις χάριτος καὶ πίστεως
καὶ ἐλπίδος, οἱ μετανοοῦντες ἐπὶ τῷ λόγῳ ἡμῶν ὄψονται τὸν βασιλέα ἐν τῇ δόξῃ
αὐτοῦ.   11. ὁ Ἰησοῦς εἶπε τοῖς γραμματεῦσι τοῖς ἀκολουθοῦσιν ὅτι εἰσέρχεται
εἰς τὴν πόλιν τὴν ἁγίαν.   12. εἰ ἀγαπῶμεν τοὺς ἀδελφούς, καὶ εὐλογήσομεν
τὸν πέμψαντα αὐτοὺς εἰς τὰ ἔθνη.   13. ὁ βασιλεὺς εἶπε τῷ πατρί μου ὅτι οἱ
ἀρχιερεῖς καὶ φαρισαῖοι θέλουσιν ἀποκτεῖναι τοὺς ἀκολουθοῦντας (τῷ) Ἰησοῦ.
14. λαλοῦντος (τοῦ) Ἰησοῦ ταῦτα ἐν ἐκείνῃ τῇ πόλει τῇ κακῇ, οἱ ἀρχιερεῖς
συνῆγον τοὺς στρατιώτας ἵνα ἀποκτείνωσιν αὐτόν.   15. οἱ μὴ ἔχοντες τὴν
χάριν τοῦ θεοῦ ἐν ταῖς καρδίαις αὐτῶν ἔχουσιν οὐδὲ ζωὴν οὐδὲ ἐλπίδα.   16. ἐὰν
εἰσέλθητε εἰς ἐκείνας τὰς πόλεις καὶ κώμας, ὄψεσθε τὸν βασιλέα τὸν ἀποκτείναντα
τοὺς πατέρας ὑμῶν καὶ τὰς μητέρας ὑμῶν.

Lesson XXVI

383.I. 1. When he had remained with him for three years, he came into that
        city.   2.   Having seen those who were in the large city, he wrote to
those who were in the small (city) also.   3.   And/but when the sons of James
had gone about five furlongs, they saw Jesus and all the disciples who were
with him.   4.   And/but after they had heard all these things, those who were

in the synagogue said that they wanted to see the one who was doing these things. 5. All the crowd marvelled as they saw the things which were being done by Jesus. 6. The man who after two years saw the apostle who had told him the Gospel did not remain one day. 7. While the chief priests were in that great city, Jesus remained in the village about five or six days. 8. It is necessary for those (who are) in the cities to go out into the mountains. 9. When the one who had been carried to Him by the four men had been healed by Jesus, all those who were in the house glorified the One who had done these great things. 10. Before those who were from the cities came, Jesus was with his disciples in the desert. 11. On the one hand the world was made through Him, and all the things which are in it, but He (himself) on the other hand became like a servant on account of us. 12. This He did in order that He might save all those who were believing on Him. 13. Every one who loves God loves the brethren also. 14. All those who were in the city were gathered together, in order that they might hear the things which were being said by the apostles. 15. Those who were in the house were saying these things to all the chief priests and scribes, because they knew all the things concerning Jesus. 16. The king of the Jews was doing these things, for he was wanting to kill the children in the village. 17. No one knows all things which are in the world, except the One who made all things. 18. No one will be saved, except through faith, for no one has kept all the commandments of God. 19. Let us (continually) pray for those who persecute us, in order that we may become sons of our Father who is in heaven. 20. Blessed are the pure, for they (emphatic) shall see God.

383.II. 1. οἱ ἀρχιερεῖς εἶδον ὅτι ἀληθῆ (εἰσιν) πάντα τὰ λαλούμενα ὑπὸ τοῦ Ἰησοῦ. 2. ἐν ἐκείνῳ τῷ τόπῳ ἦσαν ὡς πεντακισχίλιοι μετὰ πολλῶν δώρων καὶ πολλῶν ἱματίων. 3. πολλοί (εἰσιν) οἱ καταβαίνοντες εἰς τὴν ὁδὸν τὴν κακήν, ἀλλ᾽ ὀλίγοι (εἰσίν) οἱ περιπατοῦντες ἐν ταῖς ὁδοῖς τῆς ζωῆς. 4. ἐὰν γένησθε μαθηταί μου, δηλώσω ὑμῖν πάντα. 5. τῇ χάριτι τοῦ θεοῦ πάντες (ἡμεῖς) ἐγενόμεθα μαθηταὶ Ἰησοῦ. 6. διὰ (τῆς) πίστεως ἐγενόμεθα τέκνα τοῦ πατρὸς ἡμῶν τοῦ ἐν οὐρανῷ, ὁ γὰρ Ἰησοῦς ἔσωσεν ἡμᾶς. 7. ποιῶμεν πάντα τὰ ἐν τῷ νόμῳ, κατὰ τὰ λαλούμενα ἡμῖν ὑπὸ τῶν προφητῶν. 8. ἐν τῇ μεγάλῃ πόλει ἐκείνῃ εἴδομεν μαθητὰς τρεῖς τοῦ κυρίου προσευχομένους τῷ πατρὶ αὐτῶν τῷ ἐν οὐρανῷ. 9. καλέσας ἕνα τῶν τριῶν τῶν ἐν τῷ πλοίῳ ἐλάλησεν ὁ Ἰησοῦς αὐτῷ πάντα τὰ περὶ τῆς βασιλείας τοῦ θεοῦ. 10. ἦμεν ἐν τῇ αὐτῇ πόλει ἔτος ἕν, ὁ δὲ Ἰησοῦς ἀπέστειλεν ἡμᾶς εἰς πάσας τὰς κώμας τὰς ἐν Γαλιλαίᾳ. 11. ποιήσαντος (τοῦ) Ἰησοῦ πάντα ταῦτα τὰ μεγάλα, οἱ φαρισαῖοι εἶπον ὅτι δαιμόνιον ἐστίν ἐν αὐτῷ (εἶναι ἐν αὐτῷ δαιμόνιον). 12. λαλήσας πάντα ταῦτα τοῖς ὄχλοις τοῖς ἐν ταῖς πόλεσι καὶ κώμαις ἀπέστειλε ὁ Ἰησοῦς τοὺς μαθητας ἵνα κηρύσσ/(ξωσιν) καὶ ἐν ταῖς ἄλλαις πόλεσιν. 13. ὄψονται πᾶσαι αἱ ἐκκλησίαι τὸν διὰ χάριτος αὐτοῦ σώσαντα αὐτας καὶ ἀποστείλαντα πρὸς αὐτας τοὺς ἀποστόλους. 14. πολλοὶ βασιλεῖς καὶ ἱερεῖς ἐροῦσι ὅτι ἀληθῆ (εἰσιν) πάντα τὰ λαληθέντα ὑπὸ τοῦ Ἰησοῦ. 15. εἴδομεν οὐδένα ἐν ἐκείνῃ τῇ μεγάλῃ πόλει ἐὰν μὴ μαθητὴν ἕνα καὶ παιδία ὀλίγα. 16. οἱ τοῦ Ἰησοῦ ἀπέθανον διὰ τὴν πίστιν αὐτῶν.

Lesson XXVII

402.I. 1. Whoever does not receive you, this one the king will not receive.
2. Whatever (things) we do to you, also you (shall) do to us; or, ... even you... . 3. When a certain one had asked them what he should eat, they

answered him saying that he had to (i.e., it was necessary for him to) eat the bread which was in the house.   4. Whose (i.e., belonging to whom) shall all these things be in the last day?   5. When(ever) the Son of man comes, who shall the believers be?   6. Whoever breaks (should break) one of the command-ments does what is not lawful to do.   7. The things which the prophet said to you, while he was still with you, these things even those who told us the Good News will say.   8. If anyone goes (should go) to them from the dead, they will repent.   9. Whoever does not hear the prophets, neither will he repent if he should see someone of/from the dead.   10. Whatever persons say things which are not true will not receive any fruit of/from their work.   11. He was saying (said repeatedly) that if someone be raised from the dead they will repent.   12. Those who were in Galilee asked the prophet if the dead would hear the voice of the Lord.   13. He said therefore to them that in the judgment all men would hear the Lord.   14. When the Pharisees had come into a certain village, they asked those who were in it saying, "Where are those who belong to the prophet, for the things which the men who are in Galilee say concerning them are not true."   15. And the one who had been asked kept saying (was saying), "Why do you ask me?   For I do not want to answer you anything."   16. Therefore a certain one of the disciples was saying to the apostle, "What shall this man do?"   But the apostle immediately answered him saying, "God will do what (what things, the things which) He wills, and all things which He wills are good."   17. What things (the things which) he was seeing the Lord doing, these things he also (or, he himself also) was wishing to do (continually).

402.II. 1. ὃ οἳ ἐν τῇ αὐτῇ πόλει ᾔτησαν ἐποιήσαμεν.   2. οἱ ἱερεῖς οὓς εἴδομεν ἔτι ὄντας ἐκεῖ ᾔτησαν ἡμᾶς τίνες εἰσὶν ἐκεῖνοι οἱ μαθηταί.   3. ὃς ἂν μὴ ποιήσῃ/ποιῇ ἃ λέγω οὐ λήμψεται ἀπ᾽ ἐμοῦ ἃ αἰτεῖ.   4. ἦλθεν γραμματεύς τις εἰς τὴν πόλιν ἵνα λάβῃ τὰ βιβλία ἃ οἱ προφῆται ἔγραψαν.   5. εἰς ὃ ἐὰν ἔθνος εἰσέλθημεν, ζητῶμεν τοὺς μαθητὰς τοὺς ἐν αὐτῷ.   6. τί ἐροῦμεν περὶ πάντα ταῦτα;   7. ἠρώτησαν ἡμᾶς τί λέγωσι περὶ τῶν ἐν τῇ πόλει.   8. ἐλθὼν πρὸς (τὸν) Ἰησοῦν, εἶπέν τις ὅτι θέλει θεραπευθῆναι.   9. ὃς (ε)ἂν αἰτήσῃ τι λήμψεται ἃ/ὃ αἰτεῖ.   10. ἠρώτησαν Ἰησοῦν τί ἐστιν τὸ θέλημα τοῦ θεοῦ.   11. ὃς (ε)ἂν ἀποκτείνῃ τὸν ἀδελφὸν αὐτοῦ ἐλεύσεται εἰς τὴν κρίσιν.   12. τί οὖν ἐσθίετε ὃ οὐκ ἔξεστιν φαγεῖν;   13. ὃς ἂν μὴ διδάσκηται ὑπὸ τοῦ κυρίου, οὐ γνώσεται αὐτόν.   14. ὅτε εἶδον οἱ ἀρχιερεῖς ὃ ὁ Ἰησοῦς ἐποίει, ἀπέστειλαν ἄγγελόν τινα πρὸς τοὺς φαρισαίους.   15. ποῦ μενῶμεν; ἡ γὰρ νὺξ ἔρχεται καὶ οὐδεὶς εἶπεν ἡμῖν ὃν ποιήσομεν.

Lesson XXVIII

424.I.   1. And if he does not listen, take with you still one or two (men, witnesses).   2. Whatever you see the Christ (Messiah) doing, this do you also.   3. Lord, be merciful to us, for we have not done what (things) you commanded.   4. Let the one in the mountain not enter into the city.   5. Thus therefore you (continually) pray, "Our Father who is in heaven (the heavens); let your name be hallowed; let your kingdom come; let your will be done, as in heaven, upon earth also."   6. Dismiss the multitudes, then, Lord; for the night is already coming.   7. Let no one go out into the mountains, but let all (men) pray to their Father who is in the heavens.   8. When you

have taken (arrested) him, bring (him) to us.   9. Tell to no one what you
saw/have seen.   10. Arise and do not be afraid (or stop fearing); for
the Lord will save you.   11. Do and keep (continually) therefore all things,
whatsoever they say to you, but according to their works do not do (continually);
for they say and do not do/act.   12. A certain disciple was saying (kept
saying) to Him, "Lord, command me to come to you upon the waters." And Jesus
said, "Come!"   13. What(so)ever you hear with your ears and see with your
eyes tell (even) to the Gentiles also.   14. Whatever you hear in the darkness,
proclaim in the light.   15. Whoever shall eat bread in the kingdom of God
is blessed.   16. In that city are evil priests, who do not do the will of
God.   17. Having gone out (when you have gone out) tell (to) all the nations
which are upon all the earth what (things) God has done for those who love
Him.   18。 Whenever you are called by someone, go!   19. Whenever you see
these things happening, you will know that the judgment is near.   20. See,
you all, my hands! For these hands have not done anything (or, have done
nothing) of which those men tell.

424.II。 1. εἴπετε πᾶσιν τοῖς ἔθνεσιν ἃ εἶπον (ἐγὼ) ὑμῖν.   2. μὴ εἴπητε ἐν
          τῇ καρδίᾳ ὑμῶν ὅτι οὐ θέλετε ποιεῖν ἃ κελεύει ὁ βασιλεύς.   3. μηδεὶς
φοβείσθω ἐκείνους τοὺς ἱερεῖς τοὺς πονηρούς, ὅστις γὰρ ποιῇ τὸ θέλημα τοῦ
θεοῦ ἐξελεύσεται σὺν τῇ χαρᾷ.   4. ἐλεησάτω ἡμᾶς ὁ σώσας ἡμᾶς διὰ τοῦ αἵματος
αὐτοῦ ἐν ταυταῖς ταῖς ἡμέραις ταῖς κακαῖς.   5. ὃς ἐὰν ἀγαπᾷ τὸν θεὸν ἐλεύσεται
εἰς τὸ φῶς, ὁ δὲ μὴ ἀγαπῶν αὐτὸν ἐν σκότει περιπατήσει.   6. ὅσα ἐὰν ποιήσητε
ἐν τῷ φωτὶ ποιήσατε, ἵνα ἁγιάζηται τὸ ὄνομα τοῦ θεοῦ.   7。 βαπτισθήτωσαν οὗτοι,
χριστὸς γὰρ ἔσωσεν αὐτοὺς διὰ τοῦ λόγου αὐτοῦ.   8. προσεύχου τῷ πατρί σου
τῷ ἐν τῷ οὐρανῷ, ποιήσει γὰρ ὅσα ἐὰν αἰτῇς/ἐρωτᾷς.   9. μὴ λεγέτω ὁ βασιλεὺς
τοῦτο, πιστοὶ γὰρ πάντες ἡμεῖς.   10. μὴ ποιήσωμεν ἃ εἶπον οἱ πονηροὶ ἡμῖν.
11. ἐλέει πάντας, ὁ γὰρ κύριος ἐλέησέ σε.   12. ὅσα ἐὰν ὦσιν ἀγαθὰ ποιήσατε˙
ὅσα δὲ ἐὰν (ὦσιν) πονηρὰ περὶ τούτων μηδὲ εἴπητε。   13. οἱ μαθηταὶ ἐρώτησαν
τὸν ἀπόστολον τί ἐσθίωσιν, καὶ εἶπεν ὁ ἀπόστολος αὐτοῖς, Εἰσέλθετε εἰς τὰς
κώμ καὶ φάγετε τὸν ἄρτον τὸν ἐν αὐταῖς.   14。 μὴ ἄρξητε λέγειν ἐν ἑαυτοῖς
ὅτι οὐ γινώσκετε τὴν ἀλήθειαν.   15. μὴ εἰς τοὺς οἴκους αὐτῶν ὑποστρεφέτωσαν
οἱ ἐν τοῖς ἀγροῖς。   16. κύριε, σῶσόν με, ἐγὼ γὰρ ἔλυσα τὰς ἐντολάς σου.

Lesson XXIX

454.I.   1. No one is righteous according to the law except the one who has
          done all the things which stand written in the book of the law.
2. He told all the people the Good News, saying that the kingdom of heaven
is come near.   3. What we have seen and (have) heard we say also to you, in
order that you may believe in the Christ.   4. And in this we know that we
have come to know him, if his commands we (continually) keep.   5. The one
who loves Him who begot loves the One begotten of/from Him.   6. Everyone
who is (stands) born of God does not sin, but the one who was begotten of
God keeps him.   7. This thing is come to pass, because thus it stands written
through the prophet.   8. The thing begotten of the flesh is flesh, and the
thing begotten of the Spirit is spirit.   9. And/but this is the judgment, that
(the) light is come into the world, and men loved the darkness.   10. Therefore
the Jews were saying to the man who was healed, "It is not lawful to do this."

11. I am come in the name of my Father, and you do not receive me. 12. But I said to you that you have (both/even) seen me (also) and do not believe. 13. If you do not eat the flesh of the Son of Man and drink His blood, you do not have life in yourselves. 14. The words which I have spoken to you are spirit and are life. 15. Peter answered Him, "Lord, to whom shall we go? You have words of life, and we (have come to) believe and know that you are the Holy One of God (God's Holy One)." 16. As He was speaking these things, many believed on Him. 17. It is written that the testimony of two men is true. 18. These things He said to the Jews who believed on Him. 19. And/but now you are seeking to kill me, a man who has told you the truth which I heard from God. (Check NTGFB note 2 here.) English requires third person in this relative clause. 20. Blessed is the one who comes in the name of the Lord.

454.II. 1. ποῦ ἔστιν ὁ ἱερεύς ἤδη ἐλήλυθεν. 2. πάντες οἱ μαθηταὶ οἱ βεβαπτισμένοι (εἰσιν) ἐν τῇ μικρᾷ πόλει. 3. βεβαπτισμένοι οἱ ἱερεῖς συνῆλθον εἰς τὸν αὐτὸν οἶκον. 4. ποῦ ἔστιν τὸ πλῆθος; ἤδη ἔγγικεν. 5. τί (ἐστιν) ἐν τῇ καρδίᾳ σου; πεπίστευκα εἰς τὸν κύριον. 6. εἶ πιστός; ἐγὼ τετήρηκα τὴν πίστιν. 7. γέγραπται διὰ τοῦ προφήτου ὅτι ὁ χριστὸς ἔρχεται ἐν ταύταις ταῖς ἡμέραις, καὶ ἐγνώκαμεν/γινώσκομεν ὅτι ἤγγικεν ἡ βασιλεία αὐτοῦ. 8. παιδία ἠγαπημένα ὑπὸ τοῦ πατρὸς ὑμῶν, εἰσέλθετε εἰς τὴν χαρὰν τὴν τετηρημένην ἐν τῷ οὐρανῷ τοῖς πεπιστευκόσιν/ὑπὲρ τῶν πεπιστευκότων εἰς τὸν χριστόν. 9. τίς (ἐστιν) οὗτος; αὐτός ἐστιν τέκνον γεγεννημένον ὑπὸ τοῦ θεοῦ. 10. σταυρωθεὶς ὑπὸ τῶν στρατιωτῶν ὁ κύριος ἀπέθανεν, ἀλλὰ νῦν ἐγήγερται. 11. ἀδελφοὶ ἠγαπημένοι ὑπὸ πάντων τῶν μαθητῶν, τί οὐκ ἐλεεῖτε τοὺς μικρούς. 12. οἱ ἐξεληλυθότες ἐκ (τοῦ) σκότους εἰς τὸ φῶς γινώσκουσι/ ἔγνωκαν ὅτι ὁ θεὸς ποιήσει πάντα τὰ γεγραμμένα ἐν τῷ νόμῳ καὶ τοῖς προφήταις. 13. πάντα τὰ γεγραμμένα ἢ λελαλημένα διὰ τούτου τοῦ προφήτου ἐστιν ἀληθη (ἀληθη ἐστιν). 14. τοῦτο γέγονεν ἵνα πεπλήρωται/πληρωθῇ τὸ λελαλημένον ὑπὸ τοῦ κυρίου διὰ τοῦ προφήτου. 15. εἰ ἤδη λέλυσαι, εὐχαριστεῖ τῷ λυσαντί σε. 16. ποῦ ἔστιν ὁ προφήτης ὃν οἱ στρατιῶται ἐδίωξαν; γέγονε βασιλεὺς πόλεων πολλῶν.

Lesson XXX

480.I. 1. And/but I beseech/exhort you that you all say the same thing (i.e., agree). 2. Whatsoever you wish that men should do to you, thus also do you; for this is the law and the prophets. 3. Command, therefore, the body to be kept by the soldiers, lest coming the disciples should take it and say to the people that he has risen/been raised from the dead (lest the disciples come and take ...). 4. A servant is not greater than the one who sent him. 5. No one has love greater than this, that someone should die for (the) others. 6. Again he sent other servants more than the first (ones). 7. If it is (a) righteous (thing) in the sight of God to listen to you more than God, you judge. 8. And/but I say to you, "Love (continually) your enemies and pray (continually) for those who persecuted you, in order that you may become sons of your Father who is in heaven." 9. Jesus said to them that it was lawful to do (regularly) good on the Sabbath. 10. And/but Jesus stayed there because the place was near the city. 11. Then will be gathered together before Him all the nations.

12. Do not (continue to) do this! For I am not worthy that you should enter (into) my house.   13. When the soldiers had come by night they took the man, and having led him out, they killed (him).   14. On the one hand you are not with us with respect to the flesh, but, with respect to the heart, you are near.   15. Do we walk according to the flesh? (No!) Do we not have God's Spirit? (Yes!); or, We do not walk..., do we? We do have..., don't we?   16. He entered the house of the chief priest in order that he might be near the place where Jesus was.   17. Unto His own (things) He came, and His own (people) did not receive Him.   18. I am come in the name of my father, and you do not receive me; if another should come in his own name, that one you will receive.   19. Have I done my own will? (No!) Have I not rather done <u>yours</u> (your will)? (Yes!)   20. If they have persecuted me, they will persecute you also; if they have kept my word, they will keep yours also.

480.II.   1. οἱ ποιήσαντες καλῶς ἕνα ἔργον ποιήσουσι καὶ μείζονα.   2. ὅστις ἄρχεται καλῶς τὸν ἴδιον οἶκον ποιεῖ μεῖζον ἢ ὁ πολλὰς πόλεις λαμβάνων (ὅς...λαμβάνει).   3. τί ποιεῖτε ταῦτα; μὴ βασιλεῖς καὶ ἱερεῖς ἐστέ; οὐκ δοῦλοί ἐστε;   4. οἳ ἐν τῷ σκότει παρεκάλεσαν ἡμᾶς ἵνα ἐλεήσωμεν αὐτοὺς καὶ μὴ ἐκβάλωμεν αὐτούς.   5. οἱ ἐμοὶ εἰσιν ἐν τῇ πόλει καὶ οἱ σοί εἰσιν ἔξω αὐτῆς, πάντες δὲ ἡμεῖς ἐσόμεθα ἐνώπιον τοῦ θεοῦ.   6. ἰσχυρότερος/οι εἶ/ἐστὲ ἢ ὁ ποιήσας τὴν γῆν καὶ πάντα τὰ ἐν αὐτοῖς; (Or ἰσχυρότερος/οι τοῦ ποιήσαντος).   7. μὴ φοβεῖσθε τὸν ἀποκτείνοντα τὸ σῶμα, μᾶλλον δὲ φοβεῖσθε τὸν ποιήσαντα πάντα.   8. ὅτε εἴδετε τοὺς σοὺς ἀδελφοὺς ἐλεύσεσθε καὶ πρὸς τὰ ἔθνη.   9. ἔχομεν δούλους πλείονας ἢ ὑμεῖς, οἱ δὲ ἡμέτεροι οὐκ (εἰσιν) ἱκανοὶ ἵνα εὐαγγελίσωσι πάντα τὰ ἔθνη.   10. οἱ προσκυνοῦντες τὸν κύριον ἡμέρας καὶ νυκτὸς ἔσονται ἰσχυρότεροι ἢ οἱ διώκοντες αὐτούς (ἰσχυρότεροι τῶν διωκόντων αὐτούς).   11. πλείονές εἰσιν οἱ μεθ' ἡμῶν ἢ οἱ μετ' αὐτῶν.   12. ὄντες μεθ' ὑμῶν τῇ καρδίᾳ οὐ τῷ προσώπῳ, παρεκαλέσαμεν ὑμᾶς ἵνα ποιήσητε καλῶς πάντα ἃ ἐκελεύσαμεν ὑμᾶς.   13. ἐξῆλθον οἱ ἱερεῖς ἐκ τῆς πόλεως, μήποτε οἱ γραμματεῖς ἴδωσιν αὐτοὺς ποιοῦντας ὃ οὐκ ἔξεστιν ποιεῖν.   14. ἐάν τις (ὅς ἐστίν) μείζων ἡμῶν (ἢ ἡμεῖς) ἔλθῃ κατὰ ἡμᾶς, οὐ μενοῦμεν ἐν τῇ πόλει ἡμῶν.   15. Ἰησοῦ θεραπεύσαντός τινα τῷ σαββάτῳ, οἱ γραμματεῖς ἐφοβοῦντο μὴ ποιήσῃ ὁ λαὸς αὐτὸν βασιλέα.   16. (τὸ) ἀποθανεῖν ὑπὲρ τῶν ἀδελφῶν κρεῖσσον ἢ (τὸ) ποιῆσαι ὃ οἱ ἀπόστολοι παρεκάλεσαν ἡμᾶς ἵνα μὴ ποιήσωμεν.

Lesson XXXI

522.I.   1. For I delivered to you in the first (things) what I received also, that Christ died for our sins according to the Scriptures.   2. Since he had nothing (with which) to pay, his Lord dismissed/released him (literally, "He, not having to pay back...").   3. And all the people answered and said, "His blood (be) upon us and upon our children."   4. And/but I wish to give to this last person as even to you (also).   5. And while they were eating, Jesus, when He had taken bread and pronounced a blessing, broke (it) and having given to the disciples, said, "Take, eat; this is my body." and when He had taken a cup and given thanks, He gave to them saying, "All of you drink of it."   6. And they spoke saying to him, "Tell us by what sort of authority you are doing these things, or who it is who has given you this authority." And He answered and said to them, "I also will ask (you) a matter, and you tell me." 7. For the bread of God is the One who comes down from heaven and gives life to the world. 8. He said/says to them, "Whom do you say me to be (who do you say that I am)?" And Simon Peter answered and said, "You are the Messiah, the Son of the God who is alive." 9. Jesus said/says to him, "Go! Your son is alive." The man believed the word which Jesus said to him and was going (i.e. started out on his way). 10. Watch continually, lest some one repay evil for evil to anyone. 11. The hour has come; behold the Son of Man is being betrayed into the hands of sinners. Arise, let us be going; behold the one who is betraying me is at hand (is come near). 12. And behold one came and said to Him, "Teacher, what good thing should I do in order that I might have eternal life?" And He said to him, "Why are you asking me about the good? One person is the Good One. But if you want to enter into life, keep continually the commandments." 13. And the tempter came and said (and having come, the tempter said) to Him, "If as a matter of fact you are God's Son (a son of God), say/command that these stones become bread." But He answered and said "It stands written, 'Not by bread alone shall man live.'" 14. And the disciples came (and having come) and said to Him, "Why are you speaking to them in parables?" And He answered and said, "To you it is granted to know the mysteries of the kingdom of heaven, but to those it is not granted." 15. The disciples kept saying (were saying) to Him, "Dismiss them!" But He answered and said to them, "You give to them to eat!"

522.II. 1. ἡ γυνὴ παρεκάλεσε τὸν ἀπόστολον ἵνα δῷ τι αὐτῇ. ὁ δὲ ἀπεκρίθη αὐτῇ οὐδέν. 2. εἶπαν οἱ ἀποκτείναντες τὴν γυναῖκα ὅτι ἔγνωκαν τὸν βασιλέα. ὁ δὲ ἀποκριθεὶς εἶπεν ὅτι οὐ θέλει δοῦναι αὐτοῖς ὃ ἠρώτησαν. 3. εἰ πιστεύομεν εἰς τὸν ἀγαπήσαντα ἡμᾶς καὶ ἑαυτὸν δόντα ὑπὲρ ἡμῶν, ἕξομεν ζωὴν αἰώνιαν ἀντὶ θανάτου. 4. διδόντος τοῦ ἀποστόλου τοῖς τέκνοις ἃ ἠρώτησαν, αἱ γυναῖκες ἐδίδοσαν δῶρα ἡμῖν. 5. παρέδωκεν ὁ κύριος τοῖς ἀποστόλοις τὸ εὐαγγέλιον, οἱ δὲ παρέδωκαν τοῖς ἔθνεσιν αὐτό. 6. τί ἀποδῶμεν τῷ δόντι ἑαυτὸν ὑπὲρ ἡμῶν; 7. ἰδοὺ δίδωσιν ἡμῖν ζωὴν αἰώνιον. ποιῶμεν οὖν τὸ θέλημα αὐτοῦ. 8. τί ἀποδώσει τις ἀντὶ τῆς ψυχῆς αὐτοῦ; 9. ὃ ἐὰν (ἀπὸ) διδῶμεν αὐτῷ οὐκ ἔσται ἱκανόν. 10. ὃ ἐὰν θέλῃς ἵνα οἱ ἄνθρωποι (ἀπὸ) διδωσί σοι, δίδου καὶ σὺ αὐτοῖς. 11. εὐχαριστείτωσαν τοῖς παραδοῦσιν αὐτοῖς τὸ εὐαγγέλιον. 12. ἠρώτησαν τὸν κύριον τί ἀποδῶσιν αὐτῷ. ὁ δὲ ἀποκριθεὶς εἶπεν αὐτοῖς ὅτι ποιεῖν τὸ θέλημα τοῦ θεοῦ (ἐστὶν) μεῖζον πάντων τῶν δώρων. 13. ἐκεῖναι (αἱ γυναῖκες) ἀποδιδόασι τοῖς παιδίοις ἃ ἔλαβον ἀπ' αὐτῶν, μὴ ἐκβάλῃ ὁ βασιλεὺς αὐτὰς ἐκ τῆς πόλεως. 14. εἰπόντων τῶν ἱερέων ταῦτα τοῖς ἐν τῇ πόλει, ἀπῆλθεν ὁ ἀπόστολος. 15. τοῦτο τί ἐστιν; δώσει ἡμῖν τὴν σάρκα αὐτοῦ; 16. ὃ ἐὰν ἐρωτήσῃ δώσω. ὁ δὲ ἔδωκέ μοι ζωὴν αἰώνι.

Lesson XXXII

537.I. 1. On account of this the father loves me, because I am laying down my life in order that I may take it again. No one took it from me, but I (emphatic) lay it down of myself. I have authority to lay it down, and I have authority to take it (back) again. This command I received from my father. 2. This is my (own) commandment, that you love (continually) one another just as I have loved you. No one has greater love than this, that someone should lay down his life for his friends. 3. But come (having come), lay your hand upon her, and she shall live. 4. And Jesus said, "Permit the little children to come to me and do not hinder them; for of such ones is the kingdom of heaven." And when He had laid (His) hands upon them, He went thence (away from there). 5. And when they had prayed they placed (their) hands upon them. 6. Then they were laying (their) hands upon them, and they were receiving the Holy Spirit. 7. And when they heard, they were baptized in the name of the Lord Jesus; and when Paul had laid hands on them the Holy Spirit came upon them. 8. The Son of God makes alive whom He wills/wishes. 9. Let what you have heard from the beginning remain in/among you. If what you have heard from the beginning remains in you, you also will remain in the Son and in the Father. 10. And he became like a dead man, so that many were saying that he (had) died. 11. Stay (be!) there until I tell you; for Herod is going to seek the child in order to destroy it. 12. Lord, save (us); we are perishing. 13. And He opened the scroll and found the place. 14. The things which come out of the mouth come out of the heart. 15. And not only concerning these do I ask, but also concerning those who believe in me through their word, that all may be one, just as you, Father, (are) in me and I in you, that they also may be in us, in order that the world may believe that you sent me. 16. Therefore Jesus said, "Yet a little time I am with you, and I am going to the One who sent me." 17. When the (regular) time of fruits drew near, he sent forth his servants. 18. And/but he himself shall be saved, but thus as through (a) fire.

537.II. 1. ταύτην τὴν ἐντολὴν ἐπέθηκεν αὐτοῖς, ἵνα τιθῶσι/θῶσι τὰς ψυχὰς αὐτῶν ὑπὲρ τῶν ἀδελφῶν αὐτῶν. 2. ἐὰν ἀφῆτε τοῖς διώκουσιν ἡμᾶς, καὶ ἐγὼ ἀφήσω ὑμᾶς. 3. εὑρόντες τὸν ποιήσαντα τοῦτο ἀφῆκαν αὐτὸν καὶ ἀπῆλθον. 4. θεὶς τὸ σῶμα εἰς τὸ μνημεῖον ἀπῆλθεν. 5. εἴδομεν τοὺς ἐπιτιθέντας τὰς ψυχὰς αὐτῶν ὑπὲρ τῶν παιδίων. 6. εἶδον αἱ γυναῖκες ὅπου τὸ σῶμα ἐτέθη. 7. ἐρωτήσομεν αὐτὸν ἕως ἂν ἀποκρίνηται ἡμῖν. 8. ὀφείλομεν εὐχαριστεῖν τῷ ἄφεντι ἡμῖν τὰς ἁμαρτίας ἡμῶν. 9. οὐκ ἔγνωμεν, αὐτὸς/ὁ δὲ ἔγνω ἡμᾶς. 10. δός μοι τὸ σῶμα, ἵνα θῶ αὐτὸ εἰς μνημεῖον. 11. ἔδειξε πάντα ὑμῖν, ἵνα (τι) θῆς αὐτὰ ἐν ταῖς καρδίαις ὑμῶν. 12. ἀποκριθεὶς ὁ ἀπόστολος εἶπε τοῖς ἐρωτῶσιν αὐτὸν ὅτι οὐ θήσω ταῦτα τὰ δῶρα εἰς τὸ ἱερόν. 13. ἰδόντες τὸ σημεῖον ὃ ἔδειξεν ὁ Ἰησοῦς ἡμῖν, ἐπιστεύσαμεν εἰς αὐτόν.

Lesson XXXIII

554.I. .1. On account of this the world does not know us, because it did not know Him. Beloved, now we are God's children, and what we shall be has not yet been manifested. We know that if He should appear we will be like Him, because we shall see Him (just) as He is. 2. Therefore they kept saying to Him, "Where is your Father?" Jesus answered, "You know neither me nor my Father; if you had known me, you would have known my Father also." 3. You will seek me and will not find, and where I am going you are unable to go. 4. And the crowd was coming together again, so that they could not (i.e. were not able to) even eat bread. 5. You have heard that I said to you, "I am going away and am coming to you. If you had been loving me, you would have rejoiced that I am going to the Father, because the Father is greater than I." 6. He found others standing and said (says) to them, "Why do you stand here all day?" 7. The Lord God will raise up for you from your brethren a

prophet like me; him you will hear according to all things what ever he
speaks to you. 8. And the high priest stood and said to Him, "Do you not
answer a thing?" 9. Then therefore the other disciple also who had come first
to the tomb entered, and he saw and believed; for they did not yet know the
Scripture, that it was necessary for him to rise from the dead. 10. If the
miracles which have occurred in you had been done in Sodom, it would have remained until today. 11. He gave to them power and authority over all the
demons. 12. And it came to pass that while all the people were being
baptized and when Jesus also had been baptized and was praying, the heaven
was opened and the Holy Spirit came down. 13. And it came to pass (happened)
in those days that He went out into the mountains to pray. 14. And/but they
went out to see the thing which had come to pass, and they came to Jesus and
found the man from whom the demons had departed, sitting. 15. And it came
to pass that while He was in a certain place praying, as He ceased, a certain
one of His disciples said to Him, "Lord, teach us to pray, just as John taught
his disciples." 16. But He said to him, "You shall love the Lord your God
with your whole heart." 17. Do you think that I have come to give/grant
peace in the earth? 18. Concerning whom does the prophet say this?
Concerning himself or concerning some other one? 19. He (emphatic) will
baptize you with (the) Holy Spirit and fire.

554.II. 1. ἀφῆκε τοὺς ἀνάσταντας κατὰ τοῦ βασιλέως αὐτῶν. 2. οἴδαμεν ὅτι
οἱ καθήμενοι ἐν τῷ οἴκῳ οὐκ ἐκπορεύσονται ἕως ἂν ἴδωσι τὸν ἀπόστόλον.
3. καταβάντος τοῦ Ἰησοῦ ἐκ τοῦ ὄρους, οἱ μαθηταὶ εἶδον τὸν ἄνθρωπον
καθήμενον ἐν τῷ οἴκῳ. 4. εἴδομεν τοὺς ἀποστόλους ἑστῶτας ἔμπροσθεν τῶν
ἀρχιερέων. 5. παραγενόμεναι εἰς τὴν πόλιν αἱ γυναῖκες εἶδον τὸν Ἰησοῦν
ποιοῦντα δυνάμεις πολλάς. 6. ἀνέστη ἐν ἐκείναις ταῖς ἡμέραις βασιλεύς τις
ὃς ἡμᾶς οὐκ ἔγνω. 7. τοῖς καθημένοις ἐν τῷ σκότει ἐφανέρωσας σεαυτόν.
8. ἰδὼν ταῦτα οὐκ ᾔδει ὃ ἔλεγεν. 9. οὐ δυνάμεθα εἰδέναι πάντα ταῦτα ἐὰν
μὴ ὁ κύριος φανερώσῃ αὐτὰ ἡμῖν. 10. εὕρομεν τὸν δυνάμενον ἆραι τὰς ἁμαρτίας
ἡμῶν. 11. οἴδαμεν ὅτι δύναται οὐδεὶς ποιεῖν ὃ ὁ βασιλεὺς ποιεῖ.

This index includes only items which either cannot or probably would not be found by using the index in NTGFB itself. References are to the paragraphs in the Study Guide.